EVERYMAN'S LIBRARY
EDITED BY ERNEST RHYS

FICTION

TARTARIN OF TARASCON
& TARTARIN ON THE ALPS
BY ALPHONSE DAUDET

THE PUBLISHERS OF *EVERYMAN'S LIBRARY* WILL BE PLEASED TO SEND FREELY TO ALL APPLICANTS A LIST OF THE PUBLISHED AND PROJECTED VOLUMES TO BE COMPRISED UNDER THE FOLLOWING TWELVE HEADINGS:

TRAVEL ❦ SCIENCE ❦ FICTION
THEOLOGY & PHILOSOPHY
HISTORY ❦ CLASSICAL
FOR YOUNG PEOPLE
ESSAYS ❦ ORATORY
POETRY & DRAMA
BIOGRAPHY
ROMANCE

IN TWO STYLES OF BINDING, CLOTH, FLAT BACK, COLOURED TOP, AND LEATHER, ROUND CORNERS, GILT TOP.

LONDON: J. M. DENT & SONS, LTD.
NEW YORK: E. P. DUTTON & CO.

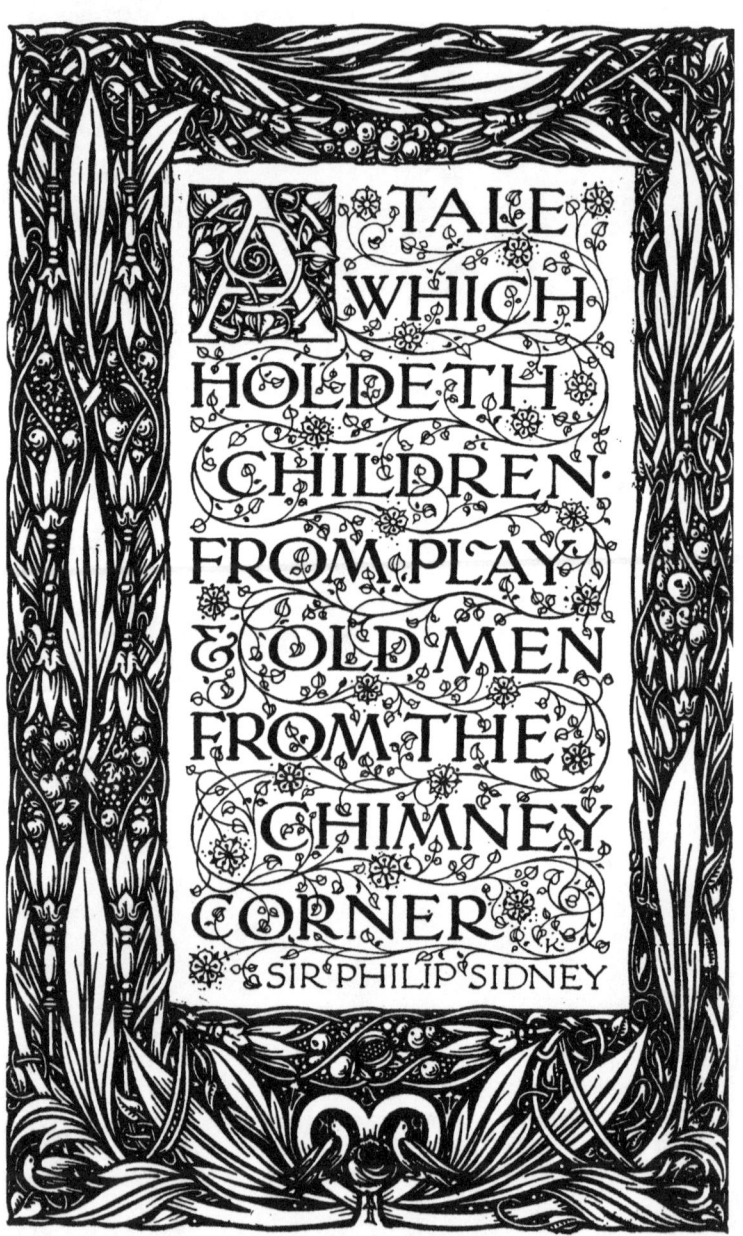

INTRODUCTION

THE younger contemporary of Alphonse Daudet, who said that a cynic was a sentimentalist turned inside out, may have been led to that idea by a comparison of his books in the two different veins of *Tartarin* and *Jack*. If there is too much sentiment in the second of these, which was his own favourite book, in the first Daudet found the perfect opening he needed for the play of his satiric wit and mercurial imagination. There the very qualities that prevented his full success, when he would have expressed his contemporary world as a serious novelist, only helped to wing and operate his invention. In the creation of *Tartarin* it may be said that his Provençal blood moved as it could never do to any northern impulse. It seemed that his mind must laugh, to be freely and delightfully inventive; when he became reflective, he was too apt to lose the light logic of gaiety without acquiring any compensatory force or graver human momentum. *Tartarin*, then, was his masterpiece; the one decisive creation of his fantasy, which, whether it be in the second rank or no of the world's humorous romances, was of a kind which only he could have invented. *Tartarin* has been called "an heroical farce," and "a comedy written with white wine"; it has been likened, on Daudet's own suggestion, to *Don Quixote*. But comparative criticism is always hazardous. It is enough to read the book for what it is—a delicious extravaganza into which, as was once said by a critic not really sympathetic to Daudet—Mr. Arthur Symons—he had put much of the sunshine and all the exterior qualities of the Provençal south; *les gestes, frénésies et ebullitions de notre soleil*, as he said himself.

Les Aventures Prodigieuses de Tartarin de Tarascon first appeared in 1872. Alphonse Daudet's was then a practised faculty that had tried many forms of prose and

viii   Tartarin

verse. Born at Nîmes in 1840, he had gone to Paris to join his elder brother Ernest when he was a boy of seventeen. He wrote articles for the *Figaro ;* his first poems, *Les Amoureuses,* appeared when he was still under twenty. The *Figaro* articles were afterwards collected, we may note, under title, *Le Chaperon Rouge ;* more poetry, and some dramas in collaboration, which were acted, followed; and under the pseudonyms of " Jehan de L'Isle," and " Gaston Marie," he published (in *Petit Moniteur*) *Lettres sur Paris* and (in *L'Evénement*) *Lettres de mon Moulin.* He was fortunate in obtaining a post, which he held for five years, as private secretary to M. de Morny, and he profited by the information thus gained of public affairs in several of his succeeding novels of contemporary Paris, notably in *Le Nabab,* which appeared between the earlier and later *Tartarin* books in 1877. Two other novels which help to fill the same interval, and which show his other art of fiction in its most effective output, are *Les Rois en Exil* and *Numa Roumestan.*

Alphonse Daudet died in Paris, December 17, 1897.

E. R.

The following table gives the chronology of his books:—

Les Amoureuses (Poésies), 1858; La Double Conversion (a tale in verse), 1861; Le Roman du Chaperon-Rouge, 1862; Lettres sur Paris (*Petit Moniteur*), 1865; Le Petit Chose, Histoire d'un Enfant, 1868; Letters de Mon Moulin (Evénement), 1869; Lettres à un Absent, 1870-71; Aventures Prodigieuses de Tartarin de Tarascon, 1872; Les Petits Robinsons du Cave, ou le Siège de Paris, raconté par une petite fille de huit ans, 1872; Contes du Lundi, 1873; Contes et Récits (chiefly tales which had already appeared in Lettres à un Absent, and Contes du Lundi), 1873; Les Femmes d'Artistes, 1874; Fromont Jeune et Risler Aîné, 1874; Robert Helmont, Etudes et Paysages, 1874; Jack, 1876; Contes Choisis, 1877; Le Nabab, 1877; Les Rois en Exit, 1879; La Fantaisie et l'Histoire, 1879; Numa Roumestan, 1881; L'Evangéliste, 1883; Les Cigognes (for children), 1883; Sapho, 1884; Tartarin sur les Alpes, 1885; La Belle Nibernaise. Histoire d'un vieux bateau, etc., 1886; Trente Ans de Paris à travers ma Vie et mes Livres, 1888; L'Immortel, 1888; Souvenirs d'un Homme de Lettres, 1888; Port-Tarascon, 1890; Rose et Ninette, 1892; Entre les Frises et la Rampe, 1894; La Petite Paroisse, 1895; Contes d'Hiver, 1896; Trois Souvenirs, 1896; L'Enterrement d'une Etoile, 1896; La Fédor, Pages de la Vie, 1897; Le Trésor d'Arlatan, 1897; Soutien de Famille, 1898; Notes sur la Vie, 1899; My First Voyage, My First Lie, A Reminiscence of an Imaginative Childhood.

Bibliography

Related to R. H. Sherard, by whom it is now published in M. Daudet's own words in English, 1901.

DRAMA.—La Dernière Idole, 1862; Les Absents, 1863; L'Œillet Blanc, 1865; Le Frère Aîné, 1868; Le Sacrifice, 1869; L'Arlésienne, 1872; Lise Tavernier, 1872; Le Char, 1878; La Lutte pour la Vie, 1890; L'Obstacle, 1891. Many of Daudet's novels were also dramatised.

An Edition Définitive of Daudet's works was published in 1899 (with a literary biography by H. Céard).

Separate English translations of the novels have been published, and a complete translation of works by H. Frith, L. Ensor, E. Barton, etc., 1896, 1902.

LIFE.—J. Clarétie, 1883; H. Le Roux, Notre Patron: Alphonse Daudet, 1888; R. Doumic, Portraits d'Ecrivains, 1892; R. H. Sherard, 1894; L. A. Daudet, 1898; A. Hermant, 1903; W. A. Munro, Charles Dickens et A. Daudet, 1908.

CONTENTS

TARTARIN OF TARASCON

EPISODE THE FIRST
IN TARASCON

CHAP.		PAGE
I.	THE GARDEN ROUND THE GIANT TREES	1
II.	A GENERAL GLANCE BESTOWED UPON THE GOOD TOWN OF TARASCON, AND A PARTICULAR ONE ON "THE CAP-POPPERS"	3
III.	"NAW! NAW! NAW!" THE GENERAL GLANCE PROTRACTED UPON THE GOOD TOWN	6
IV.	"THEY!"	8
V.	HOW TARTARIN WENT ROUND TO HIS CLUB	10
VI.	THE TWO TARTARINS	13
VII.	TARTARIN—THE EUROPEANS AT SHANGHAI—COMMERCE—THE TARTARS — CAN TARTARIN OF TARASCON BE AN IMPOSTOR?—THE MIRAGE	14
VIII.	MITAINE'S MENAGERIE—A LION FROM THE ATLAS AT TARASCON—A SOLEMN AND FEARSOME CONFRONTATION	16
IX.	SINGULAR EFFECTS OF MENTAL MIRAGE	19
X.	BEFORE THE START	22
XI.	"LET'S HAVE IT OUT WITH SWORDS, GENTLEMEN, NOT PINS!"	23
XII.	A MEMORABLE DIALOGUE IN THE LITTLE BAOBAB VILLA	25
XIII.	THE DEPARTURE	27
XIV.	THE PORT OF MARSEILLES—"ALL ABOARD, ALL ABOARD!"	29

Tartarin of Tarascon

EPISODE THE SECOND
AMONG "THE TURKS"

CHAP.		PAGE
I.	The Passage—The five Positions of the Fez—The third Evening out—Mercy upon us!	33
II.	"To Arms! to Arms!"	35
III.	An Invocation to Cervantes—The Disembarkation—Where are the Turks?—Not a sign of them—Disenchantment	37
IV.	The first Lying in Wait	39
V.	Bang! Bang!	41
VI.	Arrival of the Female—A terrible Combat—"Game Fellows Meet Here!"	44
VII.	About an Omnibus, a Moorish Beauty, and a Wreath of Jessamine	46
VIII.	Ye Lions of the Atlas, repose in Peace!	48
IX.	Prince Gregory of Montenegro	50
X.	"Tell me your Father's Name, and I will tell you the Name of that Flower"	53
XI.	Sidi Tart'ri Ben Tart'ri	56
XII.	The latest Intelligence from Tarascon	58

EPISODE THE THIRD
AMONG THE LIONS

I.	What becomes of the old Stage-coaches	62
II.	A little Gentleman drops in and "drops upon" Tartarin	65
III.	A Monastery of Lions	68
IV.	The Caravan on the March	71
V.	The Night-watch in a Poison-tree Grove	74
VI.	Bagged him at last	78
VII.	Catastrophes upon Catastrophes	82
VIII.	Tarascon again!	85

Contents xiii

TARTARIN ON THE ALPS

CHAP.		PAGE
I.	AN APPARITION ON THE RIGI-KULM—WHO IS HE?—WHAT WAS SAID AT THE TABLE D'HÔTE—RICE AND PRUNES—AN IMPROVISED BALL—THE UNKNOWN SIGNS HIS NAME IN THE HOTEL REGISTER—P. C. A.	91
II.	TARASCON, FIVE MINUTES' STOPPAGE — THE ALPINE CLUB—EXPLANATION OF P. C. A.—RABBITS OF THE WARREN AND OF THE CABBAGE-GARDEN—" THIS IS MY WILL "—THE SIROP DE CADAVRE—FIRST ASCENT—TARTARIN MOUNTS HIS SPECTACLES	102
III.	AN ALARM ON THE RIGI—BE COOL! BE COOL!—THE ALPINE HORN — WHAT TARTARIN FOUND ON HIS LOOKING-GLASS WHEN HE AWOKE—PERPLEXITY—HE ASKS FOR A GUIDE BY TELEPHONE	116
IV.	ON BOARD THE STEAMER—RAIN—THE HERO OF TARASCON SALUTES THE SHADES—THE TRUTH ABOUT WILLIAM TELL — DISILLUSION — TARTARIN OF TARASCON NEVER EXISTED!—" TÉ! BOMPARD! "	124
V.	CONFIDENCES IN A TUNNEL	135
VI.	THE PASS OF THE BRÜNIG—TARTARIN FALLS INTO THE HANDS OF THE NIHILISTS—DISAPPEARANCE OF AN ITALIAN TENOR AND AN AVIGNON ROPE—NEW EXPLOITS OF A CHASSEUR DE CASQUETTES—PAN! PAN!	141
VII.	NIGHT AT TARASCON—WHERE IS HE?—ANXIETY—THE CIGALES DU COURS DEMAND TARTARIN—MARTYRDOM OF A TARASCON SAINT—THE ALPINE CLUB—WHAT HAPPENED AT THE CHEMIST'S—HELP! BÉZUQUET.	153
VIII.	MEMORABLE DIALOGUE BETWEEN THE JUNGFRAU AND TARTARIN—A NIHILIST SALON—THE DUEL WITH HUNTING-KNIVES—HORRIBLE NIGHTMARE—" 'TIS I WHOM YOU SEEK, GENTLEMEN! "—STRANGE RECEPTION OF THE TARASCON DELEGATES AT THE HÔTEL MEYER	162
IX.	AT THE SIGN OF " THE FAITHFUL CHAMOIS "	172

CHAP.		PAGE
X.	THE ASCENT OF THE JUNGFRAU—VÉ! THE OXEN!—THE KENNEDY CRAMPONS DO NOT ANSWER; NEITHER DOES THE LAMP—APPEARANCE OF MASKED MEN AT THE CHALET—THE PRESIDENT IN THE CREVASSE—HE LEAVES HIS SPECTACLES BEHIND HIM—ON THE PEAKS —TARTARIN A DEITY	180
XI.	EN ROUTE FOR TARASCON!—THE LAKE OF GENEVA— TARTARIN SUGGESTS A VISIT TO BONNIVARD'S CELL— A SHORT DIALOGUE AMID THE ROSES—ALL THE BAND UNDER LOCK AND KEY—THE UNFORTUNATE BONNI- VARD—A CERTAIN ROPE MADE IN AVIGNON COMES TO LIGHT	191
XII.	THE HÔTEL BALTET AT CHAMONIX—THAT SMELL OF GARLIC!—CONCERNING THE USES OF THE CORD IN ALPINE EXCURSIONS—SHAKE HANDS!—A PUPIL OF SCHOPENHAUER'S—AT THE GRANDS-MULETS—" TAR- TARIN, I MUST SPEAK TO YOU "	203
XIII.	THE CATASTROPHE	215
XIV.	EPILOGUE	225

TARTARIN OF TARASCON

TARTARIN OF TARASCON

EPISODE THE FIRST

IN TARASCON

I

THE GARDEN ROUND THE GIANT TREES

My first visit to Tartarin of Tarascon has remained a never-to-be-forgotten date in my life; although quite ten or a dozen years ago, I remember it better than yesterday.

At that time the intrepid Tartarin lived in the third house on the left as the town begins, on the Avignon road. A pretty little villa in the local style, with a front garden and a balcony behind, the walls glaringly white and the venetians very green; and always about the doorsteps a brood of little Savoyard shoeblackguards playing hop-scotch, or dozing in the broad sunshine with their heads pillowed on their boxes.

Outwardly the dwelling had no remarkable features, and none would ever believe it the abode of a hero; but when you stepped inside, ye gods and little fishes! what a change! From turret to foundation-stone—I mean, from cellar to garret,—the whole building wore a heroic front; even so the garden!

O that garden of Tartarin's! there's not its match in Europe! Not a native tree was there—not one flower of France; nothing but exotic plants, gum-trees, gourds, cotton-woods, cocoa and cacao, mangoes, bananas, palms, a baobab, nopals, cacti, Barbary figs—well, you would believe yourself in the very midst of Central Africa, ten thousand leagues away. It is but fair to say that these were none of full growth; indeed, the cocoa-palms were no bigger

A

than beetroot, and the baobab (*arbos gigantea*—" giant tree," you know) was easily enough circumscribed by a window-pot; but, notwithstanding this, it was rather a sensation for Tarascon, and the townsfolk who were admitted on Sundays to the honour of contemplating Tartarin's baobab, went home chokeful of admiration.

Try to conceive my own emotion, which I was bound to feel on that day of days when I crossed through this marvellous garden; and that was capped when I was ushered into the hero's sanctum.

His study, one of the lions—I should say, lions' dens—of the town, was at the end of the garden, its glass door opening right on to the baobab.

You are to picture a capacious apartment adorned with firearms and steel blades from top to bottom: all the weapons of all the countries in the wide world—carbines, rifles, blunderbusses, Corsican, Catalan, and dagger knives, Malay kreeses, revolvers with spring-bayonets, Carib and flint arrows, knuckle-dusters, life-preservers, Hottentot clubs, Mexican lassoes,—now, can you expect me to name the rest? Upon the whole fell a fierce sunlight, which made the blades and the brass butt-plate of the muskets gleam as if all the more to set your flesh creeping. Still, the beholder was soothed a little by the tame air of order and tidiness reigning over the arsenal. Everything was in place, brushed, dusted, labelled, as in a museum; from point to point the eye descried some obliging little card reading:—

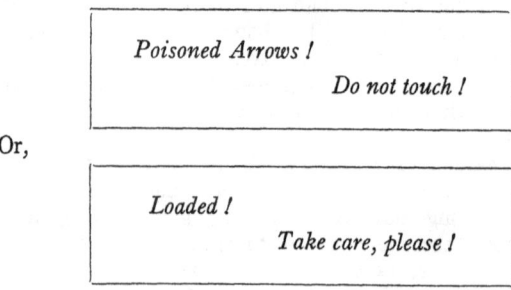

Or,

If it had not been for these cautions I never should have dared venture in.

In Tarascon

In the middle of the room was an occasional table, on which stood a decanter of rum, a siphon of soda-water, a Turkish tobacco-pouch, *Captain Cook's Voyages*, the Indian tales of Fenimore Cooper and Gustave Aimard, stories of hunting the bear, eagle, elephant, and so on. Lastly, beside the table sat a man of between forty and forty-five, short, stout, thick-set, ruddy, with flaming eyes and a strong stubbly beard; he wore flannel tights, and was in his shirt sleeves; one hand held a book, and the other brandished a very large pipe with an iron bowl-cap. Whilst reading heaven only knows what startling adventure of scalp-hunters, he pouted out his lower lip in a terrifying way, which gave the honest phiz of the man living placidly on his means the same impression of kindly ferocity which abounded throughout the house.

This man was Tartarin himself—the Tartarin of Tarascon, the great, dreadnought, incomparable Tartarin of Tarascon.

II

A GENERAL GLANCE BESTOWED UPON THE GOOD TOWN OF TARASCON, AND A PARTICULAR ONE ON "THE CAP-POPPERS"

AT the time I am telling of, Tartarin of Tarascon had not become the present-day Tartarin, the great one so popular in the whole South of France; but yet he was even then the cock of the walk at Tarascon.

Let us show whence arose this sovereignty.

In the first place you must know that everybody is shooting mad in these parts, from the greatest to the least. The chase is the local craze, and so it has ever been since the mythological times when the *Tarasque*, as the country dragon was called, flourished himself and his tail in the town marshes, and entertained shooting parties got up against him. So you see the passion has lasted a goodish bit.

It follows that, every Sunday morning, Tarascon flies to arms, lets loose the dogs of the hunt, and rushes out of its walls, with game-bag slung and fowling-piece on the shoulder, together with a hurly-burly of hounds, cracking of whips, and blowing of whistles and hunting-horns. It's splendid to see! Unfortunately, there's a lack of game, an absolute dearth.

Stupid as the brute creation is, you can readily understand that, in time, it learnt some distrust.

For five leagues around about Tarascon, forms, lairs, and burrows are empty, and nesting-places abandoned. You'll not find a single quail or blackbird, one little leveret, or the tiniest tit. And yet the pretty hillocks are mightily tempting, sweet smelling as they are of myrtle, lavender, and rosemary; and the fine muscatels plumped out with sweetness even unto bursting, as they spread along the banks of the Rhône, are deucedly tempting too. True, true; but Tarascon lies behind all this, and Tarascon is down in the black books of the world of fur and feather. The very birds of passage have ticked it off on their guide-books, and when the wild ducks, coming down towards the Camargue in long triangles, spy the town steeples from afar, the outermost flyers squawk out loudly,—

"Look out! there's Tarascon! give Tarascon the go-by, duckies!"

And the flocks take a swerve.

In short, as far as game goes, there's not a specimen left in the land save one old rogue of a hare, escaped by miracle from the massacres, who is stubbornly determined to stick to it all his life! He is very well known at Tarascon, and a name has been given him. "Rapid" is what they call him. It is known that he has his form on M. Bompard's grounds —which, by the way, has doubled, ay, tripled, the value of the property—but nobody has yet managed to lay him low. At present, only two or three inveterate fellows worry themselves about him. The rest have given him up as a bad job, and old Rapid has long ago passed into the legendary world, although your Tarasconer is very slightly superstitious naturally, and would eat cock-robins on toast, or the swallow, which is Our Lady's own bird, for that matter, if he could find any.

"But that won't do!" you will say. Inasmuch as game is so scarce, what can the sportsmen do every Sunday?

In Tarascon

What can they do?

Why, goodness gracious! they go out into the real country two or three leagues from town. They gather in knots of five or six, recline tranquilly in the shade of some well, old wall, or olive tree, extract from their game-bags a good-sized piece of boiled beef, raw onions, a sausage, and anchovies, and commence a next to endless snack, washed down with one of those nice Rhône wines, which sets a toper laughing and singing. After that, when thoroughly braced up, they rise, whistle the dogs to heel, set the guns on half-cock, and go " on the shoot "—another way of saying that every man plucks off his cap, " shies " it up with all his might, and pops it on the fly with No. 5, 6, or 2 shot, according to what he is loaded for.

The man who lodges most shot in his cap is hailed as king of the hunt, and stalks back triumphantly at dusk into Tarascon, with his riddled cap on the end of his gun-barrel, amid any quantity of dog-barks and horn-blasts.

It is needless to say that cap-selling is a fine business in the town. There are even some hatters who sell hunting-caps ready shot, torn, and perforated for the bad shots; but the only buyer known is the chemist Bézuquet. This *is* dishonourable!

As a marksman at caps, Tartarin of Tarascon never had his match.

Every Sunday morning out he would march in a new cap, and back he would strut every Sunday evening with a mere thing of shreds. The loft of Baobab Villa was full of these glorious trophies. Hence all Tarascon acknowledged him as master; and as Tartarin thoroughly understood hunting, and had read all the handbooks of all possible kinds of venery, from cap-popping to Burmese tiger-shooting, the sportsmen constituted him their great cynegetical judge, and took him for referee and arbitrator in all their differences.

Between three and four daily, at Costecalde the gunsmith's, a stout, stern pipe-smoker might be seen in a green leather-covered arm-chair in the centre of the shop crammed with cap-poppers, they all on foot and wrangling. This was Tartarin of Tarascon delivering judgment—Nimrod *plus* Solomon.

III

"NAW, NAW, NAW!" THE GENERAL GLANCE PROTRACTED UPON THE GOOD TOWN

AFTER the craze for sporting, the lusty Tarascon race cherishes one for love ballad-singing. There's no believing what a quantity of ballads is used up in that little region. All the sentimental stuff turning into sere and yellow leaves in the oldest portfolios, are to be found in full pristine lustre in Tarascon. Ay, the entire collection. Every family has its own pet, as is known to the town.

For instance, it is an established fact that this is the chemist Bézuquet's family's,—

> " Thou art the fair star that I adore! "

The gunmaker Costecalde's family's,—

> " Would'st thou come to the land
> Where the log-cabins rise? "

The official registrar's family's,—

> " If I wore a coat of invisible green,
> Do you think for a moment I could be seen? "

And so on for the whole of Tarascon. Two or three times a week there were parties where they were sung. The singularity was their being always the same, and that the honest Tarasconers had never had an inclination to change them during the long, long time they had been harping on them. They were handed down from father to son in the families, without anybody improving on them or Bowdlerising them: they were sacred. Never did it occur to Costecalde's mind to sing the Bézuquets', or the Bézuquets to try Costecalde's. And yet you may believe that they ought to know by heart what they had been singing for two-score years! But, nay! everybody stuck to his own, and they were all contented.

In ballad-singing, as in cap-popping, Tartarin was still the foremost. His superiority over his fellow-townsmen consisted in his not having any one song of his own, but in knowing the lot, the whole, mind you! But—there's a but —it was the devil's own work to get him to sing them. Surfeited early in life with his drawing-room successes, our hero preferred by far burying himself in his hunting story-books, or spending the evening at the club, to making a personal exhibition before a Nîmes piano between a pair of home-made candles. These musical parades seemed beneath him. Nevertheless, at whiles, when there was a harmonic party at Bézuquet's, he would drop into the chemist's shop as if by chance, and, after a deal of pressure, consent to do the grand duo in *Robert le Diable* with old Madame Bézuquet. Whoso never heard that, never heard anything! For my part, even if I lived a hundred years, I should always see the mighty Tartarin solemnly stepping up to the piano, setting his arms akimbo, working up his tragic mien, and, beneath the green reflection from the show-bottles in the window, trying to give his pleasant visage the fierce and satanic expression of Robert the Devil. Hardly would he fall into position before the whole audience would be shuddering with the foreboding that something uncommon was at hand. After a hush, old Madame Bézuquet would commence to her own accompaniment,—

" Robert, my love is thine!
To thee I my faith did plight,
Thou seest my affright,—
Mercy for thine own sake,
And mercy for mine! "

In an undertone she would add: " Now, then, Tartarin! " Whereupon Tartarin of Tarascon, with crooked arms, clenched fists, and quivering nostrils, would roar three times in a formidable voice, rolling like a thunder-clap in the bowels of the instrument,—

" No! no! no! " which, like the thorough southerner he was, he pronounced nasally as " Naw! naw! naw! " Then would old Madame Bézuquet again sing,—

" Mercy for thine own sake,
And mercy for mine! "

" Naw! naw! naw! " bellowed Tartarin at his loudest, and there the gem ended.

Not long, you see; but it was so handsomely voiced forth, so clearly gesticulated, and so diabolical, that a tremor of terror overran the chemist's shop, and the "Naw! naw! naw!" would be encored several times running.

Upon this Tartarin would sponge his brow, smile on the ladies, wink to the sterner sex, and withdraw upon his triumph to go remark at the club with a trifling, offhand air,—

"I have just come from the Bézuquet's, where I was forced to sing 'em the duo from *Robert le Diable*."

The cream of the joke was that he really believed it!

IV

"THEY!"

CHIEFLY to the account of these diverse talents did Tartarin owe his lofty position in the town of Tarascon. Talking of captivating, though, this deuce of a fellow knew how to ensnare everybody. Why, the army, at Tarascon, was for Tartarin. The brave commandant, Bravida, honorary captain retired—in the Military Clothing Factory Department—called him a game fellow; and you may well admit that the warrior knew all about game fellows, he played such a capital knife and fork on game of all kinds.

So was the legislature on Tartarin's side. Two or three times, in open court, the old chief judge, Ladevèze, had said, in alluding to him,—

"He is a character!"

Lastly, the masses were for Tartarin. He had become the swell bruiser, the aristocratic pugilist, the crack bully of the local Corinthians for the Tarasconers, from his build, bearing, style—that aspect of a guard's-trumpeter's charger which fears no noise; his reputation as a hero coming from nobody knew whence or for what, and some scramblings for coppers and a few kicks to the little ragamuffins basking at his doorway.

Along the waterside, when Tartarin came home from hunting on Sunday evenings, with his cap on the muzzle of

In Tarascon

his gun, and his fustian shooting-jacket belted in tightly, the sturdy river-lightermen would respectfully bob, and blinking towards the huge biceps swelling out his arms, would mutter among one another in admiration,—

" Now, there's a powerful chap if you like! he has double muscles! "

" *Double muscles !* " why, you never heard of such a thing outside of Tarascon!

For all this, with all his numberless parts, double-muscles, the popular favour, and the so precious esteem of brave Commandant Bravida, ex-captain (in the Army Clothing Factory), Tartarin was not happy: this life in a petty town weighed upon him and suffocated him.

The great man of Tarascon was bored in Tarascon.

The fact is, for a heroic temperament like his, a wild adventurous spirit which dreamt of nothing but battles, races across the pampas, mighty battues, desert sands, blizzards and typhoons, it was not enough to go out every Sunday to pop at a cap, and the rest of the time to ladle out casting-votes at the gunmaker's. Poor dear great man! If this existence were only prolonged, there would be sufficient tedium in it to kill him with consumption.

In vain did he surround himself with baobabs and other African trees, to widen his horizon, and some little to forget his club and the market-place; in vain did he pile weapon upon weapon, and Malay kreese upon Malay kreese; in vain did he cram with romances, endeavouring like the immortal Don Quixote to wrench himself by the vigour of his fancy out of the talons of pitiless reality. Alas! all that he did to appease his thirst for deeds of daring only helped to augment it. The sight of all the murderous implements kept him in a perpetual stew of wrath and exaltation. His revolvers, repeating rifles, and ducking-guns shouted " Battle! battle! " out of their mouths. Through the twigs of his baobab, the tempest of great voyages and journeys soughed and blew bad advice. To finish him came Gustave Aimard, Mayne Reid, and Fenimore Cooper.

Oh, how many times did Tartarin with a howl spring up on the sultry summer afternoons, when he was reading alone amidst his blades, points, and edges; how many times did he dash down his book and rush to the wall to unhook a deadly arm! The poor man forgot he was at home in Tarascon, in his underclothes, and with a handkerchief round his head. He would translate his readings into action, and, goading himself with his own voice, shout out whilst swinging a battle-axe or tomahawk,—

"Now, only let 'em come!"

"Them"? who were they?

Tartarin did not himself any too clearly understand. "They" was all that should be attacked and fought with, all that bites, claws, scalps, whoops, and yells—the Sioux Indians dancing around the war-stake to which the unfortunate pale-face prisoner is lashed. The grizzly of the Rocky Mountains, who wobbles on his hind legs, and licks himself with a tongue full of blood. The Touareg, too, in the desert, the Malay pirate, the brigand of the Abruzzi—in short, "they" was warfare, travel, adventure, and glory.

But, alas! it was to no avail that the fearless Tarasconer called for and defied *them;* never did they come. Odsboddikins! what would they have come to do in Tarascon?

Nevertheless, Tartarin always expected to run up against them, particularly some evening in going to the club.

V

HOW TARTARIN WENT ROUND TO HIS CLUB

LITTLE, indeed, beside Tartarin of Tarascon, arming himself cap-a-pie to go to his club at nine, an hour after the retreat had sounded on the bugle, was the Templar Knight preparing for a sortie upon the infidel, the Chinese *tiger* equipping himself for combat, or the Comanche warrior painting up for going on the war-path.

"All hands make ready for action!" as the men-of-war's men say.

In his left hand Tartarin took a steel-pointed knuckleduster; in the right he carried a sword-cane; in his left pocket a life-preserver; in the right a revolver. On his chest, betwixt outer and under garment, lay a Malay kreese.

In Tarascon

But never any poisoned arrows—they are weapons altogether too unfair.

Before starting, in the silence and obscurity of his study, he exercised himself for a while, warding off imaginary cuts and thrusts, lunging at the wall, and giving his muscles play; then he took his master-key and went through the garden leisurely; without hurrying, mark you. "Cool and calm—British courage, that is the true sort, gentlemen." At the garden end he opened the heavy iron door, violently and abruptly so that it should slam against the outer wall. If "they" had been skulking behind it, you may wager they would have been jam. Unhappily, they were not there.

The way being open, out Tartarin would sally, quickly glancing to the right and left, ere banging the door to and fastening it smartly with double-locking. Then, on the way. Not so much as a cat upon the Avignon road—all the doors closed, and no lights in the casements. All was black, except for the parish lamps, well spaced apart, blinking in the river mist.

Calm and proud, Tartarin of Tarascon marched on in the night, ringing his heels with regularity, and sending sparks out of the paving-stones with the ferule of his stick. Whether in avenues, streets, or lanes, he took care to keep in the middle of the road—an excellent method of precaution, allowing one to see danger coming, and, above all, to avoid any droppings from windows, as happens after dark in Tarascon and the Old Town of Edinburgh. On seeing so much prudence in Tartarin, pray do not conclude that Tartarin had any fear—dear, no! he only was on his guard.

The best proof that Tartarin was not scared is, that instead of going to the club by the shortest cut, he went over the town by the longest and darkest way round, through a mass of vile, paltry alleys, at the mouth of which the Rhône could be seen ominously gleaming. The poor knight constantly hoped that, beyond the turn of one of these cut-throats' haunts, "they" would leap from the shadow and fall on his back. I warrant you, "they" would have been warmly received, though; but, alack! by reason of some nasty meanness of destiny, never indeed did Tartarin of Tarascon enjoy the luck to meet any ugly customers—not so much as a dog or a drunken man—nothing at all!

Still, there were false alarms somewhiles. He would catch a sound of steps and muffled voices.

" 'Ware hawks!" Tartarin would mutter, and stop short, as if taking root on the spot, scrutinising the gloom, sniffing the wind, even glueing his ear to the ground in the orthodox Red Indian mode. The steps would draw nearer, and the voices grow more distinct, till no more doubt was possible. "They" were coming—in fact, here "they" were!

Steady, with eye afire and heaving breast, Tartarin would gather himself like a jaguar in readiness to spring forward whilst uttering his war-cry, when, all of a sudden, out of the thick of the murkiness, he would hear honest Tarasconian voices quite tranquilly hailing him with,—

"Hullo! you, by Jove! it's Tartarin! Good night, old fellow!"

Maledictions upon it! it was the chemist Bézuquet, with his family, coming from singing their family ballad at Costecalde's.

"Oh, good even, good even!" Tartarin would growl, furious at his blunder, and plunging fiercely into the gloom with his cane waved on high.

On arriving in the street where stood his club-house, the dauntless one would linger yet a moment, walking up and down before the portals ere entering. But, finally, weary of awaiting "them" and certain "they" would not show "themselves," he would fling a last glare of defiance into the shades and snarl wrathfully,—

"Nothing, nothing at all! there never is nothing!"

Upon which double negation, which he meant as a stronger affirmative, the worthy champion would walk in to play his game of bezique with the commandant.

VI

THE TWO TARTARINS

ANSWER me, you will say, how the mischief is it that Tartarin of Tarascon never left Tarascon with all this mania for adventure, need of powerful sensations, and folly about travel, rides, and journeys from the Pole to the Equator?

For that is a fact: up to the age of five-and-forty, the dreadless Tarasconian had never once slept outside his own room. He had not even taken that obligatory trip to Marseilles which every sound Provençal makes upon coming of age. The most of his knowledge included Beaucaire, and yet that's not far from Tarascon, there being merely the bridge to go over. Unfortunately, this rascally bridge has so often been blown away by the gales, it is so long and frail, and the Rhône has such a width at this spot that—well, faith! you understand! Tartarin of Tarascon preferred *terra firma*.

We are afraid we must make a clean breast of it: in our hero there were two very distinct characters. Some Father of the Church has said: " I feel there are two men in me." He would have spoken truly in saying this about Tartarin, who carried in his frame the soul of Don Quixote, the same chivalric impulses, heroic ideal, and crankiness for the grandiose and romantic; but, worse is the luck! he had not the body of the celebrated hidalgo, that thin and meagre apology for a body, on which material life failed to take a hold; one that could get through twenty nights without its breast-plate being unbuckled off, and forty-eight hours on a handful of rice. On the contrary, Tartarin's body was a stout honest bully of a body, very fat, very weighty, most sensual and fond of coddling, highly touchy, full of low-class appetite and homely requirements—the short, paunchy body on stumps of the immortal Sancho Panza.

Don Quixote and Sancho Panza in the one same man! you will readily comprehend what a cat-and-dog couple they made   what strife! what clapperclawing! Oh, the fine dialogue for Lucian or Saint-Evremond to write, between the two Tartarins—Quixote-Tartarin and Sancho-Tartarin! Quixote-Tartarin firing up on the stories of Gustave Aimard, and shouting: "Up and at 'em!" and Sancho-Tartarin thinking only of the rheumatics ahead, and murmuring: "I mean to stay at home."

THE DUET

QUIXOTE-TARTARIN.	SANCHO-TARTARIN.
(*Highly excited.*)	(*Quite calmly.*)
Cover yourself with glory, Tartarin.	Tartarin, cover yourself with flannel.
(*Still more excitedly.*)	(*Still more calmly.*)
O for the terrible double-barrelled rifle! O for bowie-knives, lassoes, and moccasins!	O for the thick knitted waistcoats! and warm knee-caps! O for the welcome padded caps with ear-flaps!
(*Above all self-control.*)	(*Ringing up the maid.*)
A battle-axe! fetch me a battle-axe!	Now, then, Jeannette, do bring up that chocolate!

Whereupon Jeannette would appear with an unusually good cup of chocolate, just right in warmth, sweetly smelling, and with the play of light on watered silk upon its unctuous surface, and with succulent grilled steak flavoured with anise-seed, which would set Sancho-Tartarin off on the broad grin, and into a laugh that drowned the shouts of Quixote-Tartarin.

Thus it came about that Tartarin of Tarascon never had left Tarascon.

VII

TARTARIN—THE EUROPEANS AT SHANGHAI—COMMERCE—THE TARTARS—CAN TARTARIN OF TARASCON BE AN IMPOSTOR?—THE MIRAGE

UNDER one conjunction of circumstances, Tartarin did, however, once almost start out upon a great voyage.

The three brothers Garcio-Camus, natives of Tarascon, established in business at Shanghai, offered him the managership of one of their branches there. This undoubtedly presented the kind of life he hankered after. Plenty of active business, a whole army of under-strappers to order about, and connections with Russia, Persia, Turkey in Asia—in short, to be a merchant prince.

In Tartarin's mouth, the title of Merchant Prince thundered out as something stunning!

The house of Garcio-Camus had the further advantage of sometimes being favoured with a call from the Tartars. Then the doors would be slammed shut, all the clerks flew to arms, up ran the consular flag, and zizz! phit! bang! out of the windows upon the Tartars.

I need not tell you with what enthusiasm Quixote-Tartarin clutched this proposition; sad to say, Sancho-Tartarin did not see it in the same light, and, as he was the stronger party, it never came to anything. But in the town there was much talk about it. Would he go or would he not? "I'll lay he will "—and " I'll wager he won't! " It was the event of the week. In the upshot, Tartarin did not depart, but the matter redounded to his credit none the less. Going or not going to Shanghai was all one to Tarascon. Tartarin's journey was so much talked about that people got to believe he had done it and returned, and at the club in the evening members would actually ask for information on life at Shanghai, the manners and customs and climate, about opium, and commerce.

Deeply read up, Tartarin would graciously furnish the particulars desired, and, in the end, the good fellow was not quite sure himself about not having gone to Shanghai, so that, after relating for the hundredth time how the Tartars came down on the trading post, it would most naturally happen him to add,—

"Then I made my men take up arms and hoist the consular flag, and zizz! phit! bang! out of the windows upon the Tartars."

On hearing this, the whole club would quiver.

"But according to that, this Tartarin of yours is an awful liar."

"No, no, a thousand times over, no! Tartarin was no liar."

"But the man ought to know that he has never been to Shanghai "——

"Why, of course, he knows that; but still "——

"But still " you see—mark that! It is high time for the law to be laid down once for all on the reputation as drawers of the long bow which Northerners fling at Southerners. There are no Baron Munchausens in the south of France, neither at Nîmes nor Marseilles, Toulouse nor Tarascon. The Southerner does not deceive but is self-deceived. He does not always tell the cold-drawn truth, but he believes he does. His falsehood is not any such thing, but a kind of mental mirage.

Yes, purely mirage! The better to follow me, you should actually follow me into the South, and you will see I am right. You have only to look at that Lucifer's own country, where the sun transmogrifies everything, and magnifies it beyond life-size. The little hills of Provence are no bigger than the Butte Montmartre, but they will loom up like the Rocky Mountains; the Square House at Nîmes—a mere model to put on your side-board—will seem grander than St. Peter's. You will see—in brief, the only exaggerator in the South is Old Sol, for he does enlarge everything he touches. What was Sparta in its days of splendour? a pitiful hamlet. What was Athens? at the most, a second-class town; and yet in history both appear to us as enormous cities. This is a sample of what the sun can do.

Are you going to be astonished after this that the same sun falling upon Tarascon should have made of an ex-captain in the Army Clothing Factory, like Bravida, the "brave commandant;" of a sprout an Indian fig-tree; and of a man who had missed going to Shanghai one who had been there?

VIII

MITAINE'S MENAGERIE—A LION FROM THE ATLAS AT TARAS-
CON—A SOLEMN AND FEARSOME CONFRONTATION

EXHIBITING Tartarin of Tarascon, as we are, in his private life, before Fame kissed his brow and garlanded him with her well-worn laurel wreath, and having narrated his heroic existence in a modest state, his delights and sorrows, his dreams and his hopes, let us hurriedly skip to the grandest pages of his story, and to the singular event which was to give the first flight to his incomparable career.

It happened one evening at Costecalde the gunmaker's, where Tartarin was engaged in showing several sportsmen the working of the needle-gun, then in its first novelty. The door suddenly flew open, and in rushed a bewildered cap-popper, howling " A lion, a lion!" General was the alarm, stupor, uproar and tumult. Tartarin prepared to resist cavalry with the bayonet, whilst Costecalde ran to shut the door. The sportsman was surrounded and pressed and questioned, and here follows what he told them: Mitaine's Menagerie, returning from Beaucaire Fair, had consented to stay over a few days at Tarascon, and was just unpacking, to set up the show on the Castle-green, with a lot of boas, seals, crocodiles, and a magnificent lion from the Atlas Mountains.

An African lion in Tarascon?

Never in the memory of living man had the like been seen. Hence our dauntless cap-poppers looked at one another how proudly! What a beaming on their sunburned visages! and in every nook of Costecalde's shop what hearty congratulatory grips of the hand were silently exchanged! The sensation was so great and unforeseen that nobody could find a word to say—not even Tartarin.

Blanched and agitated, with the needle-gun still in his fist, he brooded, erect before the counter. A lion from the Atlas Range at pistol range from him, a couple of strides off? a lion, mind you—the beast heroic and ferocious above all others, the King of the Brute Creation, the crowning game of his fancies, something like the leading actor in the ideal company which played such splendid tragedies in his mind's eye. A lion, heaven be thanked! and from the Atlas, to boot! It was more than the great Tartarin could bear.

Suddenly a flush of blood flew into his face. His eyes flashed. With one convulsive movement he shouldered the needle-gun, and turning towards the brave Commandant Bravida (formerly captain—in the Army Clothing Department, please to remember), he thundered to him,—

" Let's go have a look at him, commandant."

" Here, here, I say! that's my gun—my needle-gun you

are carrying off," timidly ventured the wary Costecalde;
but Tartarin had already got round the corner, with all the
cap-poppers proudly lock-stepping behind him.

When they arrived at the menagerie, they found a goodly
number of people there. Tarascon, heroic but too long
deprived of sensational shows, had rushed upon Mitaine's
portable theatre, and had taken it by storm. Hence the
voluminous Madame Mitaine was highly contented. In an
Arab costume, her arms bare to the elbow, iron anklets on, a
whip in one hand and a plucked though live pullet in the
other, the noted lady was doing the honours of the booth to
the Tarasconians; and, as she also had "double muscles,"
her success was almost as great as her animals'.

The entrance of Tartarin with the gun on his shoulder was
a damper.

All our good Tarasconians, who had been quite tranquilly
strolling before the cages, unarmed and with no distrust,
without even any idea of danger, felt momentary appre-
hension, naturally enough, on beholding their mighty Tartarin rush into the enclosure with his formidable engine of
war. There must be something to fear when a hero like he
was, came weaponed; so, in a twinkling, all the space along
the cage fronts was cleared. The youngsters burst out
squalling for fear, and the women looked round for the
nearest way out. The chemist Bézuquet made off altogether,
alleging that he was going home for his gun.

Gradually, however, Tartarin's bearing restored courage.
With head erect, the intrepid Tarasconian slowly and calmly
made the circuit of the booth, passing the seal's tank without
stopping, glancing disdainfully on the long box filled with
sawdust in which the boa would digest its raw fowl, and
going to take his stand before the lion's cage.

A terrible and solemn confrontation, this!

The lion of Tarascon and the lion of Africa face to face!

On the one part, Tartarin erect, with his hamstrings in
tension, and his arms folded on his gun barrel; on the other,
the lion, a gigantic specimen, humped up in the straw, with
blinking orbs and brutish mien, resting his huge muzzle and
tawny full-bottomed wig on his forepaws. Both calm in
their gaze.

Singular thing! whether the needle-gun had given him

"the needle," if the popular idiom is admissible, or that he scented an enemy of his race, the lion, who had hitherto regarded the Tarasconians with sovereign scorn, and yawned in their faces, was all at once affected by ire. At first he sniffed; then he growled hollowly, stretching out his claws; rising, he tossed his head, shook his mane, opened a capacious maw, and belched a deafening roar at Tartarin.

A yell of fright responded, as Tarascon precipitated itself madly towards the exit, women and children, lightermen, cap-poppers, even the brave Commandant Bravida himself. But, alone, Tartarin of Tarascon had not budged. There he stood, firm and resolute, before the cage, lightnings in his eyes, and on his lip that gruesome grin with which all the town was familiar. In a moment's time, when all the cap-poppers, some little fortified by his bearing and the strength of the bars, re-approached their leader, they heard him mutter, as he stared Leo out of countenance,—

"Now, this is something like a hunt!"

All the rest of that day, never a word farther could they draw from Tartarin of Tarascon.

IX

SINGULAR EFFECTS OF MENTAL MIRAGE

CONFINING his remarks to the sentence last recorded, Tartarin had unfortunately still said overmuch.

On the morrow, there was nothing talked about through town but the near-at-hand departure of Tartarin for Algeria and lion-hunting. You are all witness, dear readers, that the honest fellow had not breathed a word on that head; but, you know, the mirage has its usual effect. In brief, all Tarascon spoke of nothing but the departure.

On the Old Walk, at the club, in Costecalde's, friends accosted one another with a startled aspect,—

"And furthermore, you know the news, at least?"

"And furthermore, rather? Tartarin's setting out, at least?"

For at Tarascon all phrases begin with " and furthermore," and conclude with " at least," with a strong local accent. Hence, on this occasion more than upon others, these peculiarities rang out till the windows shivered.

The most surprised of men in the town on hearing that Tartarin was going away to Africa, was Tartarin himself. But only see what vanity is! Instead of plumply answering that he was not going at all, and had not even had the intention, poor Tartarin, on the first of them mentioning the journey to him, observed with a neat little evasive air, " Aha! maybe I shall—but I do not say as much." The second time, a trifle more familiarised with the idea, he replied, " Very likely; " and the third time, " It's certain."

Finally, in the evening, at Costecalde's and the club, carried away by the egg-nogg, cheers, and illumination; intoxicated by the impression that bare announcement of his departure had made on the town, the hapless fellow formally declared that he was sick of banging away at caps, and that he would shortly be on the trail of the great lions of the Atlas. A deafening hurrah greeted this assertion. Whereupon more egg-nogg, bravoes, hand-shaking, slappings of the shoulder, and a torchlight serenade up to midnight before Baobab Villa.

It was Sancho-Tartarin who was anything but delighted. This idea of travel in Africa and lion-hunting made him shudder beforehand; and when the house was re-entered, and whilst the complimentary concert was sounding under the windows, he had a dreadful " row " with Quixote-Tartarin, calling him a cracked head, a visionary, imprudent, and thrice an idiot, and detailing by the card all the catastrophes awaiting him on such an expedition— shipwreck, rheumatism, yellow fever, dysentery, the black plague, elephantiasis, and the rest of them.

In vain did Quixote-Tartarin vow that he had not committed any imprudence—that he would wrap himself up well, and take even superfluous necessaries with him. Sancho-Tartarin would listen to nothing. The poor craven saw himself already torn to tatters by the lions, or engulfed in the desert sands like his late royal highness Cambyses, and the other Tartarin only managed to appease him a little by explaining that the start was not immediate, as nothing pressed.

In Tarascon

It is clear enough, indeed, that none embark on such an enterprise without some preparations. A man is bound to know whither he goes, hang it all! and not fly off like a bird. Before anything else, the Tarasconian wanted to peruse the accounts of great African tourists, the narrations of Mungo Park, Du Chaillu, Dr. Livingstone, Stanley, and so on.

In them, he learnt that these daring explorers, before donning their sandals for distant excursions, hardened themselves well beforehand to support hunger and thirst, forced marches, and all kinds of privation. Tartarin meant to act like they did, and from that day forward he lived upon water broth alone. The water broth of Tarascon is a few slices of bread drowned in hot water, with a clove of garlic, a pinch of thyme, and a sprig of laurel. Strict diet, at which you may believe poor Sancho made a wry face.

To the regimen of water broth Tartarin of Tarascon joined other wise practices. To break himself into the habit of long marches, he constrained himself to go round the town seven or eight times consecutively every morning, either at the fast walk or run, his elbows well set against his body, and a couple of white pebbles in the mouth, according to the antique usage.

To get inured to fog, dew, and night coolness, he would go down into his garden every dusk, and stop out there till ten or eleven, alone with his gun, on the lookout, behind the baobab.

Finally, so long as Mitaine's wild beast show tarried in Tarascon, the cap-poppers who were belated at Costecalde's might spy in the shadow of the booth, as they crossed the Castle-green, a mysterious figure stalking up and down. It was Tartarin of Tarascon, habituating himself to hear without emotion the roarings of the lion in the sombre night.

X

BEFORE THE START

PENDING Tartarin's delay of the event by all sorts of heroic means, all Tarascon kept an eye upon him, and nothing else was busied about. Cap-popping was winged, and ballad-singing dead. The piano in Bézuquet's shop mouldered away under a green fungus, and the Spanish flies dried upon it, belly up. Tartarin's expedition had put a stopper on everything.

Ah, you ought to have seen his success in the parlours. He was snatched away by one from another, fought for, loaned and borrowed, ay, stolen. There was no greater honour for the ladies than to go to Mitaine's Menagerie on Tartarin's arms, and have it explained before the lion's den how such large game are hunted, where they should be aimed at, at how many paces off, if the accidents were numerous, and the like of that.

Tartarin furnished all the elucidation desired. He had read *The Life of Jules Gerard, the Lion-Slayer*, and had lion-hunting at his finger ends, as if he had been through it himself. Hence he orated upon these matters with great eloquence.

But where he shone the brightest was at dinner at Chief Judge Ladevèze's, or brave Commandant Bravida's (the former captain in the Army Clothing Factory, you will keep in mind), when coffee came in, and all the chairs were brought up closer together, whilst they chatted of his future hunts.

Thereupon, his elbow on the cloth, his nose over his Mocha, our hero would discourse in a feeling tone of all the dangers awaiting him thereaway. He spoke of the long moonless night lyings-in-wait, the pestilential fens, the rivers envenomed by leaves of poison-plants, the deep snow-drifts, the scorching suns, the scorpions, and rains of grasshoppers; he also descanted on the peculiarities of the great lions of the Atlas, their way of fighting, their phenomenal vigour, and their ferocity in the mating season.

Heating with his own recital, he would rise from table, bounding to the middle of the dining-room, imitating the roar of a lion and the going off of a rifle: crack! bang! the zizz of the explosive bullet—gesticulating and roaring about till he had overset the chairs.

Everybody turned pale around the board: the gentlemen looking at one another and wagging their heads, the ladies shutting their eyes with pretty screams of fright, the elderly men combatively brandishing their canes; and, in the side apartments, the little boys, who had been put to bed betimes, were greatly startled by the sudden outcries and imitated gun-fire, and screamed for lights.

Meanwhile, Tartarin did not start.

XI

"LET'S HAVE IT OUT WITH SWORDS, GENTLEMEN, NOT PINS!"

A DELICATE question: whether Tartarin really had any intention of going, and one which the historian of Tartarin would be highly embarrassed to answer. In plain words, Mitaine's Menagerie had left Tarascon over three months, and still the lion-slayer had not started. After all, blinded by a new mirage, our candid hero may have imagined in perfectly good faith that he had gone to Algeria. On the strength of having related his future hunts, he may have believed he had performed them as sincerely as he fancied he had hoisted the consular flag and fired on the Tartars, zizz, phit, bang! at Shanghai.

Unfortunately, granting Tartarin was this time again dupe of an illusion, his fellow-townsfolk were not. When, after the quarter's expectation, they perceived that the hunter had not packed even a collar box, they commenced murmuring.

"This is going to turn out like the Shanghai expedition," remarked Costecalde, smiling.

The gunsmith's comment was welcomed all over town, for nobody believed any longer in their late idol. The simpletons and poltroons—all the fellows of Bézuquet's stamp, whom a flea would put to flight, and who could not fire a shot without closing their eyes—were conspicuously pitiless. In the club-rooms or on the esplanade, they accosted poor Tartarin with bantering mien,—

"And furthermore, when is that trip coming off?"

In Costecalde's shop, his opinions gained no credence, for the cap-poppers renounced their chief!

Next, epigrams dropped into the affair. Chief Judge Ladevèze, who willingly paid court in his leisure hours to the native Muse, composed in local dialect a song which won much success. It told of a sportsman called "Master Gervais," whose dreaded rifle was bound to exterminate all the lions in Africa to the very last. Unluckily, this terrible gun was of a strange kind: "though loaded daily, it never *went off*."

"It never *went off*"—you will catch the drift.

In less than no time, this ditty became popular; and when Tartarin came by, the longshoremen and the little shoe-blacks before his door sang in chorus,—

> "Muster Jarvey's roifle
>   Allus gittin' chaarged;
> Muster Jarvey's roifle
>   'll hev to git enlaarged;
> Muster Jarvey's roifle's
>   Loaded oft—don't scoff;
> Muster Jarvey's roifle
>   Nivver do go off!"

But it was shouted out from a safe distance, on account of the double muscles.

Oh, the fragility of Tarascon's fads!

The great object himself feigned to see and hear nothing; but, under the surface, this sullen and venomous petty warfare much afflicted him. He felt aware that Tarascon was slipping out of his grip, and that popular favour was going to others; and this made him suffer horribly.

Ah, the huge bowl of popularity! it's all very well to have a seat in front of it, but what a scalding you catch when it is overturned!

Notwithstanding his pain, Tartarin smiled and peacefully jogged on in the same life as if nothing untoward had happened. Still, the mask of jovial heedlessness glued by pride on his face would sometimes be suddenly detached. Then, in lieu of laughter, one saw grief and indignation. Thus it was that one morning, when the little blackguards yelped " Muster Jarvey's Roifle " beneath his window, the wretches' voices rose even into the poor great man's room, where he was shaving before the glass. (Tartarin wore a full beard, but as it grew very thick, he was obliged to keep it trimmed orderly.)

All at once the window was violently opened, and Tartarin appeared in shirt-sleeves and nightcap, smothered in lather, flourishing his razor and shaving-brush, and roaring with a formidable voice,—

" Let's have it out with swords, gentlemen, not pins! "

Fine words, worthy of history's record, with only the blemish that they were addressed to little scamps not higher than their boot-boxes, and who were quite incapable of holding a smallsword.

XII

A MEMORABLE DIALOGUE IN THE LITTLE BAOBAB VILLA

AMID the general falling off, the army alone stuck out firmly for Tartarin. Brave Commandant Bravida (the former captain in the Army Clothing Department) continued to show him the same esteem as ever. " He's game! " he persisted in saying—an assertion, I beg to believe, fully worth the chemist Bézuquet's. Not once did the brave officer let out any allusion to the trip to Africa; but when the public clamour grew too loud, he determined to have his say.

One evening the luckless Tartarin was in his study, in a brown study himself, when he saw the commandant stride in, stern, wearing black gloves, buttoned up to his ears.

" Tartarin," said the ex-captain authoritatively, " Tartarin, you'll have to go! "

And there he dwelt, erect in the doorway frame, grand and rigid as embodied Duty. Tartarin of Tarascon comprehended all the sense in " Tartarin, you'll have to go! "

Very pale, he rose and looked around with a softened eye

upon the cosy snuggery, tightly closed in, full of warmth and tender light—upon the commodious easy chair, his books, the carpet, the white blinds of the windows, beyond which trembled the slenger twigs of the little garden. Then, advancing towards the brave officer, he took his hand, grasped it energetically, and said in a voice somewhat tearful, but stoical for all that,—

"I *am* going, Bravida."

And go he did, as he said he would. Not straight off though, for it takes time to get the paraphernalia together.

To begin with, he ordered of Bompard two large boxes bound with brass, and an inscription to be on them,—

TARTARIN, OF TARASCON.

FIREARMS, &c.

The binding in brass and the lettering took much time. He also ordered at Tastavin's a showy album, in which to keep a diary and his impressions of travel; for a man cannot help having an idea or two strike him even when he is busy lion-hunting.

Next he had over from Marseilles a down-right cargo of tinned eatables, pemmican compressed in cakes for making soup, a new pattern shelter-tent, opening out and packing up in a minute, sea-boots, a couple of umbrellas, a waterproof coat, and blue spectacles to ward off ophthalmia. To conclude, Bézuquet the chemist made him up a miniature portable medicine chest stuffed with diachylon plaister, arnica camphor, and medicated vinegar.

Poor Tartarin! he did not take these safeguards on his own behalf; but he hoped, by dint of precaution and delicate attentions, to allay Sancho-Tartarin's fury, who, since the start was fixed, never left off raging day or night.

XIII

THE DEPARTURE

EFTSOON arrived the great and solemn day. From dawn all Tarascon had been on foot, encumbering the Avignon road and the approaches to Baobab Villa. People were up at the windows, on the roofs, and in the trees; the Rhône bargees, porters, dredgers, shoe-blacks, gentry, tradesfolk, warpers and weavers, taffety-workers, the club members, in short the whole town; moreover, people from Beaucaire had come over the bridge, market-gardeners from the environs, carters in their huge carts with ample tilts, vine-dressers upon handsome mules, tricked out with ribbons, streamers, bells, rosettes, and jingles, and even, here and there, a few pretty maids from Arles, come on the pillion behind their sweethearts, with bonny blue ribbons round the head, upon little iron-grey Camargue horses.

All this swarm squeezed and jostled before our good Tartarin's door, who was going to slaughter lions in the land of the Turks.

For Tarascon, Algeria, Africa, Greece, Persia, Turkey, and Mesopotamia, all form one great hazy country, almost a myth, called the land of the Turks. They say "*Tur's,*" but that's a linguistic digression.

In the midst of all this throng, the cap-poppers bustled to and fro, proud of their captain's triumph, leaving glorious wakes where they had passed.

In front of the Indian fig-tree house were two large trucks. From time to time the door would open, and allow several persons to be spied, gravely lounging about the little garden. At every new box the throng started and trembled. The articles were named in a loud voice,—

"That there's the shelter-tent; these the potted meats; that's the physic-chest; these the gun-cases,"—the cap-poppers giving explanations.

All of a sudden, about ten o'clock, there was a great stir in the multitude, for the garden gate banged open.

" Here he is! here he is! " they shouted.

It was he indeed. When he appeared upon the threshold, two outcries of stupefaction burst from the assemblage,—

" He's a Turk! " " He's got on spectacles! "

In truth, Tartarin of Tarascon had deemed it his duty, on going to Algeria, to don the Algerian costume. Full white linen trousers, small tight vest with metal buttons, a red sash two feet wide around the waist, the neck bare and the forehead shaven, and a vast red fez, or *chechia*, on his head, with something like a long blue tassel thereto. Together with this, two heavy guns, one on each shoulder, a broad hunting-knife in the girdle, a bandolier across the breast, a revolver on the hip, swinging in its patent leather case— that is all. No, I cry your pardon, I was forgetting the spectacles—a pantomimically large pair of azure barnacles, which came in patly to temper what was rather too fierce in the bearing of our hero.

" Long life to Tartarin! hip, hip, hurrah for Tartarin! " roared the populace.

The great man smiled, but did not salute, on account of the firearms hindering him. Moreover, he knew now on what popular favour depends; it may even be that in the depths of his soul he cursed his terrible fellow-townsfolk, who obliged him to go away and leave his pretty little pleasure-house with whitened walls and green venetians. But there was no show of this.

Calm and proud, although a little pallid, he stepped out on the footway, glanced at the hand-carts, and, seeing all was right, lustily took the road to the railway-station, without even once looking back towards Baobab Villa. Behind him marched the brave Commandant Bravida, Ladevèze the Chief Judge, Costecalde the gunsmith next, and then all the sportsmen who pop at caps, preceding the hand-carts and the rag, tag, and bobtail.

Before the station the station-master awaited them, an old African veteran of 1830, who shook Tartarin's hand many times with fervency.

The Paris-to-Marseilles express was not yet in, so Tartarin and his staff went into the waiting-rooms. To prevent the place being overrun, the station-master ordered the gates to be closed.

In Tarascon

During a quarter of an hour, Tartarin promenaded up and down in the rooms in the midst of his brother marksmen, speaking to them of his journey and his hunting, and promising to send them skins; they put their names down in his memorandum-book for a lionskin apiece, as waltzers book for a dance.

Gentle and placid as Socrates on the point of quaffing the hemlock, the intrepid Tarasconian had a word and a smile for each. He spoke simply, with an affable mien; it looked as if, before departing, he meant to leave behind him a wake of charms, regrets, and pleasant memories. On hearing their leader speak in this way, all the sportsmen felt tears well up, and some were stung with remorse, to wit, Chief Judge Ladevèze and the chemist Bézuquet. The railway employés blubbered in the corners, whilst the outer public squinted through the bars and bellowed: "Long live Tartarin!"

At length the bell rang. A dull rumble was heard, and a piercing whistle shook the vault.

"The Marseilles express, gen'lemen!"

"Good-bye, Tartarin! Good luck, old fellow!"

"Good-bye to you all!" murmured the great man, as, with his arms around the brave Commandant Bravida, he embraced his dear native place collectively in him. Then he leaped out upon the platform, and clambered into a carriage full of Parisian ladies, who were ready to die with fright at sight of this stranger with so many pistols and rifles.

XIV

THE PORT OF MARSEILLES—"ALL ABOARD, ALL ABOARD!"

UPON the 1st of December 18—, in clear, brilliant, splendid weather, under a south winter sun, the startled inhabitants of Marseilles beheld a *Turk* come down the Canebière, or their Regent Street. A *Turk*, a regular Turk—never had such a one been seen; and yet, Heaven knows, there is no lack of Turks at Marseilles.

The Turk in question—have I any necessity of telling you it was the great Tartarin of Tarascon?—waddled along the quays, followed by his gun-cases, medicine-chest, and tinned comestibles, to reach the landing-stage of the Touache Company and the mail steamer the *Zouave*, which was to transport him over the sea.

With his ears still ringing with the home applause, intoxicated by the glare of the heavens and the reek of the sea, Tartarin fairly beamed as he stepped out with a lofty head, and between his guns on his shoulders, looking with all his eyes upon that wondrous, dazzling harbour of Marseilles, which he saw for the first time. The poor fellow believed he was dreaming. He fancied his name was Sinbad the Sailor, and that he was roaming in one of those fantastic cities abundant in the *Arabian Nights*. As far as eye could reach there spread a forest of masts and spars, cris-crossing in every way.

Flags of all countries floated—English, American, Russian, Swedish, Greek and Tunisian.

The vessels lay alongside the wharves—ay, head on, so that their bowsprits stuck up out over the strand like rows of bayonets. Over it, too, sprawled the mermaids, goddesses, madonnas, and other figure-heads in carved and painted wood which gave names to the ships—all worn by sea-water, split, mildewed, and dripping. Ever and anon, between the hulls, a patch of harbour like watered silk splashed with oil. In the intervals of the yards and booms, what seemed swarms of flies prettily spotted the blue sky. These were the ship-boys, hailing one another in all languages.

On the waterside, amidst thick green or black rivulets coming down from the soap-factories loaded with oil and soda, bustled a mass of custom-house officers, messengers, porters, and truckmen with their *bogheys*, or trolleys, drawn by Corsican ponies.

There were shops selling quaint articles, smoky shanties where sailors were cooking their own queer messes, dealers in pipes, monkeys, parrots, ropes, sailcloth, fanciful curios, amongst which were mingled higgledy-piggledy old culverins, huge gilded lanterns, worn-out pulley-blocks, rusty flukeless anchors, chafed cordage, battered speaking-trumpets, and marine glasses almost contemporary with the Ark. Sellers of mussels and clams squatted beside their heaps of shellfish and yawped their goods. Seamen rolled by with tar-pots, smoking soup-bowls, and big baskets full of cuttlefish, from which they went to wash the ink in the milky waters of the fountains.

Everywhere a prodigious collection of all kinds of goods: silks, minerals, wood in stacks, lead in pigs, cloths, sugars, caruba wood logs, colza seed, liquorice sticks, sugar-canes. The East and the West cheek by jowl, even to pyramids of Dutch cheeses which the Genoese were dyeing red by contact with their hands.

Yonder was the corn market: porters discharging sacks down the shoots of lofty elevators upon the pier, and loose grain rolling as a golden torrent through a blonde dust. Men in red skullcaps were sifting it as they caught it in large asses'-skin sieves, and loading it upon carts which took their millward way, followed by a regiment of women and youngsters with wisps and gleaning-baskets. Farther on, the dry docks, where large vessels were laid low on their sides till their yards dipped in the water; they were singed with thorn-bushes to free them of sea-weed; there rose an odour of pitch, and the deafening clatter of the sheathers coppering the bottoms with broad sheets of yellow metal.

At whiles a gap in between the masts, in which Tartarin could see the haven mouth, where the vessels came and went: a British frigate off for Malta, dainty and thoroughly washed down, with the officer in primrose gloves, or a large home-port brig hauling out in the midst of uproar and oaths, whilst the fat captain, in a high silk hat and frockcoat, ordered the operations in *Provençal* dialect. Other craft were making forth under all sail, and, still farther out, more were slowly looming up in the sunshine as if they were sailing in the air.

All the time a frightful riot, the rumbling of carts, the " Haul all, haul away! " of the shipmen, oaths, songs, steamboat whistles, the bugles and drums in Forts Saint Jean and Saint Nicolas, the bells of the Major, the Accoules, and Saint Victor; with the mistral atop of all, catching up the noises and clamour, and rolling them up together with a furious shaking, till confounded with its own voice, which entoned a mad, wild, heroic melody like a grand charging tune—one that filled hearers with a longing to be off, and the farther the better—a craving for wings.

It was to the sound of this splendid blast that the intrepid Tartarin of Tarascon embarked for the land of lions.

EPISODE THE SECOND

AMONG "THE TURKS"

I

THE PASSAGE—THE FIVE POSITIONS OF THE FEZ—THE THIRD
EVENING OUT—MERCY UPON US!

JOYFUL would I be, my dear readers, if I were a painter—a great artist, I mean—in order to set under your eyes, at the head of this second episode, the various positions taken by Tartarin's red cap in the three days' passage it made on board of the *Zouave*, between France and Algeria.

First would I show you it at the steaming out, upon deck, arrogant and heroic as it was, forming a glory round that handsome Tarasconian head. Next would I show you it at the harbour-mouth, when the bark began to caper upon the waves; I would depict it for you all of a quake in astonishment, and as though already experiencing the preliminary qualms of sea-sickness.

Then, in the Gulf of the Lion, proportionably to the nearing the open sea, where the white caps heaved harder, I would make you behold it wrestling with the tempest, and standing on end upon the hero's cranium, with its mighty mane of blue wool bristling out in the spray and breeze.

Position Fourth: at six in the afternoon, with the Corsican coast in view; the unfortunate *chechia* hangs over the ship's side, and lamentably stares down as though to plumb the depths of ocean. Finally and lastly, the Fifth Position: at the back of a narrow state-room, in a box-bed so small it seemed one drawer in a nest of them, something shapeless rolled on the pillow with moans of desolation. This was the fez—the fez so defiant at the sailing, now reduced to the vulgar conditions of a nightcap, and pulled down over the very ears of the head of a pallid and convulsed sufferer.

How the people of Tarascon would have kicked themselves for having constrained the great Tartarin to leave home, if they had but seen him stretched in the bunk in the dull, wan gleam through the dead-light, amid the sickly odour of cooking and wet wood—the heart-heaving perfume of mailboats; if they had but heard him gurgle at every turn of the screw, wail for tea every five minutes, and swear at the steward in a childish treble!

On my word of honour as a story-teller, the poor *Turk* would have made a pasteboard dummy pity him.

Suddenly, overcome by the nausea, the hapless victim had not even the power to undo the Algerian girdle-cloth, or lay aside his armoury; the lumpy-handled hunting-sword pounded his ribs, and the leather revolver-case made his thigh raw. To finish him arose the taunts of Sancho-Tartarin who never ceased to groan and inveigh,—

"Well, for the biggest kind of imbecile, you are *the* finest specimen! I told you truly how it would be. Ha, ha! you were bound to go to Africa, of course! Well, old merriman, now you are going to Africa, how do you like it?"

The cruellest part of it was that, from the retreat where he was moaning, the hapless invalid could hear the passengers in the grand saloon laughing, munching, singing, and playing at cards. On board the *Zouave* the company was as jolly as numerous, composed of officers going back to join their regiments, ladies from the Marseilles Alcazar Music Hall, strolling-players, a rich Mussulman returning from Mecca, and a very jocular Montenegrin prince, who favoured them with imitations of the low comedians of Paris. Not one of these jokers felt the sea-sickness, and their time was passed in quaffing champagne with the steamer captain, a good fat born Marseillais, who had a wife and family as well at Algiers as at home, and who answered to the merry name of Barbassou.

Tartarin of Tarascon hated this pack of wretches; their mirthfulness deepened his ails.

At length, on the third afternoon, there was such an extraordinary hullabaloo on the deck that our hero was roused out of his long torpor. The ship's bell was ringing, and the seamen's heavy boots ran over the planks.

"Go ahead! Stop her! Turn astern!" barked the

hoarse voice of Captain Barbassou; and then, "Stop her dead!"

There was an abrupt check of movement, a shock, and no more, save the silent rolling of the boat from side to side like a balloon in the air. This strange stillness alarmed the Tarasconian.

"Heaven ha' mercy upon us!" he yelled in a terrifying voice, as, recovering his strength by magic, he bounded out of his berth, and rushed upon deck with his arsenal.

II

"TO ARMS! TO ARMS!"

ONLY the arrival, not a foundering.

The *Zouave* was just gliding into the road-stead—a fine one of black, deep water, but dull and still, almost deserted. On elevated ground ahead rose Algiers, the White City, with its little houses of a dead cream-colour huddling against one another lest they slid into the sea. It was like Meudon slope with a laundress's washing hung out to dry. Over it a vast blue satin sky—and such a blue!

A little restored from his fright, the illustrious Tartarin gazed on the landscape, and listened with respect to the Montenegrin prince, who stood by his side, as he named the different parts of the capital, the Kasbah, the upper town, and the Rue Bab-Azoon. A very finely-brought-up prince was this Montenegrin; moreover, knowing Algeria thoroughly, and fluently speaking Arabic. Hence Tartarin thought of cultivating his acquaintance.

All at once, along the bulwark against which they were leaning, the Tarasconian perceived a row of large black hands clinging to it from over the side. Almost instantly a negro's woolly head shot up before him, and, ere he had time to open his mouth, the deck was overwhelmed on every side by a hundred black or yellow desperadoes, half naked, hideous, and fearsome. Tartarin knew who these pirates were—"they" of course, the celebrated "they" who had too often been hunted after by him in the by-ways of Tarascon.

At last they had decided to meet him face to face. At the outset surprise nailed him to the spot. But when he saw the outlaws fall upon the luggage, tear off the tarpaulin covering, and actually commence the pillage of the ship, then the hero awoke. Whipping out his hunting-sword, "To arms! to arms!" he roared to the passengers; and away he flew, the foremost of all, upon the buccaneers.

"*Ques aco?* What's the stir? What's the matter with you?" exclaimed Captain Barbassou, coming out of the 'tweendecks.

"About time you did turn up, captain! Quick, quick, arm your men!"

"Eh, what for? dash it all!"

"Why, can't you see?"

"See what?"

"There, before you, the corsairs"——

Captain Barbassou stared, bewildered. At this juncture a tall blackamoor tore by with our hero's medicine-chest upon his back.

"You cut-throat! just wait for me!" yelled the Tarasconer as he ran after, with the knife uplifted.

But Barbassou caught him in the spring, and holding him by the waist-sash, bade him be quiet.

"*Tron de ler!* by the throne on high! they're no pirates. It's long since there were any pirates hereabout. Those dark porters are light porters. Ha, ha!"

"P—p—porters?"

"Rather, only come after the luggage to carry it ashore. So put up your cook's galley knife, give me your ticket, and walk off behind that nigger—an honest dog, who will see you to land, and even into a hotel, if you like."

A little abashed, Tartarin handed over his ticket, and falling in behind the representative of the Dark Continent, clambered down by the hanging-ladder into a big skiff dancing alongside. All his effects were already there—boxes, trunks, gun-cases, tinned food,—so cramming up the boat that there was no need to wait for any other passengers. The African scrambled upon the boxes, and squatted there like a baboon, with his knees clutched by his hands. Another negro took the oars. Both laughingly eyed Tartarin, and showed their white teeth.

Standing in the stern-sheets, making that terrifying face which had daunted his fellow-countrymen, the great Tarasconian feverishly fumbled with his hunting-knife haft; for, despite what Barbassou had told him, he was only half at ease as regarded the intention of these ebony-skinned porters, who so little resembled their honest mates of Tarascon.

Five minutes afterwards the skiff landed Tartarin, and he set foot upon the little Barbary wharf, where, three hundred years before, a Spanish galley-slave yclept Miguel Cervantes devised, under the cane of the Algerian taskmaster, a sublime romance which was to bear the title of *Don Quixote*.

III

AN INVOCATION TO CERVANTES—THE DISEMBARKATION— WHERE ARE THE TURKS?—NOT A SIGN OF THEM—DISENCHANTMENT

O MIGUEL CERVANTES SAAVEDRA, if what is asserted be true, to wit, that wherever great men have dwelt some emanation of their spirits wanderingly hovers until the end of ages, then what remained of your essence on the Barbary coast must have quivered with glee on beholding Tartarin of Tarascon disembark, that marvellous type of the French Southerner, in whom was embodied both heroes of your work, Don Quixote and Sancho Panza.

The air was sultry on this occasion. On the wharf, ablaze with sunshine, were half a dozen revenue officers, some Algerians expecting news from France, several squatting Moors who drew at long pipes, and some Maltese mariners dragging large nets, between the meshes of which thousands of sardines glittered like small silver coins.

But hardly had Tartarin set foot on earth before the quay sprang into life and changed its aspect. A horde of savages, still more hideous than the pirates upon the steamer, rose between the stones on the strand and rushed upon the newcomer. Tall Arabs were there, nude under woollen blankets, little Moors in tatters, negroes, Tunisians, Port Mahonese,

M'zabites, hotel servants in white aprons, all yelling and shouting, hooking on his clothes, fighting over his luggage, one carrying away the provender, another his medicine-chest, and pelting him in one fantastic medley with the names of preposterously-entitled hotels.

Bewildered by all this tumult, poor Tartarin wandered to and fro, swore and stormed, went mad, ran after his property, and not knowing how to make these barbarians understand him, speechified them in French, Provençal, and even in dog Latin: "*Rosa*, the rose; *bonus, bona, bonum!*"—all that he knew—but to no purpose. He was not heeded. Happily, like a god in Homer, intervened a little fellow in a yellow-collared tunic, and armed with a long running-footman's cane, who dispersed the whole riff-raff with cudgel-play. He was a policeman of the Algerian capital. Very politely, he suggested Tartarin should put up at the Hotel de l'Europe, and he confided him to its waiters, who carted him and his *impedimenta* thither in several barrows.

At the first steps he took in Algiers, Tartarin of Tarascon opened his eyes widely. Beforehand he had pictured it as an Oriental city—a fairy one, mythological, something between Constantinople and Zanzibar; but it was back into Tarascon he fell. Cafés, restaurants, wide streets, four-storey houses, a little market-place, macadamised, where the infantry band played Offenbachian polkas, whilst fashionably clad gentlemen occupied chairs, drinking beer and eating pancakes, some brilliant ladies, some shaby ones, and soldiers —more soldiers—no end of soldiers, but not a solitary Turk, or, better to say, there was a solitary Turk, and that was he.

Hence he felt a little abashed about crossing the square, for everybody looked at him. The musicians stopped, the Offenbachian polka halting with one foot in the air.

With both guns on his shoulders, and the revolver flapping on his hip, as fierce and stately as Robinson Crusoe, Tartarin gravely passed through the groups; but on arriving at the hotel his powers failed him. All spun and mingled in his head: the departure from Tarascon, the harbour of Marseilles, the voyage, the Montenegrin prince, the corsairs. They had to help him up into a room and disarm and undress him. They began to talk of sending for a medical adviser; but hardly was our hero's head upon the pillow than he set to snoring, so loudly and so heartily that the landlord judged the succour of science useless, and everybody considerately withdrew.

IV

THE FIRST LYING IN WAIT

THREE o'clock was striking by the Government clock when Tartarin awoke. He had slept all the evening, night, and morning, and even a goodish piece of the afternoon. It must be granted, though, that in the last three days the red fez had caught it pretty hot and lively!

Our hero's first thought on opening his eyes was, " I am in the land of the lions! " And—well, why should we not say it?—at the idea that lions were nigh hereabouts, within a couple of steps, almost at hand's reach, and that he would have to disentangle a snarled skein with them, ugh! a deadly chill struck him, and he dived intrepidly under the coverlet.

But, before a moment was over, the outward gaiety, the blue sky, the glowing sun that streamed into the bedchamber, a nice little breakfast that he ate in bed, his window wide open upon the sea, the whole flavoured with an uncommonly good bottle of Crescia wine—it very speedily restored him his former pluckiness.

"Let's out and at the lion!" he exclaimed, throwing off the clothes and briskly dressing himself.

His plan was as follows: he would go forth from the city without saying a word to a soul, plunge into the great desert, await nightfall to ambush himself, and bang away at the first lion who walked up. Then would he return to breakfast in the morning at the hotel, receive the felicitations of the natives, and hire a cart to bring in the quarry.

So he hurriedly armed himself, attached upright on his back the shelter-tent (which, when rolled up, left its centre pole sticking out a clear foot above his head), and descended to the street as stiffly as though he had swallowed it. Not caring to ask the way of anybody, from fear of letting out his project, he turned fairly to the right, and threaded the Bab-Azoon arcade to the very end, where swarms of Algerian Jews watched him pass from their corner ambushes like so many spiders; crossing the Theatre place, he entered the outer ward, and lastly came upon the dusty Mustapha highway.

Upon this was a quaint conglomeration: omnibuses, hackney coaches, *corricolos*, the army service waggons, huge hay-carts drawn by bullocks, squads of Chasseurs d'Afrique, droves of microscopic asses, trucks of Alsatian emigrants, spahis in scarlet cloaks—all filed by in a whirlwind cloud of dust, amidst shouts, songs, and trumpet-calls, between two rows of vile-looking booths, at the doors of which lanky *Mahonnais* women might be seen doing their hair, drinking dens filled with soldiers, and shops of butchers and knackers.

"What rubbish, to din me about the Orient!" grumbled the great Tartarin; "there are not even as many *Turks* here as at Marseilles."

All of a sudden he saw a splendid camel strut by him quite closely, stretching its long legs and puffing out its throat like a turkey-cock, and that made his heart throb. Camels already, eh? Lions could not be far off now; and, indeed, in five minutes' time he did see a whole band of lion-hunters coming his way under arms.

"Cowards!" thought our hero as he skirted them; "downright cowards, to go at a lion in companies and with dogs!"

For it never could occur to him that anything but lions were objects of the chase in Algeria. For all that, these Nimrods wore such complacent phizzes of retired tradesmen, and their style of lion-hunting with dogs and game-bags was so patriarchal, that the Tarasconian, a little perplexed, deemed it incumbent to question one of the gentlemen.

"And furthermore, comrade, is the sport good?"

"Not bad," responded the other, regarding the speaker's imposing warlike equipment with a scared eye.

"Killed any?"

"Rather! Not so bad—only look."

Whereupon the Algerian sportsman showed that it was rabbits and woodcocks stuffing out the bag.

"What! do you call that your bag? Do you put such like in your bag?"

"Where else should I put 'em?"

"But it's such little game."

"Some run small and some run large," observed the hunter.

In haste to catch up with his companions, he joined them with several long strides. The dauntless Tartarin remained rooted in the middle of the road with stupefaction.

"Pooh!" he ejaculated, after a moment's reflection, "these are jokers. They haven't killed anything whatever;" and he went his way.

Already the houses became scarcer, and so did the passengers. Dark came on and objects were blurred, though Tartarin walked on for half an hour more, when he stopped, for it was night. A moonless night, too, but sprinkled with stars. On the highroad there was nobody. The hero concluded that lions are not stage-coaches, and would not of their own choice travel the main ways. So he wheeled into the fields, where there were brambles and ditches and bushes at every step, but he kept on nevertheless.

But suddenly he halted.

"I smell lions about here!" said our friend, sniffing right and left.

V

BANG, BANG!

CERTAINLY a great wilderness, bristling with odd plants of that Oriental kind which look like wicked creatures. Under the feeble starlight their magnified shadows barred the ground in every way. On the right loomed up confusedly the heavy mass of a mountain—perhaps the Atlas range. On the heart-hand, the invisible sea hollowly rolling. The very spot to attract wild beasts.

With one gun laid before him and the other in his grasp, Tartarin of Tarascon went down on one knee and waited an hour, ay, a good couple, and nothing turned up. Then he bethought him how, in his books, the great lion-slayers never went out hunting without having a lamb or a kid along with them, which they tied up a space before them, and set bleating or baa-ing by jerking its foot with a string. Not having any goat, the Tarasconer had the idea of employing an imitation, and he set to crying in a tremulous voice,—

"Baa-a-a!"

At first it was done very softly, because at bottom he was a little alarmed lest the lion should hear him; but as nothing came, he baa-ed more loudly. Still nothing. Losing patience, he resumed many times running at the top of his voice, till the "Baa, baa, baa!" came out with so much power that the goat began to be mistakable for a bull.

Unexpectedly, a few steps in front, some gigantic black thing appeared. He was hushed. This thing lowered its head, sniffed the ground, bounded up, rolled over, and darted off at the gallop, but returned and stopped short. Who could doubt it was the lion? for now its four short legs could plainly be seen, its formidable mane and its large eyes gleaming in the gloom.

Up went his gun into position. Fire's the word! and bang, bang! it was done. And immediately there was a leap back and the drawing of the hunting-knife. To the Tarasconian's shot a terrible roaring replied.

"He's got it!" cried our good Tartarin as, steadying himself on his sturdy supporters, he prepared to receive the brute's charge.

But it had more than its fill, and galloped off, howling. He did not budge, for he expected to see the female mate appear, as the story-books always lay it down she should.

Unhappily, no female came. After two or three hours' waiting the Tarasconian grew tired. The ground was damp, the night was getting cool, and the sea-breeze pricked sharply.

"I have a good mind to take a nap till daylight," he said to himself.

To avoid catching rheumatism, he had recourse to his patent tent. But here's where Old Nick interfered! This tent was of so very ingenious a construction that he could not manage to open it. In vain did he toil over it and perspire an hour through—the confounded apparatus would not come unfolded. There are some umbrellas which amuse themselves under torrential rains with just such tricks upon you. Fairly tired out with the struggle, the victim dashed down the machine and lay upon it, swearing like the regular Southron he was.

"*Tar, tar, rar, tar! tar, rar, tar!*"

"What on earth's that?" wondered Tartarin, suddenly aroused.

It was the bugles of the Chasseurs d'Afrique sounding the turn-out in the Mustapha barracks. The stupefied lion-slayer rubbed his eyes, for he had believed himself out in the boundless wilderness; and do you know where he really was?—in a field of artichokes, between a cabbage-garden and a patch of beets. His Sahara grew kitchen vegetables.

Close to him, on the pretty verdant slope of Upper Mustapha, the snowy villas glowed in the rosy rising sun: anybody would believe himself in the neighbourhood of Marseilles, amongst its *bastides* and *bastidons*.

The commonplace and kitchen-gardenish aspect of this sleep-steeped country much astonished the poor man, and put him in bad humour.

"These folk are crazy," he reasoned, "to plant artichokes in the prowling-ground of lions; for, in short, I have not been dreaming. Lions have come here, and there's the proof."

What he called the proof was blood-spots left behind the beast in its flight. Bending over this ruddy trail, with his eye on the look-out and his revolver in his fist, the valiant Tarasconian went from artichoke to artichoke up to a little field of oats. In the trampled grass was a pool of blood, and in the midst of the pool, lying on its flank, with a large wound in the head, was a—guess what?

"A lion, of course!"

Not a bit of it! An ass!—one of those little donkeys so common in Algeria, where they are called *bourriquots*.

VI

ARRIVAL OF THE FEMALE—A TERRIBLE COMBAT—" GAME FELLOWS MEET HERE!"

LOOKING on his hapless victim, Tartarin's first impulse was one of vexation. There is such a wide gap between a lion and poor Jack! His second feeling was one of pity. The poor *bourriquot* was so pretty and looked so kindly. The hide on his still warm sides heaved and fell like waves. Tartarin knelt down, and strove with the end of his Algerian sash to stanch the blood; and all you can imagine in the way of touchingness was offered by the picture of this great man tending this little ass.

At the touch of the silky cloth the donkey, who had not twopennyworth of life in him, opened his large grey eye and winked his long ears two or three times, as much as to say, " Oh, thank you!" before a final spasm shook it from head to tail, whereafter it stirred no more.

" Noiraud! Blackey!" suddenly screamed a voice, choking with anguish, as the branches in a thicket hard by moved at the same time.

Tartarin had no more than enough time to rise and stand upon guard. This was the female!

She rushed up, fearsome and roaring, under form of an old Alsatian woman, her hair in a kerchief, armed with large red umbrella, and calling for her ass, till all the echoes of Mustapha rang. It certainly would have been better for Tartarin to have had to deal with a lioness in fury than this old virago. In vain did the luckless sportsman try to make her understand how the blunder had occurred, and he had mistaken " *Noiraud* " for a lion. The harridan believed he was making fun of her, and uttering energetical " *Der Teufels !* " fell upon our hero to bang him with the gingham. A little bewildered, Tartarin defended himself as best he could, warding off the blows with his rifle, streaming with perspiration, panting, jumping about, and crying out,—

" But, Madame, but "——

Much good his buts were! Madame was dull of hearing, and her blows continued hard as ever.

Fortunately a third party arrived on the battlefield, the Alsatian's husband, of the same race; a roadside innkeeper, as well as a very good ready-reckoner, which was better. When he saw what kind of a customer he had to deal with —a slaughterer who only wanted to pay the value of his victim—he disarmed his better-half, and they came to an understanding.

Tartarin gave two hundred francs, the donkey being worth about ten—at least that is the current price in the Arab markets. Then poor Blackey was laid to rest at the root of a fig-tree, and the Alsatian, raised to joviality by the colour of the Tarascan ducats, invited the hero to have a quencher with him in his wine-shop, which stood only a few steps off on the edge of the highway. Every Sunday the sportsmen from the city came there to regale of a morning, for the plain abounded with game, and there was no better place for rabbits for two leagues around.

"How about lions?" inquired Tartarin.

The Alsatian stared at him, greatly astounded.

"Lions!"

"Yes, lions. Don't you see them sometimes?" resumed the poor fellow, with less confidence.

The Boniface burst out in laughter.

"Ho, ho! bless us! lions! What would we do with lions here?"

"Are there, then, none in Algeria?"

"'Pon my faith, I never saw any, albeit I have been twenty years in the colony. Still, I believe I have heard tell of such a thing—leastwise, I fancy the newspapers said —but that is ever so much farther inland—down South, you know"——

At this point they reached the hostelry, a suburban pot-house, with a withered green bough over the door, crossed billiard-cues painted on the wall, and this harmless sign over a picture of wild rabbits feeding,—

"*GAME FELLOWS MEET HERE.*"

"Game fellows!" It made Tartarin think of Captain Bravida.

VII

ABOUT AN OMNIBUS, A MOORISH BEAUTY, AND A WREATH OF JESSAMINE

COMMON people would have been discouraged by such a first adventure, but men of Tartarin's mettle do not easily get cast down.

"The lions are in the South, are they?" mused the hero. "Very well, then. South I go."

As soon as he had swallowed his last mouthful he jumped up, thanked his host, nodded good-bye to the old hag without any ill-will, dropped a final tear over the hapless Blackey, and quickly returned to Algiers, with the firm intention of packing up and starting that very day for the South.

The Mustapha highroad seemed, unfortunately, to have stretched since overnight; and what a sun and dust there were, and what a weight in that shelter-tent! Tartarin did not feel to have the courage to walk to the town, and he beckoned to the first omnibus coming along, and climbed in.

Oh, our poor Tartarin of Tarascon! how much better it would have been for his name and fame not to have stepped into that fatal ark on wheels, but to have continued on his road afoot, at the risk of falling suffocated beneath the burden of the atmosphere, the tent, and his heavy double-barrelled rifles.

When Tartarin got in the 'bus was full. At the end, with his nose in his prayer-book, sat a large and black-bearded vicar from town; facing him was a young Moorish merchant smoking coarse cigarettes, and a Maltese sailor and four or five Moorish women muffled up in white cloths, so that only their eyes could be spied. These ladies had been to offer up prayers in the Abdel Kader cemetery; but this funereal visit did not seem to have much saddened them, for they could be heard chuckling and chattering between themselves under their coverings whilst munching pastry. Tartarin fancied that they watched him narrowly. One in particular, seated over against him, had fixed her eyes upon his, and never took them off all the drive. Although the dame was veiled, the liveliness of the big black eyes, lengthened out by *k'hol;* a delightfully slender wrist loaded with gold bracelets, of which a glimpse was given from time to time among the folds; the sound of her voice, the graceful, almost childlike, movements of the head, all revealed that a young, pretty, and lovable creature bloomed underneath the veil. The unfortunate Tartarin did not know where to shrink. The fond, mute gaze of these splendrous Oriental orbs agitated him, perturbed him, and made him feel like dying with flushes of heat and fits of cold shivers.

To finish him, the lady's slipper meddled in the onslaught: he felt the dainty thing wander and frisk about over his heavy hunting boots like a tiny red mouse. What could he do? Answer the glance and the pressure, of course. Ay, but what about the consequences? A loving intrigue in the East is a terrible matter! With his romantic southern nature, the honest Tarasconian saw himself already falling into the grip of the eunuchs, to be decapitated, or better— we mean, worse—than that, sewn up in a leather sack and sunk in the sea with his head under his arm beside him. This somewhat cooled him. In the meantime the little slipper continued its proceedings, and the eyes, widely open opposite him like twin black velvet flowers, seemed to say,—

" Come, cull us! "

The 'bus stopped on the Theatre place, at the mouth of the Rue Bab-Azoon. One by one, embedded in their voluminous trousers, and drawing their mufflers around them with wild grace, the Moorish women alighted. Tartarin's confrontatress was the last to rise, and in doing so her countenance skimmed so closely to our hero's that her breath enveloped him—a veritable nosegay of youth and freshness, with an indescribable after-tang of musk, jessamine, and pastry.

The Tarasconian stood out no longer. Intoxicated with love, and ready for anything, he darted out after the beauty. At the rumpling sound of his belts and boots she turned, laid a finger on her veiled mouth, as who would say, " Hush! " and with the other hand quickly tossed him a little wreath of sweet-scented jessamine flowers. Tartarin of Tarascon stooped to pick it up; but as he was rather clumsy, and much overburdened with implements of war, the operation took rather long. When he did straighten up, with the jessamine garland upon his heart, the donatrix had vanished.

VIII

YE LIONS OF THE ATLAS, REPOSE IN PEACE!

LIONS of the Altas, sleep!—sleep tranquilly at the back of your lairs amid the aloes and cacti. For a few days to come, any way, Tartarin of Tarascon will not massacre you. For the time being, all his warlike paraphernalia, gun-cases, medicine-chest, alimentary preserves, dwelt peacefully under cover in a corner of room 36 in the Hotel de l'Europe.

Sleep with no fear, great red lions, the Tarasconian is engaged in looking up that Moorish charmer. Since the adventure in the omnibus, the unfortunate swain perpetually fancied he felt the fidgeting of that petty red mouse upon his huge backwoods trapper's foot; and the sea-breeze fanning his lips was ever scented, do what he would, with a love-exciting odour of sweetcakes and patchouli.

He hungered for his indispensable light of the harem! and he meant to behold her anew.

But it was no joke of a task. To find one certain person in a city of a hundred thousand souls, only known by the eyes, breath, and slipper,—none but a son of Tarascon, panoplied by love, would be capable of attempting such an adventure.

The plague is that, under their broad white mufflers, all the Moorish women resemble one another; besides, they do not go about much, and to see them, a man has to climb up into the native or upper town, the city of the " Turks," and that is a regular cut-throat's den.

Little black alleys, very narrow, climbing perpendicularly up between mysterious house-walls, whose roofs lean to touching and form a tunnel; low doors, and sad, silent little casements well barred and grated. Moreover, on both hands, stacks of darksome stalls, wherein ferocious " Turks " smoked long pipes stuck between glittering teeth in piratical heads with white eyes, and mumbled in undertones as if hatching wicked attacks.

To say that Tartarin traversed this grisly place without any emotion would be putting forth falsehood. On the contrary, he was much affected, and the stout fellow only went up the obscure lanes, where his corporation took up all the width, with the utmost precaution, his eye skinned, and his finger on his revolver trigger, in the same manner as he went to the clubhouse at Tarascon. At any moment he expected to have a whole gang of eunuchs and janissaries drop upon his back, yet the longing to behold that dark damsel again gave him a giant's strength and boldness.

For a full week the undaunted Tartarin never quitted the high town. Yes; for all that period he might have been seen cooling his heels before the Turkish bath-houses, awaiting the hour when the ladies came forth in troops, shivering and still redolent of soap and hot water; or squatting at the doorways of mosques, puffing and melting in trying to get out of his big boots in order to enter the temples.

Betimes at nightfall, when he was returning heart-broken at not having discovered anything at either bagnio or mosque, our man from Tarascon, in passing mansions, would hear monotonous songs, smothered twanging of guitars, thumping of tambourines, and feminine laughter-peals, which would make his heart beat.

"Haply she is there!" he would say to himself.

Thereupon, granting the street was unpeopled, he would go up to one of these dwellings, lift the heavy knocker of the low postern, and timidly rap. The songs and merriment would instantly cease. There would be audible behind the wall nothing excepting low, dull flutterings as in a slumbering aviary.

"Let's stick to it, old boy," our hero would think. "Something will befall us yet."

What most often befell him was the contents of the cold-water jug on the head, or else peel of oranges and Barbary figs; never anything more serious.

Well might the lions of the Atlas Mountains doze in peace.

IX

PRINCE GREGORY OF MONTENEGRO

It was two long weeks that the unfortunate Tartarin had been seeking his Algerian flame, and most likely he would have been seeking after her to this day if the little god kind to lovers had not come to his help under the shape of a Montenegrin nobleman.

It happened as follows.

Every Saturday night in winter there is a masked ball at the Grand Theatre of Algiers, just as at the Paris Opera-House. It is the undying and ever tasteless county fancy dress ball—very few people on the floor, several castaways from the Parisian students' ball-rooms or midnight dance-houses, Joans of Arc following the army, faded characters out of the Gavarni costume-book of 1840, and half-a-dozen laundress's underlings who are aiming to make loftier conquests, but still preserve a faint perfume of their former life —garlic and saffron sauce. The real spectacle is not there, but in the green-room, transformed for the nonce into a hall of green cloth or gaming saloon.

An enfevered and motley mob hustle one another around the long green table-covers: Turcos out for the day and staking their double halfpence, Moorish traders from the native town, negroes, Maltese, colonists from the inland, who have come forty leagues in order to risk on a turning card the price of a plough or of a yoke of oxen; all a-quivering, pale, clenching their teeth, and with that singular, wavering, sidelong look of the gamester, become a squint from always staring at the same card in the lay-out.

A little apart are the tribes of Algerian Jews, playing among acquaintances. The men are in the Oriental costume, hideously varied with blue stockings and velvet caps. The puffy and flabby women sit up stiffly in tight golden bodices. Grouped around the tables, the whole tribe wail, squeal, combine, reckon on the fingers, and play but little. Now and anon, however, after long conferences, some old patriarch, with a beard like those of saints by the Old Masters, detaches

Among "The Turks"

himself from the party and goés to risk the family *duro*. As long as the game lasted there would be a scintillation of Hebraic eyes directed on the board—dreadful black diamonds, which made the gold pieces shiver, and ended by gently attracting them, as if drawn by a thread. Then arose wrangles, quarrels, battles, oaths of every land, mad outcries in all tongues, knives flashing out, the guard marching in, and the money disappearing.

It was into the thick of this saturnalia that the great Tartarin came straying one evening to find oblivion and heart's ease.

He was roving alone through the gathering, brooding about his Moorish beauty, when two angered voices arose suddenly from a gaming-table above all the clamour and chink of coin.

"I tell you, M'sieu, that I am twenty francs short!"

"Stuff, M'sieu!"

"Stuff yourself, M'sieu!"

"You shall learn whom you are addressing, M'sieu!"

"I am dying to do that, M'sieu!"

"I am Prince Gregory of Montenegro, M'sieu."

Upon this title Tartarin, much excited, cleft the throng and placed himself in the foremost rank, proud and happy to find his prince again, the Montenegrin noble of such politeness whose acquaintance he had begun on board of the mail steamer. Unfortunately the title of Highness, which had so dazzled the worthy Tarasconian, did not produce the slightest impression upon the Chasseurs officer with whom the noble had his dispute.

"I am much the wiser!" observed the military gentleman sneeringly; and turning to the bystanders he added: "'Prince Gregory of Montenegro'—who knows any such a person? Nobody!"

The indignant Tartarin took one step forward.

"Allow me. I know the *prance*," said he, in a very firm voice, and with his finest Tarasconian accent.

The light cavalry officer eyed him hard for a moment, and then, shrugging his shoulders, returned,—

"Come, that is good! Just you two share the twenty francs lacking between you, and let us talk no more on the score."

Whereupon he turned his back upon them and mixed with the crowd. The stormy Tartarin was going to rush after him, but the prince prevented that.

"Let him go. I can manage my own affairs."

Taking the interventionist by the arm, he drew him rapidly out of doors. When they were upon the square, Prince Gregory of Montenegro lifted his hat off, extended his hand to our hero, and as he but dimly remembered his name, he began in a vibrating voice,—

"Monsieur Barbarin——"

"Tartarin!" prompted the other, timidly.

"Tartarin, Barbarin, no matter! Between us henceforward it is a league of life and death!"

The Montenegrin noble shook his hand with fierce energy. You may infer that the Tarasconian was proud.

"*Prance, prance!*" he repeated enthusiastically.

In a quarter of an hour subsequently the two gentlemen were installed in the Platanes Restaurant, an agreeable late supper-house, with terraces running out over the sea, where, before a hearty Russian salad, seconded by a nice Crescia wine, they renewed the friendship.

You cannot imagine any one more bewitching than this Montenegrin prince. Slender, fine, with crisp hair curled by the tongs, shaved "a week under" and pumice-stoned on that, bestarred with out-of-the-way decorations, he had the wily eye, the fondling gestures, and vaguely the accent of an Italian, which gave him an air of Cardinal Mazarin without his chin-tuft and moustaches. He was deeply versed in the Latin tongues, and lugged in quotations from Tacitus, Horace, and Cæsar's Commentaries at every opening.

Of an old noble strain, it appeared that his brothers had had him exiled at the age of ten, on account of his liberal opinions, since which time he had roamed the world for pleasure and instruction as a philosophical noble. A singular coincidence! the prince had spent three years in Tarascon; and as Tartarin showed amazement at never having met him at the club or on the esplanade, His Highness evasively remarked that he never went about. Through delicacy, the Tarasconian did not dare to question further. All great existences have such mysterious nooks.

To sum up, this Signor Gregory was a very genial aristocrat. Whilst sipping the rosy Crescia juice he patiently listened to Tartarin's expatiating on his lovely Moor, and he even promised to find her speedily, as he had full knowledge of the native ladies.

They drank hard and lengthily in toasts to " The ladies of Algiers " and " The freedom of Montenegro ! "

Outside, upon the terrace, heaved the sea, and its rollers slapped the strand in the darkness with much the sound of wet sails flapping. The air was warm, and the sky full of stars.

In the plane-trees a nightingale was piping.

It was Tartarin who paid the piper.

X

" TELL ME YOUR FATHER'S NAME, AND I WILL TELL YOU THE NAME OF THAT FLOWER "

PRINCES of Montenegro are the ones to find the love-bird.

On the morrow early after this evening at the Platanes, Prince Gregory was in the Tarasconian's bedroom.

" Quick! Dress yourself quickly! Your Moorish beauty is found. Her name is Baya. She's scarce twenty—as petty as a love, and already a widow."

" A widow! What a slice of luck! " joyfully exclaimed Tartarin, who dreaded Oriental husbands.

" Ay, but woefully closely guarded by her brother."

" Oh, the mischief ! "

" A savage chap who vends pipes in the Orléans bazaar."

Here fell a silence.

" A fig for that! " proceeded the prince; " you are not the man to be daunted by such a trifle; and, anyhow, this old corsair can be pacified, I daresay, by having some pipes bought of him. But be quick! On with your courting suit, you lucky dog! "

Pale and agitated, with his heart brimming over with love, the Tarasconian leaped out of his couch, and, as he hastily buttoned up his capacious nether garment, wanted to know how he should act.

"Write straightway to the lady and ask for a tryst."

"Do you mean to say she knows French?" queried the Tarasconian simpleton, with the disappointed mien of one who had believed thoroughly in the Orient.

"Not one word of it," rejoined the prince imperturbably; "but you can dictate the billet-doux, and I will translate it bit by bit."

"O prince, how kind you are!"

The lover began striding up and down the bedroom in silent meditation.

Naturally a man does not write to a Moorish girl in Algiers in the same way as to a seamstress of Beaucaire. It was a very lucky thing that our hero had in mind his numerous readings, which allowed him, by amalgamating the Red Indian eloquence of Gustave Aimard's Apaches with Lamartine's rhetorical flourishes in the *Voyage en Orient*, and some reminiscences of the *Song of Songs*, to compose the most Eastern letter that you could expect to see. It opened with,—

"*Like unto the ostrich upon the sandy waste*"—

and concluded by,—

"*Tell me your father's name, and I will tell you the name of that flower.*"

To this missive the romantic Tartarin would have much liked to join an emblematic bouquet of flowers in the Eastern fashion; but Prince Gregory thought it better to purchase some pipes at the brother's, which could not fail to soften his wild temper, and would certainly please the lady a very great deal, as she was much of a smoker.

"Let's be off at once to buy them!" said Tartarin, full of ardour.

"No, no! Let me go alone. I can get them cheaper."

"Eh, what? Would you save me the trouble? O prince, prince, you do me proud!"

Quite abashed, the good-hearted fellow offered his purse to the obliging Montenegrin, urging him to overlook nothing by which the lady would be gratified.

Unfortunately the suit, albeit capitally commenced, did not progress as rapidly as might have been anticipated. It appeared that the Moorish beauty was very deeply affected by Tartarin's eloquence, and, for that matter, three-parts won beforehand, so that she wished nothing better than to receive him; but that brother of hers had qualms, and to lull them it was necessary to buy pipes by the dozens; nay, the gross—well, we had best say by the shipload at once.

"What the plague can Baya do with all these pipes?" poor Tartarin wanted to know more than once; but he paid the bills all the same, and without niggardliness.

At length, after having purchased a mountainous stack of pipes and poured forth lakes of Oriental poesy, an interview was arranged.

I have no need to tell you with what throbbings of the heart the Tarasconian prepared himself; with what carefulness he trimmed, brilliantined, and perfumed his rough cap-popper's beard, and how he did not forget—for everything must be thought of—to slip a spiky life-preserver and two or three six-shooters into his pockets.

The ever-obliging prince was coming to this first meeting in the office of interpreter.

The lady dwelt in the upper part of the town. Before her doorway a boy Moor of fourteen or less was smoking cigarettes; this was the brother in question, the celebrated Ali. On seeing the pair of visitors arrive, he gave a double knock on the postern gate and delicately glided away.

The door opened. A negress appeared, who conducted the gentlemen, without uttering a word, across the narrow inner courtyard into a small cool room, where the lady awaited them, reclining on a low ottoman. At first glance she appeared smaller and stouter than the Moorish damsel met in the omnibus by the Tarasconian. In fact, was it really the same? But the doubt merely flashed through Tartarin's brain like a stroke of lightning.

The dame was so pretty thus, with her feet bare, and plump fingers, fine and pink, loaded with rings. Under her bodice of gilded cloth and the folds of her flower-patterned dress was suggested a lovable creature, rather blessed materially, rounded everywhere, and nice enough to eat. The amber mouthpiece of a *narghileh* smoked at her lips, and enveloped her wholly in a halo of light-coloured smoke.

On entering, the Tarasconian laid a hand on his heart and bowed as Moorlike as possible, whilst rolling his large impassioned eyes.

Baya gazed on him for a moment without making any answer; but then, dropping her pipe-stem, she threw her head back, hid it in her hands, and they could only see her white neck rippling with a wild laugh like a bag full of pearls.

XI

SIDI TART'RI BEN TART'RI

SHOULD you ever drop into the coffee-houses of the Algerian upper town after dark, even at this day, you would still hear the natives chatting among themselves, with many a wink and slight laugh, of one Sidi Tart'ri Ben Tart'ri, a rich and good-humoured European, who dwelt, a few years back, in that neighbourhood, with a buxom witch of local origin, named Baya.

This Sidi Tart'ri, who has left such a merry memory around the Kasbah, is no other than our Tartarin, as will be guessed.

How could you expect things otherwise? In the lives of heroes, of saints, too, it happens the same way—there are moments of blindness, perturbation, and weakness. The illustrious Tarasconian was no more exempt from this than another, and that is the reason during two months that, oblivious of fame and lions, he revelled in Oriental amorousness, and dozed, like Hannibal at Capua, in the delights of Algiers the White.

The good fellow took a pretty little house in the native style in the heart of the Arab town, with inner courtyard, banana-trees, cool verandahs, and fountains. He dwelt, afar from noise, in company with the Moorish charmer, a thorough woman to the manner born, who pulled at her hubble-bubble all day when she was not eating.

Stretched out on a divan in front of him, Baya would drone him monotonous tunes with a guitar in her fist; or else, to distract her lord and master, favour him with the Bee Dance, holding a hand-glass up, in which she reflected her white teeth and the faces she made.

As the Esmeralda did not know a word of French, and

Among "The Turks"   57

Tartarin none in Arabic, the conversation died away sometimes, and the Tarasconian had plenty of leisure to do penance for the gush of language of which he had been guilty in the shop of Bézuquet the chemist or that of Costecalde the gunmaker.

But this penance was not devoid of charm, for he felt a kind of enjoyable sullenness in dawdling away the whole day without speaking, and in listening to the gurgling of the hookah, the strumming of the guitar, and the faint splashing of the fountain on the mosaic pavement of the yard.

The pipe, the bath, and caresses filled his entire life. They seldom went out of doors. Sometimes, with his lady-love upon a pillion, Sidi Tart'ri would ride upon a sturdy mule to eat pomegranates in a little garden he had purchased in the suburbs. But never, without exception, did he go down into the European quarter. This kind of Algiers appeared to him as ugly and unbearable as a barracks at home, with its Zouaves in revelry, its music-halls crammed with officers, and its everlasting clank of metal sabre-sheaths under the arcades.

The sum total is, that our Tarasconian was very happy.

Sancho-Tartarin particularly, being very sweet upon Turkish pastry, declared that one could not be more satisfied than by this new existence. Quixote-Tartarin had some twinges at whiles on thinking of Tarascon and the promises of lion-skins; but this remorse did not last, and to drive away such dampening ideas there sufficed one glance from Baya, or a spoonful of those diabolical dizzying and odoriferous sweetmeats like Circe's brews.

In the evening Gregory came to discourse a little about a free Black Mountain. Of indefatigable obligingness, this amiable nobleman filled the functions of an interpreter in the household, or those of a steward at a pinch, and all for nothing—for the sheer pleasure of it. Apart from him, Tartarin received none but "Turks." All those fierce-headed pirates who had given him such frights from the backs of their black stalls turned out, when once he made their acquaintance, to be good inoffensive tradesmen, embroiderers, dealers in spice, pipe-mouthpiece turners—well-bred fellows, humble, clever, close, and first-class hands at homely card games. Four or five times a week these gentry would come and spend the evening at Sidi Tart'ri's, winning his small change, eating his cates and dainties, and delicately retiring on the stroke of ten with thanks to the Prophet.

Left alone, Sidi Tart'ri and his faithful spouse by the broomstick wedding would finish the evening on their terrace, a broad white roof which overlooked the city.

All around them a thousand of other such white flats, placid beneath the moonshine, were descending like steps to the sea. The breeze carried up tinkling of guitars.

Suddenly, like a shower of firework stars, a full, clear melody would be softly sprinkled out from the sky, and on the minaret of the neighbouring mosque a handsome muezzin would appear, his blanched form outlined on the deep blue of the night, as he chanted the glory of Allah with a marvellous voice, which filled the horizon.

Thereupon Baya would let go her guitar, and with her large eyes turned towards the crier, seem to imbibe the prayer deliciously. As long as the chant endured she would remain thrilled there in ecstasy, like an Oriental saint. The deeply impressed Tartarin would watch her pray, and conclude that it must be a splendid and powerful creed that could cause such frenzies of faith.

Tarascon, veil thy face; here is a son of thine on the point of becoming a renegade!

XII

THE LATEST INTELLIGENCE FROM TARASCON

PARTING from his little country seat, Sidi Tart'ri was returning alone on his mule on a fine afternoon, when the sky was blue and the zephyrs warm. His legs were kept wide apart by ample saddle-bags of esparto cloth, swelled out with cedrats and water-melons. Lulled by the ring of his large stirrups, and rocking his body to the swing and swaying of the beast, the good fellow was thus traversing an adorable country, with his hands folded on his paunch, three-quarters gone, through heat, in a comfortable doze. All at once, on entering the town, a deafening appeal aroused him.

"Ahoy! What a monster Fate is! Anybody'd take this for Monsieur Tartarin."

On this name, and at the jolly southern accent, the Tarasconian lifted his head, and perceived, a couple of steps away, the honest tanned visage of Captain Barbassou, master of the *Zouave*, who was taking his absinthe at the door of a little coffee-house.

"Hey! Lord love you, Barbassou!" said Tartarin, pulling up his mule.

Instead of continuing the dialogue, Barbassou stared at him for a space ere he burst into a peal of such hilarity that Sidi Tart'ri sat back dumbfounded on his melons.

"What a stunning turban, my poor Monsieur Tartarin! Is it true, what they say of your having turned Turk? How is little Baya? Is she still singing 'Marco la Bella'?"

"Marco la Bella!" repeated the indignant Tartarin. I'll have you to know, captain, that the person you mention is an honourable Moorish lady, and one who does not know a word of French."

"Baya does not know French! What lunatic asylum do you hail from, then?"

The good captain broke into still heartier laughter; but, seeing the chops of poor Sidi Tart'ri fall, he changed his course.

"Howsoever, may happen it is not the same lass. Let's reckon that I have mixed 'em up. Still, mark you, Monsieur Tartarin, you will do well, nonetheless, to distrust Algerian Moors and Montenegrin princes."

Tartarin rose in the stirrups, making a wry face.

"The prince is my friend, captain."

"Come, come, don't wax wrathy. Won't you have some bitters to sweeten you? No? Haven't you anything to say to the folks at home, neither? Well, then, a pleasant journey. By the way, mate, I have some good French 'bacco upon me, and if you would like to carry away a few pipefuls, you have only to take some. Take it, won't you? It's your beastly Oriental 'baccoes that have befogged your brain."

Upon this the captain went back to his absinthe, whilst the moody Tartarin trotted slowly on the road to his little house. Although his great soul refused to credit anything,

Barbassou's insinuations had vexed him, and the familiar adjurations and home accent had awakened vague remorse.

He found nobody at home, Baya having gone out to the bath. The negress appeared sinister and the dwelling saddening. A prey to inexpressible melancholy, he went and sat down by the fountain to load a pipe with Barbassou's tobacco. It was wrapped up in a piece of the Marseilles *Sémaphore* newspaper. On flattening it out, the name of his native place struck his eyes.

" *Our Tarascon correspondent writes :*—

" The city is in distress. There has been no news for several months from Tartarin the lion-slayer, who set off to hunt the great feline tribe in Africa. What can have become of our heroic fellow-countryman? Those hardly dare ask who know, as we do, how hot-headed he was, and what boldness and thirst for adventures were his. Has he, like many others, been smothered in the sands, or has he fallen under the murderous fangs of one of those monsters of the Atlas Range of which he had promised the skins to the municipality? What a dreadful state of uncertainty! It is true some negro traders, come to Beaucaire Fair, assert having met in the middle of the deserts a European whose description agreed with his; he was proceeding towards Timbuctoo. May Heaven preserve our Tartarin! "

When he read this, the son of Tarascon reddened, blanched, and shuddered. All Tarascon appeared unto him: the club, the cap-poppers, Costecalde's green arm-chair, and, hovering over all like a spread eagle, the imposing moustaches of brave Commandant Bravida.

At seeing himself here, as he was, cowardly lolling on a mat, whilst his friends believed him slaughtering wild beasts, Tartarin of Tarsacon was ashamed of himself, and could have wept had he not been a hero.

Suddenly he leaped up and thundered,—

" The lion, the lion! Down with him! "

And dashing into the dusty lumber-hole where mouldered the shelter-tent, the medicine chest, the potted meats, and the gun-cases, he dragged them out into the middle of the court.

Sancho-Tartarin was no more: Quixote-Tartarin occupied the field of active life.

Only the time to inspect his armament and stores, don his

harness, get into his heavy boots, scribble a couple of words to confide Baya to the prince, and slip a few bank-notes sprinkled with tears into the envelope, and then the dauntless Tarasconian rolled away in the stage-coach on the Blidah road, leaving the house to the negress, stupor-stricken before the pipe, the turban, and babooshes—all the Moslem shell of Sidi Tart'ri which spawled piteously under the little white trefoils of the gallery.

EPISODE THE THIRD

AMONG THE LIONS

I

WHAT BECOMES OF THE OLD STAGE-COACHES

COME to look closely at the vehicle, it was an old stage-coach all of the olden time, upholstered in faded deep blue cloth, with those enormous rough woollen balls which, after a few hours' journey, finally establish a raw spot in the small of your back.

Tartarin of Tarascon had a corner of the inside, where he installed himself most free-and-easily; and, preliminarily to inspiring the rank emanations of the great African felines, the hero had to content himself with that homely old odour of the stage-coach, oddly composed of a thousand smells, of man and woman, horses and harness, eatables and mildewed straw.

There was a little of everything inside—a Trappist monk, some Jew merchants, two fast ladies going to join *their* regiment, the Third Hussars, a photographic artist from Orléansville, and so on. But, however charming and varied was the company, the Tarasconian was not in the mood for chatting; he remained quite thoughtful, with an arm in the arm-rest sling-strap and his guns between his knees. All churned up his wits—the precipitate departure, Baya's eyes of jet, the terrible chase he was about to undertake, to say nothing of this European coach, with its Noah's Ark aspect, rediscovered in the heart of Africa, vaguely recalling the Tarascon of his youth, with its races in the suburbs, jolly dinners on the river-side—a throng of memories, in short.

Gradually night came on. The guard lit up the lamps. The rusty *diligence* danced creakingly on its old springs; the horses trotted and their bells jangled. From time to time in the boot arose a dreadful clank of iron: that was the war material.

Tartarin of Tarascon, nearly overcome, dwelt a moment scanning the fellow-passengers, comically shaken by the jolts, and dancing before him like the shadows in galanty-shows, till his eyes grew cloudy and his mind befogged, and only vaguely he heard the wheels grind and the sides of the conveyance squeak complainingly.

Suddenly a voice called Tartarin by his name, the voice of an old fairy godmother, hoarse, broken, and cracked.

"Monsieur Tartarin!" three times.

"Who's calling me?"

"It's I, Monsieur Tartarin. Don't you recognise me? I am the old stage-coach who used to do the road betwixt Nîmes and Tarascon twenty year agone. How many times I have carried you and your friends when you went to shoot at caps over Joncquières or Bellegarde way! I did not know you again at the first, on account of your Turk's cap and the flesh you have accumulated; but as soon as you began snoring—what a rascal is good-luck!—I twigged you straight away."

"All right, that's all right enough!" observed the Tarasconian, a shade vexed; but softening, he added, "But to the point, my poor old girl; whatever did you come out here for?"

"Pooh! my good Monsieur Tartarin, I assure you I never came of my own free will. As soon as the Beaucaire railway was finished I was considered good for nought, and shipped away into Algeria. And I am not the only one either! Bless you, next to all the old stage-coaches of France have been packed off like me. We were regarded as too much the conservative—' the slow-coaches '—d'ye see, and now we are here leading the life of a dog. This is what you in France call the Algerian railways."

Here the ancient vehicle heaved a long-drawn sigh before proceeding.

"My wheels and linchpin! Monsieur Tartarin, how I regret my lovely Tarascon! That was the good time for me, when I was young! You ought to have seen me starting off in the morning, washed with no stint of water and all a-shine, with my wheels freshly varnished, my lamps blazing like a brace of suns, and my boot always rubbed up with oil! It was indeed lovely when the postillion cracked his whip to the tune of 'Lagadigadeou, the Tarasque! the Tarasque!' and the guard, his horn in its sling and laced cap cocked well over one ear, chucking his little dog, always in a fury, upon the top, climbed up himself with a shout: 'Right—away!'

"Then would my four horses dash off to the medley of bells, barks, and horn-blasts, and the windows fly open for all Tarascon to look with pride upon the royal mail coach dart over the king's highway.

"What a splendid road that was, Monsieur Tartarin, broad and well kept, with its milestones, its little heaps of road-metal at regular distances, and its pretty clumps of vines and olive-trees on either hand! Then, again, the roadside inns so close together, and the changes of horses every five minutes! And what jolly, honest chaps my patrons were! —village mayors and parish priests going up to Nîmes to see their prefect or bishop, taffety-weavers returning openly from the *Mazet*, collegians out on holiday leave, peasants in worked smock-frocks, all fresh shaven for the occasion that morning; and up above, on the top, you gentlemen-sportsmen, always in high spirits, and singing each your own family ballad to the stars as you came back in the dark.

"Deary me! it's a change of times now! Lord knows what rubbish I am carting here, come from nobody guesses where! They fill me with small deer, these negroes, Bedouin Arabs, swashbucklers, adventurers from every land, and ragged settlers who poison me with their pipes, and all jabbering a language that the Tower of Babel itself could make nothing of! And, furthermore, you should see how they treat me—I mean, how they never treat me: never a brush or a wash. They begrudge me grease for my axles. Instead of my good fat quiet horses of other days, little Arab ponies, with the devil in their frames, who fight and bite, caper as they run like so many goats, and break my splatterboard all to smithereens with their lashing out behind. Ouch! ouch! there they are at it again!

"And such roads! Just here it is bearable, because we are near the governmental headquarters; but out a bit there's nothing, Monsieur—not the ghost of a road at all. We get along as best we can over hill and dale, over dwarf palms and mastic-trees. Ne'er a fixed change of horses, the stopping being at the whim of the guard, now at one farm, again at another.

"Somewhiles this rogue goes a couple of leagues out of the way to have a glass of absinthe or *champoreau* with a chum. After which, ' Crack on, postillion! ' to make up for the lost time. Though the sun be broiling and the dust scorching, we whip on! We catch in the scrub and spill over, but whip on! We swim rivers, we catch cold, we get swamped, we drown, but whip! whip! whip! Then in the evening, streaming—a nice thing for my age, with my rheumatics—I have to sleep in the open air of some caravan-serai yard, open to all the winds. In the dead o' night jackals and hyænas come sniffing of my body; and the marauders who don't like dews get into my compartment to keep warm.

"Such is the life I lead, my poor Monsieur Tartarin, and that I shall lead to the day when—burnt up by the sun and rotted by the damp nights until unable to do anything else —I shall fall in some spot of bad road, where the Arabs will boil their *kouskous* with the bones of my old carcass "——

"Blidah! Blidah!" called out the guard as he opened the door.

II

A LITTLE GENTLEMAN DROPS IN AND "DROPS UPON" TARTARIN

VAGUELY through the mud-dimmed glass Tartarin of Tarascon caught a glimpse of a second-rate but pretty town market-place, regular in shape, surrounded by colonnades and planted with orange-trees, in the midst of which what seemed toy leaden soldiers were going through the morning exercise in the clear roseate mist. The cafés were shedding their shutters. In one corner there was a vegetable market. It was bewitching, but it did not smack of lions yet.

"To the South! farther to the South!" muttered the good old desperado, sinking back in his corner.

At this moment the door opened. A puff of fresh air

rushed in, bearing upon its wings, in the perfume of the orange-blossoms, a little person in a brown frock-coat, old and dry, wrinkled and formal, his face no bigger than your fist, his neckcloth of black silk five fingers wide, a notary's letter-case, and umbrella—the very picture of a village solicitor.

On perceiving the Tarasconian's warlike equipment, the little gentleman, who was seated over against him, appeared excessively surprised, and set to studying him with burdensome persistency.

The horses were taken out and the fresh ones put in, whereupon the coach started off again. The little weasel still gazed at Tartarin, who in the end took snuff at it.

"Does this astonish you?" he demanded, staring the little gentleman full in the face in his turn.

"Oh, dear, no! it only annoys me," responded the other, very tranquilly.

And the fact is, that, with his shelter-tent, revolvers, pair of guns in their cases, and hunting-knife, not to speak of his natural corpulence, Tartarin of Tarascon did take up a lot of room.

The little gentleman's reply angered him.

"Do you by any chance fancy that I am going lion-hunting with your umbrella?" queried the great man haughtily.

The little man looked at his umbrella, smiled blandly, and still with the same lack of emotion, inquired,—

"Oho, then you are Monsieur "——

"Tartarin of Tarascon, lion-killer!"

In uttering these words the dauntless son of Tarascon shook the blue tassel of his fez like a mane.

Through the vehicle was a spell of stupefaction.

The Trappist brother crossed himself, the dubious women uttered little screams of affright, and the Orléansville photographer bent over towards the lion-slayer, already cherishing the unequalled honour of taking his likeness.

The little gentleman, though, was not awed.

"Do you mean to say that you have killed many lions, Monsieur Tartarin?" he asked, very quietly.

The Tarasconian received his charge in the handsomest manner.

"Is it many have I killed, Monsieur? I wish you had only as many hairs on your head as I have killed of them."

All the coach laughed on observing three yellow bristles standing up on the little gentleman's skull.

In his turn, the Orléansville photographer struck in,—

"Yours must be a terrible profession, Monsieur Tartarin. You must pass some ugly moments sometimes. I have heard that poor Monsieur Bombonnel"——

"Oh, yes, the panther-killer," said Tartarin, rather disdainfully.

"Do you happen to be acquainted with him?" inquired the insignificant person.

"Eh! of course! Know him? Why, we have been out on the hunt over twenty times together."

The little gentleman smiled.

"So you also hunt panthers, Monsieur Tartarin?" he asked.

"Sometimes, just for pastime," said the fiery Tarasconian. "But," he added, as he tossed his head with a heroic movement that inflamed the heart of the two sweethearts of the regiment, "that's not worth lion-hunting."

"When all's said and done," ventured the photographer, "a panther is nothing but a big cat."

"Right you are!" said Tartarin, not sorry to abate the celebrated Bombonnel's glory a little, particularly in the presence of ladies.

Here the coach stopped. The conductor came to open the door, and addressed the insignficant little gentleman most respectfully, saying,—

"We have arrived, Monsieur."

The little gentleman got up, stepped out, and said, before the door was closed again,—

"Will you allow me to give you a bit of advice, Monsieur Tartarin?"

"What is it, Monsieur?"

"Faith! you wear the look of a good sort of fellow, so I would, rather than not, let you have it. Get you back quickly to Tarascon, Monsieur Tartarin, for you are wasting your time here. There do remain a few panthers in the colony, but, out upon the big cats! they are too small game for you. As for lion-hunting, that's all over. There are none left in Algeria, my friend Chassaing having lately knocked over the last."

Upon which the little gentleman saluted, closed the door, and trotted away chuckling, with his document-wallet and umbrella.

"Guard," asked Tartarin, screwing up his face contemptuously, "who under the sun is that poor little mannikin?"

"What! don't you know him? Why, that there's Monsieur Bombonnel!"

III

A MONASTERY OF LIONS

At Milianah, Tartarin of Tarascon alighted, leaving the stage-coach to continue its way towards the South.

Two days' rough jolting, two nights spent with eyes open to spy out of window if there were not discoverable the dread figure of a lion in the fields beyond the road—so much sleeplessness well deserved some hours' repose. Besides, if we must tell everything, since his misadventure with Bombonnel, the outspoken Tartarin felt ill at ease, notwithstanding his weapons, his terrifying visage, and his red cap, before the Orléansville photographer and the two ladies fond of the military.

So he proceeded through the broad streets of Milianah, full of fine trees and fountains; but whilst looking up a suitable hotel, the poor fellow could not help musing over Bombonnel's words. Suppose they were true! Suppose there were no more lions in Algeria? What would be the good then of so much running about and fatigue?

Suddenly, at the turn of a street our hero found himself face to face with—with what? Guess! "A donkey, of course!" A donkey? A splendid lion this time, waiting before a coffee-house door, royally sitting up on his hindquarters, with his tawny mane gleaming in the sun.

"What possessed them to tell me that there were no more of them?" exclaimed the Tarasconian, as he made a backward jump.

On hearing this outcry the lion lowered his head, and taking up in his mouth a wooden bowl that was before him on the footway, humbly held it out towards Tartarin, who was immovable with stupefaction. A passing Arab tossed a copper into the bowl, and the lion wagged his tail. Thereupon Tartarin understood it all. He saw what emotion had prevented him previously perceiving: that the crowd was gathered around a poor tame blind lion, and that two stalwart negroes, armed with staves, were marching him through the town as a Savoyard does a marmot.

The blood of Tarascon boiled over at once.

"Wretches that you are!" he roared in a voice of thunder, "thus to debase such noble beasts!"

Springing to the lion, he wrenched the loathsome bowl from between his royal jaws. The two Africans, believing they had a thief to contend with, rushed upon the foreigner with uplifted cudgels. There was a dreadful conflict: the blackamoors smiting, the women screaming, and the youngsters laughing. An old Jew cobbler bleated out of the hollow of his stall, " Dake him to the shustish of the beace!" The lion himself, in his dark state, tried to roar as his hapless champion, after a desperate struggle, rolled on the ground among the spilt pence and the sweepings.

At this juncture a man cleft the throng, made the negroes stand back with a word, and the women and urchins with a wave of the hand, lifted up Tartarin, brushed him down, shook him into shape, and sat him breathless upon a corner-post.

"What, *prance*, is it you?" said the good Tartarin, rubbing his ribs.

"Yes, indeed, it is I, my valiant friend. As soon as your letter was received, I entrusted Baya to her brother, hired a postchaise, flew fifty leagues as fast as a horse could go, and here I am, just in time to snatch you from the brutality of these ruffians. What have you done, in the name of just Heaven, to bring this ugly trouble upon you?"

"What done, prince? It was too much for me to see this unfortunate lion with a begging-bowl in his mouth, humiliated, conquered, buffeted about, set up as a laughing-stock to all this Moslem rabble"——

"But you are wrong, my noble friend. On the contrary,

this lion is an object of respect and adoration. This is a sacred beast who belongs to a great monastery of lions, founded three hundred years ago by Mahomet Ben Aouda, a kind of fierce and forbidding La Trappe, full of roarings and wild-beastly odours, where strange monks rear and feed lions by hundreds, and send them out all over Northern Africa, accompanied by begging brothers. The alms they receive serve for the maintenance of the monastery and its mosques; and the two negroes showed so much displeasure just now because it was their conviction that the lion under their charge would forthwith devour them if a single penny of their collection were lost or stolen through any fault of theirs."

On hearing this incredible and yet veracious story Tartarin of Tarascon was delighted, and sniffed the air noisily.

"What pleases me in this," he remarked, as the summing up of his opinion, "is that, whether Monsieur Bombonnel likes it or not, there are still lions in Algeria"——

"I should think there were!" ejaculated the prince enthusiastically. "We will start to-morrow beating up the Shelliff Plain, and you will see lions enough!"

"What, prince! have you an intention to go a-hunting, too?"

"Of course! Do you think I am going to leave you to march by yourself into the heart of Africa, in the midst of ferocious tribes of whose languages and usages you are ignorant! No, no, illustrious Tartarin, I shall quit you no more. Go where you will, I shall make one of the party."

"O *prance! prance!*"

The beaming Tartarin hugged the devoted Gregory to his breast at the proud thought of his going to have a foreign prince to accompany him in his hunting, after the example of Jules Gerard, Bombonnel, and other famous lion-slayers.

IV

THE CARAVAN ON THE MARCH

LEAVING Milianah at the earliest hour next morning, the intrepid Tartarin and the no less intrepid Prince Gregory descended towards the Shelliff Plain through a delightful gorge shaded with jessamine, carouba, tuyas, and wild olive-trees, between hedges of little native gardens and thousands of merry, lively rills which scampered down from rock to rock with a singing splash—a bit of landscape meet for the Lebanon.

As much loaded with arms as the great Tartarin, Prince Gregory had, over and above that, donned a queer but magnificent military cap, all covered with gold lace and a trimming of oak-leaves in silver cord, which gave His Highness the aspect of a Mexican general or a railway station-master on the banks of the Danube.

This plague of a cap much puzzled the beholder; and as he timidly craved some explanation, the prince gravely answered,—

"It is a kind of headgear indispensable for travel in Algeria."

Whilst brightening up the peak with a sweep of his sleeve, he instructed his simple companion in the important part which the military cap plays in the French connection with the Arabs, and the terror this article of army insignia alone has the privilege of inspiring, so that the Civil Service has been obliged to put all its employés in caps, from the extra-copyist to the receiver-general. To govern Algeria (the prince is still speaking) there is no need of a strong head, or even of any head at all. A military cap does it alone, if showy and belaced, and shining at the top of a non-human *pole*, like Gessler's.

Thus chatting and philosophising, the caravan proceeded. The barefooted porters leaped from rock to rock with ape-like screams. The gun-cases clanked, and the guns themselves flashed. The natives who were passing, salaamed to the ground before the magic cap. Up above, on the ramparts

of Milianah, the head of the Arab Department, who was out
for an airing with his wife, hearing these unusual noises, and
seeing the weapons gleam between the branches, fancied
there was a revolt, and ordered the drawbridge to be raised,
the general alarm to be sounded, and the whole town put
under a state of siege.

A capital commencement for the caravan!

Unfortunately, before the day ended, things went wrong.
Of the black luggage-bearers, one was doubled up with
atrocious colics from having eaten the diachylon out of the
medicine-chest; another fell on the roadside dead drunk with
camphorated brandy; the third, carrier of the travelling-
album, deceived by the gilding on the clasps into the per-
suasion that he was flying with the treasures of Mecca, ran
off into the Zaccar on his best legs.

This required consideration. The caravan halted, and
held a council in the broken shadow of an old fig-tree.

"It's my advice that we turn up negro porters from this
evening forward," said the prince, trying without success to
melt a cake of compressed meat in an improved patent triple-
bottomed saúcepan. "There is, haply, an Arab trader
quite near here. The best thing to do is to stop there, and
buy some donkeys."

"No, no; no donkeys," quickly interrupted Tartarin,
becoming quite red at memory of Noiraud. "How can you
expect," he added, hypocrite that he was, "that such little
beasts could carry all our apparatus?"

The prince smiled.

"You are making a mistake, my illustrious friend. However weakly and meagre the Algerian *bourriquot* may appear
to you, he has solid loins. He must have them so to support
all that he does. Just ask the Arabs. Hark to how they
explain the French colonial organisation. 'On the top,'
they say, ' is Mossoo, the Governor, with a heavy club to rap
the staff; the staff, for revenge, canes the soldier; the soldier
clubs the settler, and he hammers the Arab; the Arab smites
the negro, the negro beats the Jew, and he takes it out of
the donkey. The poor *bourriquot*, having nobody to be-
labour, arches up his back and bears it all.' You see clearly
now that he can bear your boxes."

"All the same," remonstrated Tartarin, "it strikes me

that jackasses will not chime in nicely with the effect of our caravan. I want something more Oriental. For instance. if we could only get a camel "——

"As many as you like," said His Highness; and off they started for the Arab mart.

It was held a few miles away, on the banks of the Shelliff. There were five or six thousand Arabs in tatters here, grovelling in the sunshine and noisily trafficking, amid jars of black olives, pots of honey, bags of spices, and great heaps of cigars; huge fires were roasting whole sheep, basted with butter; in open air slaughter-houses stark naked negroes, with ruddy arms and their feet in gore, were cutting up kids hanging from crosspoles, with small knives.

In one corner, under a tent patched with a thousand colours, a Moorish clerk of the market in spectacles scrawled in a large book. Here was a cluster of men shouting with rage: it was a spinning-jenny game, set on a corn-measure, and Kabyles were ready to cut one another's throats over it. Yonder were laughs and contortions of delight: it was a Jew trader on a mule drowning in the Shelliff. Then there were dogs, scorpions, ravens, and flies—rather flies than anything else.

But a plentiful lack of camels abounded. They finally unearthed one, though, of which the M'zabites were trying to get rid—the real ship of the desert, the classical, standard camel, bald, woe-begone, with a long Bedouin head, and its hump, become limp in consequence of unduly long fasts, hanging melancholically on one side.

Tartarin considered it so handsome that he wanted the entire party to get upon it. Still his Oriental craze!

The beast knelt down for them to strap on the boxes.

The prince enthroned himself on the animal's neck. For the sake of the greater majesty, Tartarin got them to hoist him on the top of the hump between two boxes, where, proud, and cosily settled down, he saluted the whole market with a lofty wave of the hand, and gave the signal of departure.

Thunderation! if the people of Tarascon could only have seen him!

The camel rose, straightened up its long knotty legs, and stepped out.

Oh, stupor! At the end of a few strides Tartarin felt he was losing colour, and the heroic *chechia* assumed one by one its former positions in the days of sailing in the *Zouave*. This devil's own camel pitched and tossed like a frigate.

"*Prance! prance!*" gasped Tartarin, pallid as a ghost, as he clung to the dry tuft of the hump, "*prance*, let's go down. I find—I feel that I m—m—must get off, or I shall disgrace France."

A deal of good that talk was—the camel was on the go, and nothing could stop it. Behind it raced four thousand barefooted Arabs, waving their hands and laughing like mad, so that they made six hundred thousand white teeth glitter in the sun.

The great man of Tarascon had to resign himself to circumstances. He sadly collapsed on the hump, where the fez took all the positions it fancied, and France was disgraced.

V

THE NIGHT-WATCH IN A POISON-TREE GROVE

SWEETLY picturesque as was their new steed, our lion-hunters had to give it up, purely out of consideration for the red cap, of course. So they continued the journey on foot as before, the caravan tranquilly proceeding southwardly by short stages, the Tarasconian in the van, the Montenegrin in the rear, and the camel, with the weapons in their cases, in the ranks.

The expedition lasted nearly a month.

During that seeking for lions which he never found, the dreadful Tartarin roamed from *douar* to *douar* on the immense plain of the Shelliff, through the odd but formidable French Algeria, where the old Oriental perfumes are complicated by a strong blend of absinthe and the barracks, Abraham and "the Zouzou" mingled, something fairy-tale-like and simply burlesque, like a page of the Old Testament related by Tommy Atkins.

A curious sight for those who have eyes that can see.

A wild and corrupted people whom we are civilising by teaching them our vices. The ferocious and uncontrolled authority of grotesque bashaws, who gravely use their *grand cordons* of the Legion of Honour as handkerchiefs, and for a mere yea or nay order a man to be bastinadoed. It is the justice of the conscienceless, bespectacled cadis under the palm-tree, Mawworms of the Koran and Law, who dream languidly of promotion and sell their decrees, as Esau did his birthright, for a dish of lentils or sweetened kouskous. Drunken and libertine cadis are they, formerly servants to some General Yusuf or the like, who get intoxicated on champagne, along with laundresses from Port Mahon, and fatten on roast mutton, whilst before their tents the whole tribe waste away with hunger, and fight with the harriers for the bones of the lordly feast.

All around spread the plains in waste, burnt grass, leafless shrubs, thickets of cactus and mastic—" the Granary of France!"—a granary void of grain, alas! and rich alone in vermin and jackals. Abandoned camps, frightened tribes fleeing from them and famine, they know not whither, and strewing the road with corpses. At long intervals French villages, with the dwellings in ruins, the fields untilled, the maddened locusts gnawing even the window-blinds, and all the settlers in the drinking-places, absorbing absinthe and discussing projects of reform and the Constitution.

This is what Tartarin might have seen had he given himself the trouble; but, wrapped up entirely in his leonine-hunger, the son of Tarascon went straight on, looking to neither right nor left, his eyes steadfastly fixed on the imaginary monsters which never really appeared.

As the shelter-tent was stubborn in not unfolding, and the compressed meat-cakes would not dissolve, the caravan was obliged to stop, morn and eve, at tribal camps. Everywhere, thanks to the gorgeous cap of Prince Gregory, our hunters were welcomed with open arms. They lodged in the aghas' odd palaces, large white windowless farmhouses, where they found, pell-mell, narghilehs and mahogany furniture, Smyrna carpets and moderator lamps, cedar coffers full of Turkish sequins, and French statuette-decked clocks in the Louis Philippe style.

Everywhere, too, Tartarin was given splendrous galas,

diffas, and *fantasias,* which, being interpreted, mean feasts and circuses. In his honour whole *goums* blazed away powder, and floated their burnouses in the sun. When the powder was burnt, the agha would come and hand in his bill. This is what is called Arab hospitality.

But always no lions, no more than on London Bridge.

Nevertheless, the Tarasconian did not grow disheartened. Ever bravely diving more deeply into the South, he spent the days in beating up the thickets, probing the dwarf-palms with the muzzle of his rifle, and saying, "Boh!" to every bush. And every evening, before lying down, he went into ambush for two or three hours. Useless trouble, however, for the lion did not show himself.

One evening, though, going on six o'clock, as the caravan scrambled through a violet-hued mastic-grove, where fat quails tumbled about in the grass, drowsy through the heat, Tartarin of Tarascon fancied he heard—though afar and very vague, and thinned down by the breeze—that wondrous roaring to which he had so often listened by Mitaine's Menagerie at home.

At first the hero feared he was dreaming; but in an instant further the roaring recommenced more distinct, although yet remote; and this time the camel's hump shivered in terror, and made the tinned meats and arms in the cases rattle, whilst all the dogs in the camps were heard howling in every corner of the horizon.

Beyond doubt this was the lion.

Quick, quick! to the ambush. There was not a minute to lose.

Near at hand there happened to be an old *marabout's,* or saint's, tomb, with a white cupola, and the defunct's large yellow slippers placed in a niche over the door, and a mass of odd offerings—hems of blankets, gold thread, red hair—hung on the wall.

Tartarin of Tarascon left his prince and his camel and went in search of a good spot for lying in wait. Prince Gregory wanted to follow him, but the Tarasconian refused, bent on confronting Leo alone. But still he besought His Highness not to go too far away, and, as a measure of foresight, he entrusted him with his pocket-book, a good-sized one, full of precious papers and bank-notes, which he feared would get torn by the lion's claws. This done, our hero looked up a good place.

A hundred steps in front of the temple a little clump of rose-laurel shook in the twilight haze on the edge of a rivulet all but dried up. There it was that Tartarin went and ensconced himself, one knee on the ground, according to the regular rule, his rifle in his hand, and his huge hunting-knife stuck boldly before him in the sandy bank.

Night fell.

The rosy tint of nature changed into violet, and then into dark blue. A petty pool of clear water gleamed like a hand-glass over the river-pebbles; this was the watering-place of the wild animals.

On the other slope the whitish trail was dimly to be discerned which their heavy paws had traced in the brush—a mysterious path which made one's flesh creep. Join to this sensation that from the vague swarming sound in African forests, the swishing of branches, the velvety pads of roving creatures, the jackal's shrill yelp, and up in the sky, two or three hundred feet aloft, vast flocks of cranes passing on with screams like poor little children having their weasands slit. You will own that there were grounds for a man being moved.

Tartarin was so, and even more than that, for the poor fellow's teeth chattered, and on the cross-bar of his hunting-knife, planted upright in the bank, as we repeat, his rifle-barrel rattled like a pair of castanets. Do not ask too much of a man! There are times when one is not in the mood; and, moreover, where would be the merit if heroes were never afraid?

Well, yes, Tartarin was afraid, and all the time, too, for the matter of that. Nevertheless, he held out for an hour; better, for two; but heroism has its limits. Nigh him, in the dry part of the rivulet-bed, the Tarasconian unexpectedly heard the sound of steps and of pebbles rolling. This time terror lifted him off the ground. He banged away both barrels at haphazard into the night, and retreated as fast as his legs would carry him to the *marabout's* chapel-vault, leaving his knife standing up in the sand like a cross commemorative of the grandest panic that ever assailed the soul of a conqueror of hydras.

"Help! this way, *prance*; the lion is on me!"
There was silence.
"*Prance, prance*, are you there?"
The prince was not there. On the white moonlit wall of the fane the camel alone cast the queer-shaped shadow of his protuberance. Prince Gregory had cut and run with the wallet of bank-notes. His Highness had been for the month past awaiting this opportunity.

VI

BAGGED HIM AT LAST

It was not until early on the morrow of this adventurous and dramatic eve that our hero awoke, and acquired assurance doubly sure that the prince and the treasure had really gone off, without any prospect of return. When he saw himself alone in the little white tomb-house, betrayed, robbed, abandoned in the heart of savage Algeria, with a one-humped camel and some pocket-money as all his resources, then did the representative of Tarascon for the first time doubt. He doubted Montenegro, friendship, glory, and even lions; and the great man blubbered bitterly.

Whilst he was pensively seated on the sill of the sanctuary, holding his head between his hands and his gun between his legs, with the camel mooning at him, the thicket over the way was divided, and the stupor-stricken Tartarin saw a gigantic lion appear not a dozen paces off. It thrust out its high head and emitted powerful roars, which made the temple walls shake beneath their votive decorations, and even the saint's slippers dance in their niche.

The Tarasconian alone did not tremble.

"At last you've come!" he shouted, jumping up and levelling the rifle.

Bang, bang! went a brace of shells into its head.

It was done. For a minute, on the fiery background of the Afric sky, there was a dreadful firework display of scattered brains, smoking blood, and tawny hair. When all fell, Tartarin perceived two colossal negroes furiously running towards him, brandishing cudgels. They were his two negro acquaintances of Milianah!

Oh, misery!

This was the domesticated lion, the poor blind beggar of the Mohammed Monastery, whom the Tarasconian's bullets had knocked over.

This time, spite of Mahound, Tartarin escaped neatly. Drunk with fanatical fury, the two African collectors would have surely beaten him to pulp had not the god of chase and war sent him a delivering angel in the shape of the rural constable of the Orléansville commune. By a bypath this *garde champêtre* came up, his sword tucked under his arm.

The sight of the municipal cap suddenly calmed the negroes' choler. Peaceful and majestic, the officer with the brass badge drew up a report on the affair, ordered the camel to be loaded with what remained of the king of beasts, and the plaintiffs as well as the delinquent to follow him, proceeding to Orléansville, where all was deposited with the law-courts receiver.

There issued a long and alarming case!

After the Algeria of the native tribes which he had overrun, Tartarin of Tarascon became thence acquainted with another Algeria, not less weird and to be dreaded—the Algeria, in the towns, surcharged with lawyers and their papers. He got to know the pettifogger who does business at the back of a café—the legal Bohemian, with documents reeking of wormwood bitters and white neckcloths spotted with champoreau; the ushers, the attorneys, all the locusts of stamped paper, meagre and famished, who eat up the colonist body and boots —ay, to the very straps of them, and leave him peeled to the core like an Indian cornstalk, stripped leaf by leaf.

Before all else it was necessary to ascertain whether the lion had been killed on the civil or the military territory. In the former case the matter regarded the Tribunal of Commerce; in the second, Tartarin would be dealt with by the Council of War; and at the mere name the impressionable Tarasconian saw himself shot at the foot of the ramparts or huddled up in a casemate-silo.

The puzzle lay in the limitation of the two territories being very hazy in Algeria.

At length, after a month's running about, entanglements, and waiting under the sun in the yards of Arab Departmental offices, it was established that, whereas the lion had been killed on the military territory, on the other hand Tartarin was in the civil territory when he shot. So the case was decided in the civil courts, and our hero was let off on paying two thousand five hundred francs damages, costs not included.

How could he pay such a sum?

The few piastres escaped from the prince's sweep had long since gone in legal documents and judicial libations. The unfortunate lion-destroyer was therefore reduced to selling the store of guns by retail, rifle by rifle; so went the daggers, the Malay kreeses, and the life-preservers. A grocer purchased the preserved aliments; an apothecary what remained of the medicaments. The big boots themselves walked off after the improved tent to a dealer of curiosities, who elevated them to the dignity of " rarities from Cochin-China."

When everything was paid up, only the lion's skin and the camel remained to Tartarin. The hide he had carefully packed, to be sent to Tarascon to the address of brave Commandant Bravida, and, later on, we shall see what came of this fabulous trophy. As for the camel, he reckoned on making use of him to get back to Algiers, not by riding on him, but by selling him to pay his coach-fare—the best way to employ a camel in travelling. Unhappily the beast was difficult to place, and no one would offer a copper for him.

Still Tartarin wanted to regain Algiers by hook or crook. He was in haste again to behold Baya's blue bodice, his little snuggery and his fountains, as well as to repose on the white trefoils of his little cloister whilst awaiting money from France, So our hero did not hesitate; distressed but not downcast. he undertook to make the journey afoot and penniless by short stages.

In this enterprise the camel did not cast him off. The strange animal had taken an unaccountable fancy for his master, and on seeing him leave Orléansville, he set to striding steadfastly behind him, regulating his pace by his, and never quitting him by a yard.

At the first outset Tartarin found this touching; such fidelity and devotion above proof went to his heart, all the more because the creature was accommodating, and fed himself on nothing. Nevertheless, after a few days, the Tarasconian was worried by having this glum companion perpetually at his heels, to remind him of his misadventures. Ire arising, he hated him for his sad aspect, hump and gait of a goose in harness. To tell the whole truth, he held him as his Old Man of the Sea, and only pondered on how to shake him off; but the follower would not be shaken off. Tartarin attempted to lose him, but the camel always found him; he tried to outrun him, but the camel ran faster. He bad him begone, and hurled stones at him. The camel stopped with a mournful mien, but in a minute resumed the pursuit, and always ended by overtaking him. Tartarin had to resign himself.

For all that, when, after eight full days of tramping, the dusty and harassed Tarasconian espied the first white house-tops of Algiers glimmer from afar in the verdure, and when he got to the city gates on the noisy Mustapha Avenue, amid the Zouaves, Biskris, and Mahonnais, all swarming around him and staring at him trudging by with his camel, overtasked patience escaped him.

"No! no!" he growled, " it is not likely! I cannot enter Algiers with such an animal!"

Profiting by a jam of vehicles, he turned off into the fields and jumped into a ditch. In a minute or so he saw over his head on the highway the camel flying off with long strides and stretching his neck with a wistful air.

Relieved of a great weight thereby, the hero sneaked out of his covert, and entered the town anew by a circuitous path which skirted the wall of his own little garden.

VII

CATASTROPHES UPON CATASTROPHES

ENTIRELY astonished was Tartarin before his Moorish dwelling when he stopped.

Day was dying and the street deserted. Through the low pointed-arch doorway which the negress had forgotten to close, laughter was heard; and the clink of wine-glasses, the popping of champagne corks; and, floating over all the jolly uproar, a feminine voice singing clearly and joyously,—

> " Do you like, Marco la Bella,
>   To dance in the hall hung with bloom? "

" Throne of heaven! " ejaculated the Tarasconian, turning pale, as he rushed into the enclosure.

Hapless Tartarin! what a sight awaited him! Beneath the arches of the little cloister, amongst bottles, pastry, scattered cushions, pipes, tambourines, and guitars, Baya was singing, " Marco la Bella " with a ship captain's cap over one ear. She had on no blue vest or bodice; indeed, her only wear was a silvery gauze wrapper and full pink trousers. At her feet, on a rug, surfeited with love and sweetmeats, Barbassou, the infamous skipper Barbassou, was bursting with laughter at hearing her.

The apparition of Tartarin, haggard, thinned, dusty, his flaming eyes, and the bristling up fez tassel, sharply interrupted this tender Turkish-Marseillais orgie. Baya piped the low whine of a frightened leveret, and ran for safety into the house. But Barbassou did not wince; he only laughed the louder, saying,—

" Ha, ha, Monsieur Tartarin! What do you say to that now? You see she does know French."

Tartarin of Tarascon advanced furiously, crying,—

" Captain! "

" *Digo-li qué vengué, moun bon !*—tell him what's happened, old dear! " screamed the Moorish woman, leaning over the first floor gallery with a pretty low-bred gesture.

The poor man, overwhelmed, let himself collapse upon a drum. His genuine Moorish beauty not only knew French, but the French of Marseilles!

"I told you not to trust the Algerian girls," observed Captain Barbassou sententiously. "They're as tricky as your Montenegrin prince."

Tartarin lifted his head.

"Do you know where the prince is?"

"Oh, he's not far off. He has gone to live five years in the handsome prison of Mustapha. The rogue let himself be caught with his hand in the pocket. Anyways, this is not the first time he has been clapped into the calaboose. His Highness has already done three years somewhere, and—stop a bit! I believe it was at Tarascon."

"At Tarascon!" cried out her worthiest son, abruptly enlightened. "That's how he only knew one part of the town."

"Hey? Of course. Tarascon—a jail bird's-eye view from the state prison. I tell you, my poor Monsieur Tartarin, you have to keep your peepers jolly well skinned in this deuce of a country, or be exposed to very disagreeable things. For a sample, there's the muezzin's game with you."

"What game? Which muezzin?"

"Why your'n, of course! The chap across the way who is making up to Baya. That newspaper, the *Akbar*, told the yarn t'other day, and all Algiers is laughing over it even now. It is so funny for that steeplejack up aloft in his crow's-nest to make declarations of love under your very nose to the little beauty whilst singing out his prayers, and making appointments with her between bits of the Koran."

"Why, then, they're all scamps in this country!" howled the unlucky Tarasconian.

Barbassou snapped his fingers like a philosopher.

"My dear lad, you know, these new countries are 'rum!' But, anyhow, if you'll believe me, you'd best cut back to Tarascon at full speed."

"It's easy to say, 'Cut back.' Where's the money to come from? Don't you know that I was plucked out there in the desert?"

"What does that matter?" said the captain merrily. "The *Zouave* sails to-morrow, and if you like I will take you home. Does that suit you, mate? Ay? Then all goes well. You have only one thing to do. There are some bottles of fizz left, and half the pie. Sit you down and pitch in without any grudge."

After the minute's wavering which self-respect commanded, the Tarasconian chose his course manfully. Down he sat, and they touched glasses. Baya, gliding down at that chink, sang the finale of "Marco la Bella," and the jollification was prolonged deep into the night.

About 3 A.M., with a light head but a heavy foot, our good Tarasconian was returning from seeing his friend the captain off, when, in passing the mosque, the remembrance of his muezzin and his practical jokes made him laugh, and instantly a capital idea of revenge flitted through his brain.

The door was open. He entered, threaded long corridors hung with mats, mounted and kept on mounting till he finally found himself in a little oratory, where an openwork iron lantern swung from the ceiling, and embroidered an odd pattern in shadows upon the blanched walls.

There sat the crier on a divan, in his large turban and white pelisse, with his Mostaganam pipe, and a bumper of absinthe before him, which he whipped up in the orthodox manner, whilst awaiting the hour to call true believers to prayer. At view of Tartarin, he dropped his pipe in terror.

"Not a word, knave!" said the Tarasconian, full of his project. "Quick! Off with turban and coat!"

The Turkish priest-crier tremblingly handed over his outer garments, as he would have done with anything else. Tartarin donned them, and gravely stepped out upon the minaret platform.

In the distance the sea shone. The white roofs glittered in the moonbeams. On the sea breeze was heard the strumming of a few belated guitars. The Tarasconian muezzin gathered himself up for the effort during a space, and then, raising his arms, he set to chanting in a very shrill voice:

"*La Allah il Allah!* Mahomet is an old humbug! The Orient, the Koran, bashaws, lions, Moorish beauties—they are all not worth a fly's skip! There is nothing left but gammoners. Long live Tarascon!"

Whilst the illustrious Tartarin, in his queer jumbling of Arabic and Provençal, flung his mirthful maledictions to the four quarters, sea, town, plain and mountain, the clear, solemn voices of the other muezzins answered him, taking up the strain from minaret to minaret, and the believers of the upper town devoutly beat their bosoms.

VIII

TARASCON AGAIN!

MID-DAY has come.

The *Zouave* had her steam up, ready to go. Upon the balcony of the Valentin Café, high above, the officers were levelling telescopes, and, with the colonel at their head, looking at the lucky little craft that was going back to France. This is the main distraction of the staff. On the lower level, the roads glittered. The old Turkish cannon breaches, stuck up along the waterside, blazed in the sun. The passengers hurried. Biskris and Mahonnais piled their luggage up in the wherries.

Tartarin of Tarascon had no luggage. Here he comes down the Rue de la Marine through the little market, full of bananas and melons, accompanied by his friend Barbassou. The hapless Tarasconian left on the Moorish strand his gun-cases and his illusions, and now he had to sail for Tarascon with his hands in his otherwise empty pockets. He had barely leaped into the captain's cutter before a breathless beast slid down from the heights of the square and galloped towards him. It was the faithful camel, who had been hunting after his master in Algiers during the last four-and-twenty hours.

On seeing him, Tartarin changed countenance, and feigned not to know him, but the camel was not going to be put off. He scampered along the quay; he whinnied for his friend, and regarded him with affection.

"Take me away," his sad eyes seemed to say, "take me away in your ship, far, far from this sham Arabia, this ridiculous Land of the East, full of locomotives and stage coaches, where a camel is so sorely out of keeping that I do not know what will become of me. You are the last real Turk, and I am the last camel. Do not let us part, O my Tartarin!"

"Is that camel yours?" the captain inquired.

"Not a bit of it!" relpied Tartarin, who shuddered at the idea of entering Tarascon with that ridiculous escort; and, impudently denying the companion of his misfortunes, he spurned the Algerian soil with his foot, and gave the cutter the shoving-off start. The camel sniffed of the water, extended its neck, cracked its joints, and, jumping in behind the row-boat at haphazard, he swam towards the *Zouave* with his humpback floating like a bladder, and his long neck projecting over the wave like the beak of a galley.

Cutter and camel came alongside the mail steamer together.

"This dromedary regularly cuts me up," observed Captain Barbassou, quite affected. "I have a good mind to take him aboard and make a present of him to the Zoological Gardens at Marseilles."

And so they hauled up the camel with many blocks and tackles upon the deck, being increased in weight by the brine, and the *Zouave* started.

Tartarin spent the two days of the crossing by himself in his stateroom, not because the sea was rough, or that the red fez had too much to suffer, but because the deuced camel, as soon as his master appeared above decks, showed him the most preposterous attentions. You never did see a camel make such an exhibition of a man as this.

From hour to hour, through the cabin portholes, where he stuck out his nose now and then, Tartarin saw the Algerian blue sky pale away; until one morning, in a silvery fog, he heard with delight Marseilles bells ringing out. The *Zouave* had arrived and cast anchor.

Our man, having no luggage, got off without saying anything, hastily slipped through Marseilles for fear he was still pursued by the camel, and never breathed till he was in a third-class carriage making for Tarascon.

Deceptive security!

Hardly were they two leagues from the city before every head was stuck out of window. There were outcries and astonishment. Tartarin looked in his turn, and—what did he descry! the camel, reader, the inevitable camel, racing

along the line behind the train, and keeping up with it!
The dismayed Tartarin drew back and shut his eyes.
After this disastrous expedition of his he had reckoned
on slipping into his house *incognito*. But the presence of
this burdensome quadruped rendered the thing impossible.
What kind of a triumphal entry would he make? Good
heavens! not a sou, not a lion, nothing to show for it save
a camel!

"Tarascon! Tarascon!"
He was obliged to get down.
O amazement!
Scarce had the hero's red fez popped out of the doorway
before a loud shout of "Tartarin for ever!" made the glazed
roof of the railway station tremble. "Long life to Tartarin,
the lion-slayer!" And out burst the windings of horns and
the choruses of the local musical societies.

Tartarin felt death had come: he believed in a hoax. But,
no! all Tarascon was there, waving their hats, all of the same
way of thinking. Behold the brave Commandant Bravida,
Costecalde the armourer, the Chief Judge, the chemist, and
the whole noble corps of cap-poppers, who pressed around
their leader, and carried him in triumph out through the
passages.

Singular effects of the mirage!—the hide of the blind lion
sent to Bravida was the cause of all this riot. With that
humble fur exhibited in the club-room, the Tarasconians,
and, at the back of them, the whole South of France, had
grown exalted. The *Sémaphore* newspaper had spoken of it.
A drama had been invented. It was not merely a solitary
lion which Tartarin had slain, but ten, nay, twenty—pooh!
a herd of lions had been made marmalade of. Hence, on
disembarking at Marseilles, Tartarin was already celebrated
without being aware of it, and an enthusiastic telegram had
gone on before him by two hours to his native place.

But what capped the climax of the popular gladness was
to see a fancifully shaped animal, covered with foam and
dust, appear behind the hero, and stumble down the station
stairs.

Tarascon for an instant believed that its dragon was come
again.

Tartarin set his fellow-citizens at ease.

"This is my camel," he said.

Already feeling the influence of the splendid sun of Tarascon, which makes people tell "bouncers" unwittingly, he added, as he fondled the camel's hump:

"It is a noble beast! It saw me kill all my lions!"

Whereupon he familiarly took the arm of the commandant, who was red with pleasure; and followed by his camel, surrouned by the cap-hunters, acclaimed by all the population, he placidly proceeded towards the Baobab Villa; and, on the march, thus commenced the account of his mighty hunting:

"Once upon an evening, you are to imagine that, out in the depths of the Sahara "——

TARTARIN ON THE ALPS

TARTARIN ON THE ALPS

I

AN APPARITION ON THE RIGI-KULM—WHO IS HE?—WHAT WAS SAID AT THE TABLE D'HÔTE—RICE AND PRUNES—AN IMPROVISED BALL—THE UNKNOWN SIGNS HIS NAME IN THE HOTEL REGISTER—P. C. A.

On the 10th of August, 1880, at the fabled hour of sunset, so much belauded by Joanne's and Bædeker's Guide-Books, a thick, yellow fog, rendered more puzzling by a whirling snow-storm, enveloped the summit of the Rigi (*Regina montium*) and that immense hotel—which presents such an extraordinary appearance in the barren landscape of hills— the Rigi-Kulm, glazed like an observatory, massive as a citadel, wherein for a day and a night a crowd of sun-worshipping tourists is located.

While awaiting the second dinner-gong, the occupants of this extensive and sumptuous caravanserai, chilled in their bedrooms, or seated listlessly on the divans in the reading-room, in the damp semi-warmth of the lighted stoves, were gazing — in default of the promised splendours — at the whirling snowflakes in the air, or at the lighting of the great lamps before the entrance, whose double glasses quivered in the tempestuous wind.

Fancy having ascended so high and having come from all parts of the world for this! O Bædeker!

Suddenly something emerged from the fog and advanced towards the hotel, with the clanking of iron, an exaggeration of its movements being caused by the unusual surroundings.

At twenty paces distant through the snow, the idle tourists, with their noses flattened against the windows, the little girls,

whose hair was cut short like boys', took this apparition for
a straying cow, then for a *rétameur* carrying his tools.

At ten paces the apparition again changed its appearance,
and showed a cross-bow on its shoulder, and the casque of
an archer of the middle ages on its head, an object still less
likely to be met with on the mountains than a cow or a
pedlar.

When he reached the steps, the archer was only a fat man,
thickset, and broad-shouldered, who stopped to puff and
blow, and to shake the snow from his gaiters, which were of
yellow cloth like his cap, and from his knitted comforter,
which permitted scarcely anything to be seen of his face but
two enormous tufts of grey whisker and a pair of green
spectacles like the eye-pieces of a stereoscope. An ice-axe,
an alpenstock, a knapsack, a coil of rope, *crampons*, and iron
hooks suspended from the belt of a Norfolk jacket with deep
flaps, completed the accoutrement of this perfect Alpine
climber.

Upon the desolate summit of Mont Blanc or the Finsteraarhorn, such a "get up" would have been suitable
enough; but at the Rigi-Kulm, a few paces from the
railway!

The Alpinist, it is true, came from the side opposite to the
station, and the condition of his leggings bore witness to the
long tramp he had had through the snow and mire.

For a moment he gazed at the hotel and its dependencies,
surprised to find, at six thousand feet above the level of the
sea, a building of such a size, with its glazed galleries, its
colonnades, its seven ranges of windows, and the wide flight
of steps between two rows of lamps which gave to the top of
the mountain something of the appearance of the Place de
l'Opera in a wintry twilight.

But however greatly surprised he may have been, the
occupants of the hotel seemed much more so; and when he
entered the wide vestibule, a curious, pushing crowd filled
the doorways of the *salles*; gentlemen grasping billiard cues,
or with newspapers in their hands; ladies holding their books
or work; while at the end, up the staircase, heads were protruded over the banisters and between the chains of the
"lift."

The new-comer spoke in a loud voice, a strong basso-profundo, a *creux du Midi*, which sounded like a pair of cymbals,—

"*Coquin de sort!* Here's weather——"

Suddenly he stopped, took off his cap and spectacles. He was choking.

The glare of the lights, the heat of the gas and of the stoves, contrasting with the black cold night outside, the sumptuous appearance of the hotel, the lofty vestibule, the richly-laced porters with " REGINA MONTIUM " in gold letters on their caps, the white ties of the *maîtres d'hôtel*, and the battalion of Swiss female servants in their national costumes, who came running up at the sound of the gong—all this impressed him for a second, not for more than one.

He felt himself the cynosure of all eyes, and immediately recovered his self-possession, like a comedian before a full house.

"*Monsieur desire*—— ?"

It was the manager who asked him the question, softly; a very well got-up manager, with a striped jacket, carefully tended whiskers, and *très chic*, in fact.

The mountaineer, without any emotion, demanded a room, "a nice little room at any rate," quite as much at his ease with this majestic manager as with an old school friend.

He was very nearly putting himself out, though, when the Bernese servant approached him, candle in hand, resplendent in her gold lace and tulle-decked sleeves, to inquire whether Monsieur would like to go up in the lift. If she had suggested the commission of a crime our hero could not have been more indignant.

A lift! for him! for *him!* His exclamation and his gesture, caused his paraphernalia to rattle again.

As suddenly appeased he said to the Swiss maid in a pleasant tone: "*Pedibus cum jambis, ma belle chatte*," and he mounted behind her, his wide back occupying the width of the stairs, knocking against people on the way up, while the whole hotel rang with the question, "Who is he?" expressed in every language under the sun. Then the second dinner-bell sounded, and no one troubled himself or herself any more concerning this extraordinary individual.

A sight indeed is the *salle-à-manger* of the Rigi-Kulm.

Tartarin on the Alps

Six hundred guests seated around an immense horse-shoe table on which dishes of rice and prunes alternate in long files with green plants, reflecting in their clear or brown sauce the lights of the lustres or the gilding of the panelled ceiling.

As at all Swiss *tables d'hôte*, this rice and these prunes divide the diners into two rival factions, and the looks of hatred or covetousness bestowed upon the dessert dishes is quite sufficient to enable the spectator to divine to which party the guests belong. The Rice Party betray themselves by their pallor, the Prunes by their congested appearance.

On this particular evening the latter were in the majority, and included all the most important personages, quite European celebrities, such as the great historian Astier-Réhu of the French Academy; the Baron de Stolz, an old Austro-Hungarian diplomatist; Lord Chippendale, a member of the Jockey Club with his niece (?) (hum!); the illustrious Professor Schwanthaler, of Bonn University; a Peruvian general and his eight daughters.

To all these the Rice faction could only oppose as *vedettes* a Belgian Senator and his family; Madame Schwanthaler, the wife of the Professor aforesaid; and an Italian tenor on his way from Russia, exhibiting upon the table-cloth a pair of sleeve-links as large as saucers.

These double and opposing currents no doubt gave an air of lassitude and stiffness to the *table d'hôte*. How otherwise can we account for the silence of these six hundred persons, stiff, surly, defiant, with that supreme contempt which they affected to possess one for the other? A superficial observer would have attributed it to the stupid Anglo-Saxon reserve which now gives the tone to the travelling world.

But no! Human beings do not thus hate each other at first sight; turning up their noses at each other; sneering, and glancing superciliously at one another in the absence of introductions. There must have been something else!

Rice and Prunes, I tell you. There you have the explanation of the mournful silence that weighed down upon the dinner at the Rigi-Kulm, which, considering the number and the varied nationalities of the guests, ought to have

At the Table d'Hôte

been very animated and noisy; something like what one would imagine a meal at the foot of the Tower of Babel might have been.

The mountaineer entered the room—a little perplexed in this assembly of Trappists beneath the glare of the lustres—coughed loudly without any one taking any notice of him, and seated himself in his place next the last comer, at the end of the table. Unaccoutred now, he was simply an ordinary tourist, but of a very amiable appearance; bald, rotund, his beard thick and pointed, a fine nose, thick and somewhat fierce eyebrows, with a pleasant manner and appearance.

Rice or Prune! No one knew yet.

Scarcely had he seated himself, when, quitting his place with a bound, he exclaimed, "*Outre!* a draught!" and rushed to an empty chair turned down at the centre of the table.

He was stopped by one of the Swiss female attendants, a native of the canton of Uri, wearing little silver chains and white stomacher.

"Monsieur, that is engaged."

Then, from the table, a young lady, of whom he could see nothing but a mass of fair hair relieved by a neck white as virgin snow, said, without turning round, and with a foreign accent:

"This seat is at liberty; my brother is not well, and will not come down to dinner."

"Ill?" asked the mountaineer, with an interested, almost affectionate, manner, as he seated himself. "Ill? Not dangerously, *au moins?*"

He pronounced the last words *au mouain*, and they reasserted themselves with some other vocal parasites "*hé, qué, té, zou, vé, vaï, allons,*" etc., that still further accentuated his southern tongue, which was no doubt displeasing to the youthful blonde; for she only replied to him with a stony stare—from eyes of deep, dark blue.

The neighbour on his right was not encouraging either. He was the Italian tenor, with a low forehead, very moist eyes, and Hectoring moustaches which he twirled in an irritable manner, for had he not been separated from his pretty neighbour? But the good mountaineer had a habit of talking while he was eating—he thought it good for his digestion.

"*Vé!* What pretty buttons," he remarked aloud to himself, as he glanced at the Italian's sleeve-studs. "Those notes of music, inlaid with the jasper, have a charming effect"—"*un effet charmain*"!

His strident tones rang through the silent *salle*, without producing the least echo.

"Surely monsieur is a singer, *qué?*"

"*Non capisco*," growled the Italian through his moustache.

For a moment the man devoted himself to his dinner without speaking—but the food choked him. At length, as his opposite neighbour, the Austro-Hungarian diplomatist, attempted to reach the mustard-pot with his small, aged, shaking hands, enveloped in mittens, our hero passed it politely to him, saying, "*A votre service, monsieur le baron*," for he had heard him thus addressed.

Unfortunately poor M. de Stoltz, notwithstanding the cunning and ingenious air which he had contracted in the pursuit of Chinese diplomacy, had long ago lost his speech and his ideas, and was travelling around the mountains with the view of finding them again. He opened his eyes wide and gazed at the unknown face, and then shut them again without saying anything. It would have taken ten old diplomats of his intellectual power to find the formula of acknowledgment.

At this new failure the mountaineer made a grimace, and the rough manner in which he seized the bottle gave one the idea that he was going to break, with it, the cracked head of the old diplomatist. But no such thing. It was merely to offer his neighbour a glass of wine, but she did not hear him, being lost in a murmured conversation—a chirping, sweet and lively, in an unknown tongue—with two young people close by. She leaned forward, she became animated. He could see her little curls shimmer in the light against a tiny ear, transparent and rosy-tinted. Polish? Russian? Norwegian? Well, certainly Northern; and a pretty little song of his native district escaped the lips of the Southerner, who quietly began to hum,—

Rice and Prunes

" O coumtesso gènto,
Estelo dou Nord
Qué la neu argento,
Qu'Amour friso en or."

Everybody at table turned round: they all thought he had gone mad. He blushed and kept himself quiet in his place, not moving except to push violently away the dish of sacred fruit which they passed to him.

" Prunes! Never in my life! "

This was too much.

There was a great movement of chairs. The Academician, Lord Chippendale, the Professor of Bonn, and some other notables of the party, rose and quitted the room by way of protest.

The Rice Party almost immediately followed them when they perceived the stranger push away from him the other dessert dish as violently as the former.

Neither Rice nor Prune! What then?

All the guests retired, and the silence was truly glacial as the people, with bowed heads and with the corners of their mouths disdainfully drawn down, passed in front of the unhappy individual who remained alone in the immense dining-room, inclined *de faire une trempette* after the manner of his country, but kept down by the universal disdain!

My friends, never despise any one. Contempt is the resource of upstarts, of *parvenus*, of ugly people, of fools,—the mask beneath which they hide their insignificance, sometimes their poverty, and which dispense with mind, with judgment, with goodness. All hump-backed people are contemptuous; all the wry-nosed ones scowl and display disdain when they meet with a straight nose!

Our good mountaineer knew that. Having passed his fortieth year some time before—that " *palier du quatrième* " where man finds and picks up the magic key which opens life to him to the very end, showing him the monotonous and deceptive perspective of years, becoming cognisant, besides, of his worth, the importance of his mission, and of the great name that he bears—the opinion of such people scarcely affected him. Besides he had only to mention his name—to cry out, " It is I "—to change into profound respect all these haughty lips. But the *incognito* amused him.

He only suffered because he could not talk and make a noise, give vent to his opinions, shake hands, tap people familiarly on the shoulder, and call them by their Christian names. That is what oppressed him at the Rigi-Kulm.

But above all was the fact that he had no one to talk to!

"It will give me the pip, I am quite sure of that," he said to himself, as he wandered about the hotel, not knowing what to do with himself.

He entered the *café*, as empty as a church on a week-day, called the waiter "my good friend," ordered a "mocha without sugar—*qué*." As the waiter did not ask, "Why without sugar?" the Alpinist added quickly, "That is a habit I contracted in Algeria when I was hunting there."

He was going to tell him about it, but the man had fled away like a phantom to Lord Chippendale, who was stretched upon a couch and demanding in a melancholy voice, "Tchimppègne, Tchimppègne." The cork popped cheerfully, and then nothing more was heard but the roaring of the wind in the massive chimney and the chilling click of the snow against the window-panes.

Very doleful also was the reading-room; all the papers engaged. Those hundreds of heads bent around the long green tables under the reflectors. From time to time was heard a sneeze or a cough, or the rustling of a page turned by a reader. Standing upright and motionless, looking down upon the calm of the reading-room, with their backs to the stove, were the two pontiffs of official history, Schwanthaler and Astier-Réhu—equally solemn and equally dry—whom a curious fatality had brought together at the top of the Rigi after a lapse of thirty years, during which period they had been vilifying each other, and pulling each other to pieces in abusive notes, as Schwanthaler the blockhead, and Astier-Réhu *vir ineptissimus*.

You may imagine the reception the benevolent Alpinist had when he took a seat at the corner of the fire-place, to hear a few instructive words. From the height of the two Caryatids fell suddenly upon him one of those cold currents which he so greatly dreaded: he rose, paced the room, as much for appearance sake as to warm himself; then he opened the bookcase. Some English novels were in it, mixed

up with heavy Bibles and some well-thumbed volumes of
the Swiss Alpine Club: he took one of these, with the intention of reading it in bed, but he was stopped at the door,
as the regulations of the hotel do not permit any one to
carry books up stairs to the bedrooms.

Then, continuing to wander about, he opened the door of
the billiard-room, where the Italian tenor was playing by
himself, bending himself into graceful attitudes, and displaying his wristbands for the edification of his pretty neighbour,
who was seated on a divan between two young men, to whom
she was reading a letter. As the mountaineer entered she
paused, and one of the young fellows got up—he was the
taller, a sort of *moujik, homme-chien*, with hairy hands, and
black locks, flat and shiny, joined to an untrimmed beard.
He made two paces towards the new-comer, and looked at
him so provokingly and so ferociously that the kindly
Alpinist, without demanding any explanation, executed a
half-turn to the right prudently and with dignity.

" They are not very pleasant people in the North," he said
aloud, as he slammed the door behind him loudly to let the
savage perceive that he was not afraid of him.

The *salon* was now his only remaining refuge. He entered
it. *Coquin de sort!* The Morgue, good people, the Morgue
of Mont St. Bernard—wherein the monks exhibit the unfortunate travellers who have been found in the snow in the
various attitudes in which they were frozen to death—that
was what the *salon* of the Rigi-Kulm was!

All the ladies, in frozen silence, in groups upon the circular
seats, or had fallen even on isolated chairs, here and there.
All the young ladies, immovable, under the lamps on the
round tables, still holding in their hands the album, the
magazine, or the embroidery which they were holding when
the cold seized them; and amongst them were the daughters
of the general, the eight little Peruvians with their saffron
complexions, their tresses in disorder, the bright-coloured
ribbons of their dresses contrasting with the more subdued
tones of the English fashions, poor little *pays-chauds* whom
one can imagine grinning and grimacing at the tops of the
cocoa-nut trees, and whom, more than the other victims, it
pained one to see in that state of silence and congelation.
Then at the end of the room, at the piano, was the death's-

head profile of the old diplomatist, his little mitten-covered hands lay motionless upon the key-board, his face reflecting the yellow tinge of the keys.

Betrayed by his strength and his memory, lost in a polka of his own composition, which he always recommenced at the same movement in default of recollecting the *coda*, the unhappy de Stoltz had gone to sleep while playing it, and with him all the elderly ladies of the Rigi, nodding, in their sleep, their curls, or those lace caps like the crust of a *vol-au-vent* of which Englishwomen are so fond, and which is part of the *cant voyageur*.

The entrance of the Alpinist did not wake them, and he himself was creeping into a seat, overcome by the glacial atmosphere, when some loud and cheering sounds proceeded from the vestibule, where three musicians (a harp, violin, and flute—those wandering minstrels of such piteous mien, with long coats down to their heels, who frequent Swiss hotels) were tuning their instruments. At the very first notes our hero jumped up as if galvanised.

"*Zou!* bravo! Go ahead with the music!"

There he was in an instant, opening the doors, treating the musicians liberally to champagne, feeling somewhat intoxicated himself, though he drank nothing, with this music, which gave him life. He imitated the cornet, he imitated the harp, snapped his fingers together above his head, rolled his eyes, cut a few capers, to the profound astonishment of the tourists who had rushed from all sides at the uproar. Then, roughly, at the first notes of one of Strauss's waltzes, which the musicians attacked with the fury of veritable Tzigans, the Alpinist, perceiving at the door of the *salon* the wife of Professor Schwanthaler, a little chubby Viennese lady, sprightly in appearance and still young—notwithstanding her hair was sprinkled with grey—rushed at her, seized her round the waist, and dragged her out, calling at the same time to the others, "Come, then! waltz away!"

The impetus was given; the entire hotel, thawed and tumultuous now, was carried away by it. They danced in the vestibule, in the *salon*, around the long green table in the reading-room. And it was this devil of a fellow who had set them all going! Nevertheless he danced no more;

he was out of breath after a few turns; but he superintended the ball, pressed the musicians, made up the couples for the dances, threw the Professor of Bonn into the arms of an old Englishwoman, and the most frisky of the Peruvian young ladies upon the austere Astier-Réhu.

Resistance was impossible. This terrible Alpinist carried you away in a perfect whirlwind! "*Et zou! et zou!*" No more disdain, no more hatred. There were now neither Rices nor Prunes! All were waltzers. The madness quickly spread and reached every story; and in the enormous bay of the staircase might have been seen, up to the sixth *étage*, turning around the pilasters with the rigidity of the automata outside a musical *chalet*, the heavy coloured gowns of the Swiss female servants!

Ah, the wind may blow now if it please! let it shake the lamps, let it moan and whistle through the telegraph wires, and whirl the snow in spiral storms over the deserted summit of the mountain! Here all is warm and comfortable; and all were settled for the night.

"All the same, I will go to bed myself," thought the worthy mountaineer.

He seizes his key and his chamber candlestick; at the first floor he pauses a moment to enjoy the sight of his work, to watch the crowd of stuck-up people whom he has compelled to amuse and unstiffen themselves.

A Swiss woman, out of breath with her interrupted dance, presented him a pen and the hotel register.

"If I may venture to request monsieur to inscribe his name—?"

He hesitated an instant. Must he do so? Cannot he preserve his *incognito*?

After all, what matter? Suppose that the intelligence of his arrival at the Rigi should reach the valleys, no one will know for what reason he had come to Switzerland. And then what a joke it would be in the morning.

He took the pen, and with a careless hand, beneath the names of Astier-Réhu, Schwanthaler, and all the other illustrious personages, he signed that name which eclipsed them all—his own: then he ascended to his bedroom without even turning round to see the effect which he was confident he had made.

Behind him the Swiss waitress was reading—

TARTARIN DE TARASCON ;

and underneath it—
P. C. A.

She read that, this Bernese young woman—and was not overcome. She did not know what P. C. A. signified. She had never heard of " Dardarin."

Savage! *vaï !*

II

TARASCON, FIVE MINUTES' STOPPAGE—THE ALPINE CLUB—EXPLANATION OF P. C. A.—RABBITS OF THE WARREN AND OF THE CABBAGE-GARDEN—" THIS IS MY WILL "—THE " SIROP DE CADAVRE " — FIRST ASCENT — TARTARIN MOUNTS HIS SPECTACLES

WHEN the name of " Tarascon " vibrates along the Paris, Lyons, and Mediterranean Line, and in the clear blue vault of the Provençal sky, heads of curious people are protruded from the windows of the carriages of the express train, and from compartment to compartment the travellers say to each other—

" Ah, this is Tarascon! let us see something of Tarascon."

What they do see of it is, however, nothing out of the common: a small, quiet, clean town, some turrets, some roofs, a bridge over the Rhone. But the Tarascon sunlight and its wonderful mirage effects, so fruitful in surprises, in inventions, in bewildering *cocasseries ;* the cheerful little inhabitants, scarcely bigger than a chick-pea, who reflect and epitomise the instincts of all the French people of the South, are lively, brisk, chatty, imaginative, comic, impressionable, —that is what the passengers by the express get a glimpse of, and that is what makes the place popular.

In certain memorable pages which our modesty prevents us from particularising, the historiographer of Tarascon formerly attempted to depict those pleasant days at the little club, singing its " romances "—every one his own—and in default of game, organising curious shooting-parties *à la casquette*.[1] Then the war came—the " black times," as they call it at Tarascon—its heroic defence, the torpedo-lined esplanade, the club and the Café de la Comédie rendered impregnable; all the inhabitants enrolled as Free Companions —embellished with death's heads and cross-bones, all beards grown, and such a display made of hatchets, cutlasses, and American revolvers, that the unfortunate inhabitants were afraid to venture out in the streets for fear of each other.

Many years have passed since the war, many almanacs have been burned, but Tarascon has not been forgotten; and renouncing the futile distractions of a past time, only considers how to turn its blood and muscle to profit in future revenge.

At length the old club itself, abjuring *bouillotte* and besigue, was transformed into the Alpine Club, after the pattern of the famous Alpine Club in London, whose members have sustained its renown even in the Indies.

There is, however, this difference between the clubs—that the Tarasconnais, instead of expatriating themselves with the view of conquering strange and distant mountains, are content with what they have in their hands, or rather under their feet, at the gates of their town.

The Alps of Tarascon? No, but the *Alpines*, that chain of little hills perfumed with thyme and lavender; neither very difficult nor very high (some 450 to 600 feet in elevation above the level of the sea), which form a horizon of blue waves to the Provençal roads, and which the local imagination has supplied with fabulous and characteristic names, such as *le Mont-Terrible, le Bout-du-Monde, le Pic-des-Geánts*, etc.

It is a pleasant sight on a Sunday morning to see the Tarasconnais fully accoutred, with ice-axe, knapsack, and

[1] This is what was said of the local sport in the *Prodigious Adventures of Tartarin of Tarascon* :
" After a good breakfast in the open country each one of the sportsmen took his cap, threw it with all his strength into the air, and fired at it ' flying ' with No. 5, No. 6, or No. 2 shot, according to the regulations. He who hit his cap oftenest was proclaimed King of the Sport, and returned in the evening to Tarascon in triumph—his riddled cap at the end of his gun—amidst the barking of dogs and the flourish of trumpets."

tent on his back, go forth, preceded by clarions, to make the ascent of which the *Forum*—the local journal—gives such a flourishing and descriptive account, with an exaggeration of epithets, " abysses, ravines, terrible gorges," as if it were describing an ascent in the Himalayas. Just think that in this pastime the natives have acquired new strength, the " double muscles " formerly the attributes of the good, brave, heroic Tartarin only.

If Tarascon epitomised the South, Tartarin epitomised Tarascon. He was not only the first citizen of the town, he was its soul, its genius; he knew all about it. He was acquainted with its ancient exploits, its triumphs of song (oh that duet from *Robert le Diable* at the chemist's!), with the astounding Odyssey of its lion-hunts from which he brought back that splendid camel, the last in Algeria, which has since died full of years and honours, the skeleton of which is in the town museum amongst the Tarasconnais curiosities.

Tartarin himself had not deteriorated; he had still good teeth, a bright eye, notwithstanding his fifty years; and always conserved that extraordinary imagination which brought near and enlarged objects with the power of a telescope. It was of him that the brave commander Bravida said, " *C'est un lapin.*"

Two rabbits, rather. For in Tartarin, as in all the Tarasconnais, there is a warren and a cabbage breed, very clearly marked. The rabbit of the warren is a rover—an adventurous animal; the cabbage-rabbit is domesticated—a stay-at-home, having an extraordinary horror of fatigue, of draughts, and of all the contingencies which may bring death in their train.

We all know that this prudence never prevented him from showing himself brave, and ever heroic, on occasion; but it is quite permissible to inquire what business he had on the Rigi (*Regina montium*) at his age, when he had so dearly purchased the right to his ease and comfort.

To such a question the infamous Costecalde only could reply.

Costecalde, a gun-maker by trade, represented a type rare in Tarascon. Envy—base, malignant envy—visible in the curl of the thin lips, and in a kind of yellow steam which, rising from the liver in puffs, swelled his large, shaven face into uneven ridges as if produced by the blows of a hammer—like an ancient medal of Tiberius or Caracalla. Envy with him was a disease which he did not even attempt to hide, and with that fine Tarasconic temperament, which is gushing enough, he used to say when speaking of his infirmity, " You do not know how bad it is! "

Costecalde's tormentor naturally was Tartarin. All that glory for one man! To him ever; always to him! And slowly, surely, like the termite in the gilded wood of the idol, for twenty years he had been sapping and undermining this great reputation, moth-eating it as it were. When in the evening, at the club, Tartarin would relate his combats with the lion, his hunting in the Sahara, Costecalde would indulge in little sniggering laughs, and incredulous shakes of the head.

" But the skins at least, Costecalde, the lion-skins which he sent us, which are yonder in the club-room? "

" Té! pardi. And the furs; do not you think that there is any want of them in Algeria? "

" But the marks of the bullets, quite round, in the heads? "

" And on the other hand, was it not at the time of our cap-hunting that we used to find, in the hatters' shops, caps with bullet-holes, and riddled with shot, for the unskilful marksmen? "

No doubt the fame of Tartarin, the beast-slayer, remained superior to these attacks; but the Alpinist in his own house listened to all the criticism, and Costecalde did not spare him, furious that they had named as President of the Alpine Club a man who was ageing visibly, and whose habits, contracted in Algeria, disposed him to laziness.

Rarely did Tartarin take part in any of the ascents; he contented himself by accompanying the climbers with his good wishes, and in reading to the full assembly, with much rolling of eyes, and emphasis which made ladies grow pale, the dramatic records of the expeditions.

Costecalde, on the contrary, dry, muscular, nervous, " *Jambe de coq*," as they called him, always climbed first of all: he had made all the ascents of the *Alpines* one by one, and had planted upon their lofty summits the flag of the club, the silver-spangled *Tarasque* or dragon. Nevertheless, he was only the Vice-President (V. P. C. A.), but he was working so well that evidently at the next election Tartarin would be ousted.

Advised of this by his associates, our hero was at first terribly disgusted; the evil spirit which ingratitude and injustice will raise in the best minds seized upon him. He had a great mind to give the whole thing up—to emigrate —to cross the bridge, and live in Beaucaire amongst the Volsques. But he grew calmer after a while.

To leave his little house, his garden, his cherished habits, to renounce his chair as President of the Alpine Club he had founded, to give up the majestic P. C. A. which embellished and distinguished his card, his writing paper, even the lining of his hat! It was not to be thought of! It was impossible! *Vé!* Then suddenly there occurred to him a perfectly miraculous notion.

As a matter of fact the exploits of Costecalde were confined to his expeditions in the *Alpines*. Why should not Tartarin, during the three months which must intervene between that time and the election, attempt some grand adventure? why should not he plant upon the highest summits in Europe (the Jungfrau and Mont Blanc for instance) the banner of his club?

What a triumph would await him on his return, what a slap in the face it would be for Costecalde when the *Forum* would have published the narrative of the ascent! How after that could he dare to dispute the possession of the chairmanship?

With all speed he went to work: he had sent to him secretly from Paris a number of special works, such as Whymper's *Scrambles in the Alps,* Tyndall's *Among the Glaciers,* Stephen d'Arve's *Mont Blanc,* the *Alpine Journals* (both Swiss and English); and he fuddled his brain with a string of Alpine terms,—chimneys, *couloirs, moulins, névé, séracs, moraines, rotures,*—without knowing precisely what they all meant.

At night his dreams were disturbed by interminable *glissades,* and sheer falls into bottomless crevasses! Avalanches overwhelmed him; *arêtes* of ice impaled his body on the way; and long after he was awake and had consumed his morning chocolate, which he always took in bed, he retained the agony and the oppression of the nightmare. But that did not deter him, once he had got up, from devoting his morning to the laborious exercise of getting into training.

There is all around Tarascon a road planted with trees, which in the local parlance is called "*le tour de ville.*" Every Sunday, in the afternoon, the residents, who despite their imaginativeness are a regular people, always make the tour of the town, and always in the same way. Tartarin trained himself by doing it eight or ten times in the morning, and often even in the opposite direction! He proceeded with his hands behind his back, taking short steps as on a mountain, slow and sure, and the stall-keepers, horrified at this infraction of the local custom, lost themselves in speculations of the most complicated character.

At home, in his own garden, he practised leaping crevasses by jumping over the little basin wherein some water-lilies floated; on two occasions he fell in, and was obliged to go and change his clothes. These drawbacks only excited him to fresh effort, and, risking vertigo, he walked along the narrow rim of the basin, to the manifest alarm of the old servant, who could by no means understand all these performances.

At the same time he ordered from Avignon *crampons*, such as are recommended by Whymper, for his boots, and an ice-axe of the Kennedy pattern; he also procured a cooking-lamp, two waterproof coverings, and two hundred feet of rope of his own invention, twisted with iron wire.

The arrival of these different articles, the mysterious comings and goings which their manufacture necessitated, exercised the Tarasconnais very greatly. It was reported in the town that the President was preparing a *coup*. But of what nature? Something great for certain, for according to the brave and sententious commandant Bravida, a retired captain who only dealt in apophthegms, "The eagle does not hunt flies!"

With his most intimate friends Tartarin remained impenetrable; but at the club meetings they would remark the trembling of his voice and his flashing eyes when he spoke to Costecalde—an indirect result of this new expedition, of which the dangers and fatigues became more accentuated as the time drew nearer. The unlucky man did not conceal them from himself, and he looked at them in such lugubrious colours that he put his affairs in order and wrote his last wishes, the expression of which costs the Tarasconnais, who love their lives, so much that they generally die intestate!

So one morning in June, a bright, sunny day, without a cloud in the sky, the door of the study open to the neat little garden with its sanded walks, on which the exotic plants threw clearly-defined shadows, in which a tiny jet of water trickled amid the joyous cries of the Savoyards who were playing at *marelle* before the gate,—on that morning see Tartarin in slippers, and easy flannel costume, happy, satisfied, smoking a favourite pipe, and reading aloud as he wrote,—

"This is my will."

One had need to have a heart firm in its place and solidly fixed; these are cruel moments! Nevertheless, neither his hand nor his voice shook, while he devised to the citizens all the ethnographical riches treasured in his little house, carefully dusted and kept in first-rate order,—

"To the Alpine Club, the baobab (*Arbos gigantea*), to be placed on the chimney-piece of the hall of science.

"To Bravida, my fowling-pieces, revolvers, hunting-knives, Malay knives, tomahawks, and other deadly weapons.

"To Excourbaniès, all my pipes, calumets, *narghilés*, and little pipes for kif and opium smoking.

"To Costecalde—yes, Costecalde himself had his legacy—the famous poisoned arrows. (Mind you don't touch them!)"

Perhaps Tartarin had a secret hope that the man would touch them and die, but no such idea was evidenced in the will, which closed with these words of divine mansuetude,—

"I beg my dear Alpinists not to forget their president. I hope they will forgive my mortal enemy as I forgive him, although it is he, nevertheless, who has occasioned my death."

Here Tartarin was compelled to stop, blinded by his tears. For one moment he seemed to see himself a mangled mass at the foot of some lofty mountain, picked up in a wheelbarrow, and his shapeless remains carried to Tarascon. Oh, power of the Provençal imagination! he was assisting at his own funeral, listening to the chants for the dead, the discourse at the grave. "Poor Tartarin! *péchère!*" And lost amid the crowd of his friends, he began to weep for himself!

But almost immediately the sight of his study, filled with sunlight, glittering with weapons and rows of pipes, the song of the little *jet d'eau* in the garden, brought him back to the reality of things. On the other hand, why should he die? why even go away? Who compelled him to do so, if not his own self-respect? To risk his life for a presidential chair and three letters!

But this was only weakness, and did not last longer than the other impression. At the end of five minutes the will was finished, signed, and sealed with an enormous black seal, and the great man then made the last preparations for his departure.

Once again Tartarin of the warren had triumphed over Tartarin of the cabbage-garden. And we might say of this Tarascon hero what was said of Turenne: "His body was not always ready to go into battle, but his soul carried him there in spite of himself."

On the evening of that very day, as the last stroke of ten was sounding from the *maison de ville*, and the streets, already deserted, were clear except for here and there a belated one knocking for admission, a gruff voice half strangled with fear cried in the dark, "Good-night, *au mouain*," and then, with a sudden closing of the door, a pedestrian glided through the darkened town where the fronts of the houses were only illuminated by the red and green tints brightly reflected from the bottles in Bézuquet's shop, which were projected with the silhouette of the chemist himself, with his elbows on his desk, and sleeping on the Codex. He indulged in a little nap every evening in this manner, from nine till ten, so that—as he said—he might be all the fresher at night, should any one require his services. Between ourselves, this was a mere Tarasconnade, for no one ever called him up, and indeed he had himself severed the wire of the night-bell in order that he might sleep the more soundly.

Suddenly Tartarin entered, wrapped up, his travelling-bag in his hand, and so pale, so discomposed, that the chemist, with that vivid local imagination of which the shop did not deprive him, believed that some fearful and terrible thing had happened.

"Unhappy man!" he exclaimed, "what is the matter? You have been poisoned? Quick, quick, the ipecacuanha!"

He was hurrying off, upsetting his bottles, when Tartarin, to stop him, was obliged to hold him round the body: "Just listen now, *qué diable!*"—and in his sharp tones the spitefulness of the actor who has made a bad entrance was manifest. The chemist once again brought back to his counter by an iron hand, Tartarin whispered,—

"Are we alone, Bézuquet?"

"*Bé oui!*" replied the other, looking about him in vague terror. "Pascalon has gone to bed (Pascalon was his pupil), and mother also—But why?"

"Shut your shutters," said Tartarin in a commanding tone, without replying to the question. "They can see us from outside."

Bézuquet obeyed, trembling. He was an old bachelor, living with his mother, whom he had never quitted; he was as timid and gentle as a girl, and his demeanour contrasted strangely with his swarthy face and thick lips, his immense hooked nose, which bent over his long moustache—a head of an Algerian pirate before the conquest. These antitheses are common in Tarascon, where the heads possess too much of the Roman and Saracenic character: heads with the expression of models in a school of design, unfitted to mere tradespeople and the ultra-pacific manners of the little town.

Thus it was that Excourbaniès, who had the air of one of the bold companions of Pizarro, was a mercer, and rolled flaming yellow eyes when measuring off two yards of thread; and that Bézuquet, labelling the Spanish liquorice and the *sirupus gummi*, resembled an ancient rover of the Barbary coast.

When the shutters had been closed, and fastened with bolt and bar, Tartarin said, "Listen, Ferdinand," for he had a habit of calling people by their Christian names. Then he arose and "emptied his heart," which was full of bitterness against his associates. He related the low manœuvres of "*Jambe de coq*," the trick which they wished to play him at the next election, and the manner in which he hoped to checkmate them.

Sirop de Cadavre

In the first place, it was most important to keep the matter a secret, and not reveal it until the precise moment which would determine the success of the plan had arrived, always except in case of an accident—one of those fearful catastrophes—"*Eh ! coquin de sort*, Bézuquet; don't whistle like that while I am speaking."

This was one of the chemist's little habits. Being taciturn by nature—a phenomenon in Tarascon—he gained the confidence of the President; his big lips, always like an O, preserved the habit of a continual whistling, which seemed to ridicule every one, even in the most solemn moments.

And while the hero was alluding to his possible death, and saying, as he placed the folded, sealed packet upon the table, "My last wishes are declared here, Bézuquet: I have chosen you as the executor of my will——"

"*Hu, hu, hu,*" whistled the chemist, carried away by his mania, but really very much moved, and quite appreciating the importance of the part he had to play.

Then the hour of departure approached: he wished to drink success to the enterprise—"something good, *qué ?* a glass of the Garus Elixir." After many cupboards had been opened and searched, he remembered that his mother had the keys of the Garus. It would be necessary to wake her, and tell who was there. So a substitute for the elixir was found in a glass of the syrup of Calabria, a summer beverage, modest and inoffensive, of which Bézuquet was the inventor, and which was advertised in the *Forum* as "*Sirop de Calabre*, ten sous the bottle, including a glass"! "*Sirop de Cadavre,*" that infernal Costecalde would say, for he sneered at all successes: for the rest, this abominable play upon the words only aided the sale, and the Tarasconnais were exceedingly fond of this *sirop de Cadavre*.

The libation performed, a few last words exchanged, the friends tore themselves asunder. Bézuquet was still whistling through his moustache, while great tears were rolling down his cheeks.

"Adieu, *au mouain*," said Tartarin in a rough voice, feeling as if he were about to weep also; and as the shutter of the door had been put up, the hero was obliged to leave the shop on all fours.

The trials of his journey were already commencing.

Three days later he disembarked at Vitznau, at the foot of the Rigi. As a preliminary canter to get into training for mountaineering, the Rigi attracted him because of its low altitude (1800 mètres, about ten times the height of *Mont-Terrible,* the most elevated peak of the *Alpines !*), and also because of the splendid panorama which is obtainable from the summit, all the Bernese Alps seated, white and rosy, round the lakes, waiting till the climber shall make his choice, and throw his ice-axe at one of them.

Sure of being recognised *en route,* and perhaps followed—for it was a weakness of his to fancy he was as well-known throughout France as he was celebrated and popular in Tarascon—he had made a wide *détour* to reach Switzerland, and did not " harness " himself until he had crossed the frontier. It was a good thing he did not, as his " armament " could never be contained in a French railway compartment.

But, however commodious the Swiss railway carriages may be, the Alpinist, embarrassed by implements to the use of which he was quite unaccustomed, stabbed people's toes with the point of his alpenstock, harpooned others with his *crampons,* and everywhere he went, in the railway stations, the hotels, or on the steamer, he excited as much astonishment as cursing, elbowing, and angry looks, which he could not understand, and which were torture to his candid and affectionate nature. To sum up, there was a leaden sky, heavy clouds, and a pelting rain.

It rained at Bâle, where the houses are washed and re-washed by servants and the water from heaven; it rained at Lucerne, on the quay where the mails and luggage seemed to be just recovered from a wreck; and when he reached Vitznau, on the brink of the Lake of the Four Cantons, there was the same deluge falling upon the green slopes of the Rigi, encircled by black clouds, with torrents dashing over the rocks, making cascades in dust-like spray, dropping from all the stones and from every fir-branch. Tartarin had never seen so much water before.

He entered an *auberge,* and was served with some *café au lait,* honey, and butter, the only really good things that he had so far enjoyed in his journey. Then, once more refreshed, his beard cleared of some honey by means of a corner of his *serviette,* he made preparations to attempt his first ascent.

The First Ascent

"And now," said he, as he was packing up his *sac*, "how long will it take me to get to the top of the Rigi?"

"An hour or an hour and a quarter, monsieur. But you must make haste; the train will start in five minutes."

"A train up the Rigi! You are joking!"

Through the leaden-sashed window of the *auberge* she showed him the train which was about to ascend. Two large covered waggons without windows, pushed by a locomotive with a short chimney and with a kettle-shaped body —a monstrous insect clinging to the mountain, and getting quite out of breath in its attempt to climb the steep sides.

The two Tartarins—the wild and the domestic species— were shocked at the idea of ascending in this hideous machine. One thought it ridiculous to climb the Alps in a lift: as for the other, the light bridges which carry the line over chasms, with the prospect of a fall of a thousand feet if the train left the metals ever so little, inspired him with all kinds of sad reflections, which found reason for the establishment of the little cemetery at Vitznau, the tombs in which are squeezed together at the bottom of the slope like the linen displayed in the courtyard of a laundry. Evidently this cemetery is established as a matter of precaution, so that in case of accident travellers may find it quite convenient.

"I'll go up on foot," said the valiant Tarasconnais. "It will give me some exercise. *Zou!*"

And so he went, very much pre-occupied by his alpenstock in the presence of the staff of the *auberge*, who ran to the door shouting to him the way, indications which he never heard. He first pursued an ascending path, paved with great pebbles, of unequal sizes, pointed, as in a Southern lane, and bordered with wooden channels to permit the escape of the rain-water.

To right and left are fine orchards, grassy meadows crossed by these same irrigating pipes made from trunks of trees. This arrangement causes a continual splashing of water from the top to the bottom of the mountain, and every time that the ice-axe of the Alpinist caught in the low branches of an oak or chestnut his cap crackled as if subjected to a shower from a watering-pot.

"*Diou!* what a quantity of water!" sighed the man of the South. But things became worse when the paved way ceased, for then he was obliged to pick his way through the torrent, to leap from one stone to another, so as not to wet his gaiters. Then the downpour hindered him, penetrating, continuous; and it seemed to get colder as he ascended. When he stopped to take breath, he could hear nothing but the rushing of the water in which he stood, half-drowned, and when he turned round he could see the black clouds united to the lake by long fine rods of glass, through which the *chalets* of Vitznau glistened like freshly varnished toy-houses.

Several men and children passed close by, some with heads bent down and backs curved under the hod of white wood containing supplies for some villa or *pension*, whose balconies could be perceived mid-way. "To the Rigi-Kulm?" asked Tartarin, to assure himself that he was in the right direction; but his extraordinary equipment, and particularly the knitted comforter which shrouded his face, alarmed those he addressed, and every one of them, after staring at him with wide-open eyes, hurried upwards without replying.

These meetings soon became few and far between: the last human being he encountered, was an old woman who was washing some linen in the trunk of a tree under the shade of an enormous red umbrella fixed in the ground.

"Rigi-Kulm?" asked the Alpinist.

The old woman raised to his a terrified and idiotic face, bearing a *goître* which hung from her neck, as large as the bell of a Swiss cow: then after having taken a long look at him she burst into a peal of inextinguishable laughter, which stretched her mouth from ear to ear, puckering up her little eyes; and every time that she opened them again, the sight of Tartarin standing before her, his ice-axe on his shoulder, seemed to redouble her mirth.

"*Tron de l'air!*" growled the Tarasconnais, "it's lucky she's a woman;" and bursting with rage he continued his *route*, losing his way in a pine wood, where his boots slipped upon the soaking moss.

Beyond that, the scene changed. No more paths, no trees nor pastures. A few mournful slopes, bare, but sustaining great boulders, which he was obliged to scale on hands and knees for fear of falling; morasses full of yellow mud, which he crossed slowly, testing the quagmire with his alpenstock,

The First Ascent

and lifting his feet like a knife-grinder. Every moment he consulted the compass which hung as a charm to his watch-chain; but, whether owing to the altitude or to the variations of the temperature, the needle seemed defective. He had no means by which he could take his bearings, for the thick yellow fog that prevented him from seeing ten paces in any direction, was penetrated by a thick, cold sleet, which made the ascent more and more laborious.

Suddenly he halted, the ground was white in front. Take care of your eyes! He had come to the snow-line!

Immediately he drew his glasses from their case and adjusted them firmly. The moment was a solemn one. Somewhat nervous, but proud all the same, Tartarin felt that at one bound he had ascended 3000 feet towards the peaks and their dangers!

He advanced with great precaution, thinking of the *crevasses* and the *rotures* of which he had read, and in his heart of hearts cursing the people of the *auberge*, who had advised him to ascend straight up without a guide.

Night would surprise him on the mountain. Could he find a hut, or only the projection of a rock, to shelter himself? Suddenly he perceived, on the wild and desolate platform, a kind of wooden *chalet*, bound with a placard bearing enormous letters, which he deciphered with difficulty: PHO—TO—GRA —PHIE DU RI—GI—KULM. At the same moment the immense hotel with its three hundred windows became visible to him a little farther on between the great lamps, which burned brightly in the fog.

III

AN ALARM ON THE RIGI—BE COOL! BE COOL!—THE ALPINE HORN—WHAT TARTARIN FOUND ON HIS LOOKING-GLASS WHEN HE AWOKE—PERPLEXITY—HE ASKS FOR A GUIDE BY TELEPHONE

"*Quès aco?* Who goes there?" cried Tartarin, listening attentively, and with eyes wide open in the dark.

The pattering of many feet was audible in the hotel—doors banged—sounds of puffing—blowing—cries of "Make haste!"—while out of doors was a blowing of horns, and a rush of flame lighted up the windows and the curtains.

Fire!

With a single bound Tartarin was out of bed, and, rapidly shod and dressed, gained the still gas-lit staircase, where he found, descending, a buzzing swarm of young ladies hastily *coiffées*, wrapped up in green shawls, woollen scarves—anything that first came to hand when they got out of bed.

Tartarin, with a view to fortifying his own courage, and to reassure the young ladies as he rushed about and ran against everybody, cried out, Keep cool! keep cool!" with the voice of a sea-gull—a thin, faint voice—one of those which one hears in dreams, which give the "creeps" to the bravest of us. Can you imagine how the young ladies almost shouted with laughter as they looked at him? only thinking him very funny indeed. They had no idea of the danger—at their age!

Fortunately the old diplomatist came after them, rapidly arrayed in a dressing-gown over white *caleçons*, and silken slippers.

At last there was a man!

Tartarin ran up to him gesticulating: "Ah, Monsieur le Baron, what a terrible mishap! Do you know anything about it? Where is it? How did it break out?"

"Who? what?" bleated the bewildered Baron, who understood nothing of all this.

"Why, the fire!"

"What fire?"

The unfortunate man was evidently so vacant and stupid that Tartarin left him to himself, and dashed out of doors to organise assistance.

"Assistance! Help!" repeated the Baron; and after him five or six waiters, who slept standing in the antechamber, stared at each other and repeated in a bewildered fashion, "Help!"

At the first step he took outside the building Tartarin perceived his mistake. There was not the least sign of a fire. A nipping cold, a dark night illuminated by pine-torches which threw a lurid glare upon the snow.

At the bottom of the steps, a man with an Alpine horn emitted his modulated lowings, a monotonous *ranz des vaches* of three notes, with which it is the fashion on the Rigi-Kulm to awake the sun-worshippers, and to announce to them the approaching appearance of the luminary.

It is stated that he shows himself sometimes, at his first rising, at the extreme edge of the mountain behind the hotel. To find his bearings Tartarin had only to follow the continual tittering of the girls, who were walking close to him. But he proceeded more slowly, still feeling very sleepy, and stiff in his limbs after his six hours' climb.

"Is that you Maniloff?" asked a clear-toned voice suddenly out of the darkness—a lady's voice: "come and help me; I have lost my shoe."

Tartarin recognised the bird-like notes of his little neighbour at the *table d'hôte*, whose graceful profile he caught in the pale light reflected from the snowy ground.

"It is not Maniloff, mademoiselle; but if I can be of any assistance——"

She uttered a little cry of surprise and fear, and made a gesture of repulsion which Tartarin did not see, for he was already stooping down and tapping the short grass, which crackled with frost beneath his fingers.

"*Té, pardi!* here it is!" he exclaimed joyfully. He shook the slender shoe, which was powdered with rime, knelt down on one knee on the cold damp ground, in the most gallant fashion, and asked that he might be rewarded by having the honour to put on Cinderella's slipper!

The lady, more unamiable than in the story, replied with

a " No " very sharply uttered, and hopping on one foot endeavoured to insert her silk stocking into the reddish-brown shoe; but she would never have succeeded without the aid of our hero, who was very much pleased to feel a little hand resting for a minute on his shoulder.

"You have very good eyes," she said by way of acknowledgment, while they proceeded groping their way in the dark side by side.

"The result of sporting habits, mademoiselle."

"Ah, then you are a sportsman!"

She said this with some raillery and a little incredulity in her voice. Tartarin had only to mention his name to convince her of the fact, but, like all illustrious people, he was discreet, and, with a kind of coquetry, wished to surprise her by degrees as it were,—

"I am a hunter, as a matter of fact!"

She continued in her ironical tone,—

"And what game do you hunt for choice, now?"

"The large carnivora and the great deer," replied Tartarin, believing he would overwhelm her.

"Do you find many of them on the Rigi?" she asked.

Always polite in his repartee, Tartarin was going to reply that on the Rigi he had met none but *gazelles*, when his remark was cut short by the approach of two shadows who called out,—

"Sonia! Sonia!"

"I am coming," she said, and then turning towards Tartarin, whose eyes, now accustomed to the obscurity, were able to distinguish her pretty pale face under a mantilla *en manola*, she added, this time seriously,—

"You are engaged in a dangerous pursuit, my good man. Take care you do not lose your life——"

And then, all of a sudden, she disappeared in the darkness with her friends.

Later on the menacing import of these words occurred to the imaginative mind of the Southerner: but at the time he was only vexed at the use of the term "good man," flung at his stoutness and grey hair, and at the careless disappearance of the young lady just as he was going to tell her who he was, and to gloat over her stupefaction.

He advanced a few paces in the direction of the group

A Rigi Sunrise

who were preceding him, with a confused murmur in his ears —the coughing, the sneezing of the assembled tourists, who were waiting with impatience the rising of the sun: some of the most adventurous climbed up into a little stand or belvedere, the supports of which, coated with snow, were distinguishable in the dying darkness of the night.

A gleam of light began to streak the eastern sky, and was saluted by another note on the Alpine horn, and with that "ah" which escapes from the overcharged bosoms of the spectators as the prompter's last bell rings for the raising of the curtain. Thin as a crack in a lid, the light gradually extended itself, widening the horizon, but at the same time raising from the valley a thick, opaque, yellow fog, which became thicker and more extended as day broke. It was like a veil between the stage and the audience.

They were obliged to give up all hope of seeing the beautiful effects described by the guide-books. On the other hand, the heterodox costumes of the dancers of the night before, hurriedly aroused from sleep, were displayed as in a magic lantern, ludicrous and eccentric; for shawls, counterpanes, even the curtains of the beds which they had occupied were worn. Beneath the varied head-dresses—silk or cotton caps, hoods, toques, night-caps—were scared, puffed faces, the heads of shipwrecked people on an island in the open sea, on the watch for a sail in the offing with all the intentness of gaze of which their widely open eyes were capable.

And nothing—all the time nothing!

Nevertheless, some of them in an access of good will made believe to distinguish the peaks from the belvedere; and the "clucking" of the Peruvian girls were heard as they surrounded a big fellow in a check ulster who was enumerating in the calmest way the invisible panoramic objects of the Bernese Alps, naming and designating, in a loud voice, the peaks which were enveloped in the fog,—

"On the left you see the Finsteraarhorn, 12,825 feet high; the Schreckhorn, the Wetterhorn, the Mönch, the Jungfrau, to the elegant proportions of which I would call the attention of the young ladies."

"*Bé!* true, that fellow does not want for impudence," said Tartarin to himself. Then as an after-thought he muttered—" But I know that voice—*pas mouain.*"

He recognised the accent—that *assent* of the South of France which is as distinguishable at a distance as the garlic is; but so pre-occupied was he in following up the fair unknown that he did not stop, continuing to inspect the groups he passed. She had, no doubt, returned to the hotel, as every one else was now doing, tired of remaining shivering in the cold and stamping their feet.

Some bent backs, some tartan-plaids, the ends of which swept the snow, disappeared into the ever-thickening fog! Very soon nothing remained on the plateau, cold and desolate in the grey dawn, but Tartarin, and the Alpine horn-blower who continued to extract melancholy howls from the instrument like a dog baying at the moon.

He was a little old man, with a long beard, wearing a Tyrolese hat embellished with green tassels which fell down his back, and bearing, like those of all the retainers of the hotel, the *Regina Montium* in letters of gold. Tartarin advanced towards him to bestow on him a *pour-boire*, as he had seen the other tourists do.

"Let us go to bed, old fellow," said he, tapping the man upon the shoulder with the Tarascon familiarity. "A regular humbug, *qué*, this Rigi sunrise!"

The old man continued to blow his horn, finishing his *ritornello* with a silent laugh which wrinkled up the corners of his eyes and shook the green tassels of his hat.

Tartarin, after all, did not regret the experience of the night. The meeting with the pretty blonde made amends to him for his interrupted sleep, for although near his fiftieth year he had still a warm heart, a romantic imagination, an ardent soul. When he again had reached his bedroom, and had shut his eyes to woo sleep, he still fancied he could feel in his hand the tiny shoe, and hear the jerky appeals of the young lady: "Is that you, Maniloff?"

Sonia! What a beautiful name. She was certainly a Russian; and these young men were travelling with her—friends of her brother no doubt. Then all became misty; the golden-curled little head went to mingle with other floating and drowsy visions—the slopes of the Rigi and the waterfalls,—and very soon the heroic snoring of the great man, sonorous and rhythmical, filled the little room and a considerable section of the corridor besides.

As he was about to go down stairs next morning, at the first sound of the breakfast-bell, Tartarin was reassuring himself that his beard had been properly brushed, and that he did not look very badly in his mountaineering costume, when suddenly he began to shake with fear. Before him, open, and stuck in the looking-glass, an anonymous letter displayed the following threatening words,—

"*Français du diable, thy disguise but ill conceals thee. We have spared thee this time, but if thou crossest our path again, beware!*"

Perfectly astounded, he read and re-read the note without comprehending it. Of whom, of what, was he to beware? How had the letter got there? Evidently while he slept, for he had not perceived it when he returned from his early morning promenade. He rang for the chambermaid, a flat-faced creature marked with small-pox like a Gruyère cheese, from whom he could elicit nothing intelligible except that she was of "*pon famille*," and never entered the rooms when a gentleman was in possession.

"What a very curious thing," said Tartarin, as he turned the note over and over. He was greatly impressed. In a moment the name of Costecalde crossed his mind, Costecalde imbued with his own plans of mountaineering, and endeavouring to turn him aside by menaces and plotting! Then he began to persuade himself that the letter was a hoax, for he soon abandoned the other theory; perhaps some of the girls who had laughed at him so merrily had perpetrated it,—they were so independent, these young English and American ladies!

The second bell sounded. He put the anonymous letter in his pocket. "After all, we shall soon see," he muttered, and the formidable *moue* which accompanied this reflection indicated the heroism of his soul.

A new surprise awaited him at the breakfast-table. Instead of the pretty little neighbour with the golden hair he perceived the vulture-like neck of an old English woman whose long "weepers" swept the cloth.

It was repeated near him that the young lady and her party had left by the early train.

"*Cré nom! je suis floué*," exclaimed the Italian tenor who the night before had declared so rudely to Tartarin that he did not understand French. He had evidently learnt it in the night!

The tenor rose from his chair, threw down his *serviette* and rushed out, leaving our hero completely dumbfounded.

A great many of the guests also took their departure. It is always thus on the Rigi, where no one remains more than four-and-twenty hours. Besides, the arrangements of the table are invariably the same, the dessert dishes in long rows separating the two factions. But that morning the Rice Party were triumphant in the large majority—reinforced by some illustrious personages; and the Prunes, as was said, did not show to advantage.

Tartarin, without taking either side, went up stairs, fastened up his knapsack, and sent for his bill. He had had quite enough of *Regina montium*, of its *table d'hôte*, and its "dummies."

Suddenly reminded of his Alpine mania by the touch of his ice-axe, the rope, and the *crampons* with which he was again accoutred, he began to burn with the desire to attack some real mountain—a peak without a lift and a photographic studio in the open. He hesitated between the more elevated Finsteraarhorn and the more celebrated Jungfrau, while the fair virginal name of the latter brought the little Russian once more to his memory.

As he was balancing these questions in his mind while his bill was being got ready, he amused himself in the large, silent, and melancholy hall, by looking at the coloured photographs on the wall, which represent the glaciers, the snow-slopes, the celebrated and dangerous passes of the mountains. Here is a party in single file, like ants in search of food, upon an ice-*arête*, steep and blue; farther on an enormous crevasse with sea-green sides, across which a ladder had been flung, and was being crossed by a lady on her knees, then by an *abbé* holding up his gown.

The mountaineer of Tarascon, resting his hands upon his ice-axe, had had no idea of such difficulties as those; but he must encounter them somehow!

Suddenly his face paled in fear.

In a black frame was an engraving after the famous picture of Gustave Doré, representing the accident on the Matterhorn. Four human bodies, on their backs or on their faces,

A Guide by Telephone

were sliding down the snow-slope, their arms extended, their hands beating the snow, seeking the broken rope on which their lives depended, and which had only served to drag them more easily to death over the precipice when they fell pellmell with ropes, axes, green veils, and all the pleasant apparatus of the ascent which had become so terribly tragic.

"*Mâtin!*" said Tartarin, speaking aloud in dismay.

One of the polite managers heard his exclamation, and thought it his duty to reassure the guest. Accidents of that kind were becoming more and more rare: prudence was one essential qualification, and, particularly, a good guide.

Tartarin inquired whether the manager could tell him of one in confidence. Not that he had any fear; but it was always best to be on the safe side.

The man considered the point with a very important air, caressing his whiskers the while. "In confidence? Ah! if monsieur had only mentioned it sooner we had here this morning the very man. The courier of a Peruvian family."

"He is acquainted with the mountain?" asked Tartarin with a knowing air.

"Oh, monsieur, with every mountain—in Switzerland, Savoy, the Tyrol, and India, in the whole world—he has done them all; he knows them by heart, and will tell you about them. He is something like! I believe they would relinquish him without making any difficulty. With such a man as he a child could go anywhere without danger!"

"Where is he? Where can he be found?"

"At the Kaltbad, monsieur, where he is arranging the rooms for his party. We can telephone."

A telephone, on the Rigi!

That was the crowning of the edifice. Tartarin was never astonished at anything after that!

In five minutes the *garçon* returned with the reply.

The Peruvians' courier was leaving for Tellsplatte, where he would certainly stay the night.

This Tellsplatte is a memorial chapel, one of the shrines established in honour of William Tell, many of which are found in Switzerland. People go there to see the frescoes which a celebrated painter of Bâle has executed on the walls of the chapel.

It was scarcely an hour by steamboat—or an hour and a

half perhaps. Tartarin did not hesitate. He might thus
lose a day, but he must pay his respects to William Tell, for
whom he had a strong predilection; and then there was the
chance to secure this wonderful guide and arrange to do the
Jungfrau with him.

En route, *zou !*

He immediately paid his bill, in which the sunrise and
sunset were included as well as the lights and attendance,
and then, preceded by the terrible clanking of iron which
disseminated fear and surprise wherever he went, he proceeded to the railway—for to descend the Rigi on foot when
he had already walked up it seemed to him waste of time,
and would, besides, be doing too much honour to that
artificial mountain.

IV

ON BOARD THE STEAMER—RAIN—THE HERO OF TARASCON
SALUTES THE SHADES—THE TRUTH ABOUT WILLIAM TELL
—DISILLUSION—TARTARIN OF TARASCON NEVER EXISTED!
—" TÉ! BOMPARD!"

HE had left snow on the Rigi-Kulm—below on the lake he
found rain, a fine close rain, a kind of mist in which the
mountains appeared like clouds.

The *Föhn* wind was blowing, making waves upon the lake,
where the gulls, flying low, seemed to be carried on by the
billows: one could almost fancy one's self at sea.

Tartarin recalled his departure from Marseilles fifteen years
before, when he was setting out to hunt lions—he thought of
that sky without a cloud, bathed in light; the blue sea, blue
as indigo, stirred up into crisp salt waves by the mistral; the
salutes of the forts, the clanging of the bells, intoxication,
joy, sun, all the fairy impressions of the first voyage!

What a contrast was it with the black deck of the almost
deserted little steamer, on which he made out as in a mist a

few passengers wrapped in ulsters or mackintoshes; and the man at the wheel, motionless abaft, hooded, grave, and sybilline, above the legend couched in three languages: "You must not speak to the man at the wheel."

This prohibition was quite unnecessary, for no one spoke on board the *Winkelried* at all,—no more on deck than in the cabins, which were crammed with passengers of melancholy mien, sleeping, reading, yawning, pell-mell, their light baggage strewn upon the benches. They appeared like a number of people being transported on the day after a *coup d'état*.

From time to time the hoarse steam whistle announced the approach to a station. A noise of footsteps and of the unloading of luggage resounded from the deck. Then the shore faded into the mist, advanced again, displaying the dark green slopes, the villas shivering amid the saturated trees, the poplars in rows along the road, bordered all its length by sumptuous hotels designated in letters of gold on their façades — the hotels Meyer, Müller, du Lac, with numbers of heads belonging to bored residents looking out of the dripping casements.

The people crossed the gangway to the shore; descended, ascended; equally dirty, soaked, and silent. On the tiny pier a crowd of umbrellas was visible: the omnibus quickly disappeared. Then the paddle-wheels churned the water into foam and the shore receded, fading into the blurred landscape with the *pensions* Meyer, Müller, du Lac,—all the windows of which, for an instant open, displaying at every story a waving of pocket handkerchiefs, and outstretched arms, as if to say: "Have mercy!—pity us! take us away —if you only knew—!"

Sometimes the *Winkelried* would pass another steamer, with its name in black letters on the white ground—*Germania, Guillaume Tell*. There was the same lugubrious deck, the same shiny waterproofs, the same lamentable passage, no matter in which direction the phantom vessel was proceeding, the same distressful glances were exchanged from one to the other.

And to think that all these people were travelling for pleasure! that they were prisoners for their own pleasure in the *pensions* of Meyer, Müller, and du Lac!

Here, as at the Rigi-Kulm, the great grievance of Tartarin,

which irritated him more than the cold rain or the leaden sky, was the impossibility of speaking!

Below, he had again found some well-known faces—the member of the Jockey Club, with his niece! The Academician, Astier-Réhu, and Professor Schwanthaler, those two implacable foes, condemned to exist side by side for a month, bound to the same itinerary, to a Cook's circular tour, with others too: but none of these illustrious Prunes would recognise the Tarasconnais, who was nevertheless easily recognisable by his comforter and his equipment, in a most indubitable manner. Every one seemed ashamed of that dance the evening before, and of the inexplicable transports into which they had been inveigled by that fat man.

Madame Schwanthaler alone came towards her partner, with the bright and rosy appearance of a little chubby fairy, and holding her skirt between two fingers as if she was about to perform a minuet, she said, "*Ballir,—dantsir,—très choli!*" Was she invoking memory, or tempting him to tread another measure? She would not let him alone; and Tartarin, to escape her importunity, went on deck again, preferring to be wet to his very bones rather than be made a laughing-stock.

And it did come down, and the sky was murky! To heighten the gloom, a whole detachment of the Salvation Army was going to Beckenried—a dozen fat girls of heavy mien, with navy-blue dresses, and coal-scuttle bonnets, under enormous red umbrellas, singing hymns, which were accompanied on the accordion by a man with wild eyes, lanky, emaciated—a kind of David Gamm. These shrill voices, spiritless and discordant as the cries of a gull, came dragging through the rain, and the smoke of the steamer which the wind beat back. Tartarin had never heard anything so deplorable in his life.

At Brunnen the detachment quitted the boat, leaving the tourists' pockets full of pious tracts; and almost immediately the accordion and the singing of these poor *larvæ* had ceased, the sky began to clear, and bits of blue became visible.

Now the steamer was entering the Bay of Uri, shaded and inclosed between wild and lofty mountain; and on the right, at the foot of Seelisberg, the tourists were shown the Grütli, where Melchtal, Fürst, and Stauffacher took the oath to deliver their land from the oppressor.

Tartarin, very much affected, reverently removed his cap, without noticing the astonishment his action aroused; he even waved his head-covering in the air three times, by way of doing homage to the *manes* of the heroes. Some passengers mistook his enthusiasm, and politely returned his salute.

At length the engine uttered a hoarse bellow, which echoed across the narrow bay. The placard which they display on deck at every landing-place—as is done at public balls at every change of dance—announced Tellsplatte. They had arrived!

The chapel is situated five minutes' walk from the landing-place, quite on the margin of the lake, on the very rock upon which William Tell leaped from Gesler's boat in the storm. Tartarin experienced a delicious emotion, while he followed the Cook's tourists along the lake, as he trod the historic ground, and recalled, and lived over again, the principal events of the great drama, the details of which he knew as well as those in his own life.

From his earliest years, William Tell had been his ideal! When, at the chemist's (at Bézuquet's), they used to write their "likes and dislikes," their favourite poet, author, tree, scent, hero or heroine, one of the papers invariably bore the following,—

"The favourite tree?—The baobab.
"The favourite scent?—Of powder.
"The favourite author?—Fenimore Cooper.
"Who would you wish to have been?—William Tell."

Then in the surgery there was only one opinion—they all cried with one voice, "That is Tartarin!"

Ask yourself, then, whether he was not happy, if his heart did not beat high, when he reached this memorial chapel erected as a mark of the gratitude of the entire nation. It seemed to him that William Tell in person, still dripping with water after his plunge in the lake, his cross-bow and arrows in his hand, would open the door to him.

"No admission. I am at work: this is not the day," shouted a voice from the interior, the tone being much increased in volume by the vaulted roof.

"Monsieur Astier-Réhu, of the French Academy."

"Herr Doctor Professor Schwanthaler."

"Tartarin de Tarascon!"

In the ogive window above the door, the artist, perched on a scaffolding, appeared in his working blouse, palette in hand.

"My *famulus* is going down to open the door to you, gentlemen," he said respectfully.

"I was sure of it," thought Tartarin. "I had only to mention my name!"

Nevertheless he had the good taste to keep back, and modestly enter after every one else.

The painter, a very fine young fellow, showing a golden head of an artist of the Renaissance, received his visitors on the wooden steps which ascended to the temporary staging erected for the painting of the chapel. The frescoes, representing the principal episodes in the life of William Tell, had been completed, all but one — the representation of the shooting at the apple in the market-place of Altorf. He was working at it then, and his young assistant—*famulus*, as he called him—his hair *à l'archange*, his legs and feet bare, beneath a smock frock of the middle ages, was posing as the son of William Tell.

All these archaic personages,—red, green, yellow, blue,—of more than human stature, in narrow streets, and intended to be seen from a distance, impressed the spectators rather tamely; but they were there to admire, and they did so. Besides, nobody there knew anything about them!

"I call that most characteristic," said the pontifical Astier-Réhu, bag in hand.

And Schwanthaler, a camp-stool under his arm, not to be outdone, quoted two verses of Schiller, half of which remained in his flowing beard. Then the ladies exclaimed their delight, and for a while nothing was to be heard but such phrases as,—

"*Schön! oh, schön!*"

"Yes; lovely!"

"*Exquis! délicieux!*"

One could have fancied one's self at a confectioner's!

Suddenly, a voice rang out like a trumpet blast in the silence which succeeded.

"That shoulder is wrong, I tell you: that cross-bow is out of drawing!"

We can picture the stupor of the artist, face to face with the critical mountaineer, who, with his staff in hand and ice-axe on his shoulder threatening to wound some one at every moment, was demonstrating energetically that the attitude of William Tell was not correctly represented.

"And I know what I am talking about, *au mouains!* I beg you to believe——"

"Who are you?"

"Who am I!" exclaimed Tartarin, very much "put out." Was it not for him that admission had been granted! Therefore, drawing himself up, he said: "Go and ask my name of the panthers of Zaccar, from the lions of the Atlas. *They* will perhaps inform you!"

There was a simultaneous recoil, a general alarm, at these words.

"But," asked the artist, at length, "in what way is my position not correct?"

"Look at me—you!"

Falling into position with a stamping which drove the dust from the staging in clouds, Tartarin shouldered his alpenstock after the manner of a cross-bow, and stood in position.

"Splendid! He is right. Don't stir."

Then the artist, addressing his *famulus*, cried, "Quick—a sheet of paper—a charcoal-pencil."

Tartarin was going to be painted as he stood, a dumpy, round-backed man, wrapped in his muffler to the chin; fixing the terrified *famulus* with his flaming little eye.

Imagination, oh what magic power you possess! He believed himself standing in the market-place of Altorf, facing his son—he who had never had one—a bolt in his cross-bow, another in his girdle to pierce the heart of the tyrant. More than that, he communicated the conviction to the spectators!

"It is William Tell himself!" said the artist, who, seated on a stool, was wielding his pencil in feverish haste. "Ah, monsieur, I wish I had known you sooner! You would have served for my model."

"Really! You see some resemblance, then?" asked Tartarin, feeling much flattered, but without disarranging his *pose*.

Yes, it was quite thus that the artist had pictured the hero.
" His head, too? " asked Tartarin.

" Oh, the head does not matter," replied the artist, as he stepped back to criticise his sketch. " A manly, energetic face is all that is necessary, since no one knows what William Tell was like—he probably never lived."

Tartarin let fall his " stock " in a kind of stupefaction.
" *Outre !* [1] Never lived! *What* is that you tell me? "
" Ask these gentlemen."

Astier-Réhu, very solemn, his three chins resting upon his white neckcloth, replied: " It is a Danish legend."

" Ice-landic," affirmed Schwanthaler, no less majestically.
" Saxo Grammaticus relates that a valiant named Tobe or Paltanoke——"
" It is written in the Viking's Saga——"
Then they proceeded, together—

| " fut condamnè par le roi de Danemark, Harold aux dents bleues——" | " dass der Isländische König Necding——" |

With fixed eyes, extended arms, without either looking at or understanding each other, they both spoke at the same time, as if " in the chair," in the dictatorial despotic tones of the professor assured of not being contradicted. They became excited, shouting names and dates: " Justinger de Berne! " " Jean de Winterthur! "

By and by the discussion became general, animated, furious; they brandished campstools, umbrellas, valises, while the unhappy artist went from one to another endeavouring to restore harmony, while trembling for the solidity of his staging. When the storm had ceased, he was desirous to resume his sketch, and sought the mysterious mountaineer; he of whom the panthers of Zaccar, and the lions of the Atlas could alone pronounce the name! But the Alpinist had disappeared!

He was striding furiously along through the birches and beeches, towards the hotel of Tellsplatte where the Peruvians'

---

[1] *Outre* and *boufre* are Tarasconnais oaths of mysterious etymology. Ladies use them at times with a softening addition—as, " *Outre ! que vous me feriez dire !* "

Disillusion

courier was to pass the night; and, smarting under the blow which had disillusioned him, he spoke aloud, driving his alpenstock furiously into the soaked pathway.

"Never lived! William Tell! William Tell a myth, a legend! And it is the painter intrusted with the decoration of Tellsplatte who calmly says that!" He inveighed against it as a sacrilege; he was angry with the *savants*, with this sceptical century, the impious upsetter, which respects nothing—neither glory nor beauty: "*coquin de sort!*"

Thus two hundred or three hundred years hence, when people speak of Tartarin, they will find Astier-Réhus and Schwanthalers to support the argument that no such person as Tartarin ever lived! that he was a Provençal or Barbary myth! He stopped, suffocated by his indignation—and the steep ascent; and seated himself upon a rustic bench.

From that place one can see, between the branches of the trees, the lake, and the white walls of the chapel like a new mausoleum. A blowing-off of steam and a rattling of a gangway indicated a new access of visitors. They were grouped on the shore of the lake, guide-book in hand, advancing and gesticulating as they read the legend. And suddenly, by a quick revulsion of thought, the comic side of the question came into Tartarin's head.

He thought of all historic Switzerland living upon this imaginary hero; raising statues and building chapels in his honour in the market-places of little towns and in the museums of great ones; organising patriotic *fêtes* at which people from all the cantons appear with banners carried before them; the banquets, the toasts, the speeches, the cheering, the singing, the tears which swell the manly bosoms —all this for a great patriot who, everybody knows, never had any existence!

Talk of Tarascon! Here was a *Tarasconnade* which never had its equal there!

Restored to good humour, Tartarin in a few good jumps regained the high road to Fluelen, on which stands the Tellsplatte hotel with its long green-shuttered *façade*. While waiting the announcement of dinner, the boarders were walking up and down before a rock-work cascade upon the ravined road, along which a number of unhorsed carriages were placed amid the copper-coloured pools of water.

Tartarin ascertained that the man he sought was there. He learnt that he was at dinner. " Lead me to him, *zou*," and he said it with such an authoritative air, that, notwithstanding the respectful repugnance to disturb so important a personage which was displayed, a female servant led the Alpinist through the hotel, where his appearance created some sensation, towards the precious courier who was eating by himself in a small room opening from the courtyard.

"Monsieur," began Tartarin, as he came in, ice-axe on shoulder. " Excuse me if——"

He stopped in surprise; while the courier, the lanky courier, his *serviette* tucked under his chin amid the savoury steam of a plateful of soup, let his spoon fall.

" *Vé !* Monsieur Tartarin."

" *Té !* Bompard."

It was Bompard, the former manager of the club: a good fellow enough, but afflicted with a vivid imagination which prevented him from uttering a single word of truth, an attribute which had gained for him in Tarascon the surname of the Impostor. Designated at Tarascon as an impostor, you may judge what he was! And this man was the incomparable guide, the climber of the Alps, the Himalayas, the Mountains of the Moon!

" Oh, then I understand! " exclaimed Tartarin, somewhat disappointed, but pleased, nevertheless, at finding a countryman, and hearing the dear delicious *accent du Cours*.

" *Différemment*, Monsieur Tartarin, you will dine with me, *qué ?* "

Tartarin at once accepted, relishing the idea of seating himself at a nice little table laid for two, without any partisan dishes, to be able to drink freely, to talk while he ate, and to enjoy many excellent courses; for *MM. les Courriers* are very well treated by inn-keepers; they dine apart, and have the best wines and the " extra " dishes.

And there was plenty of *au moins, pas moins*, and *différemment* then!

" So it is you, *mon bon*, whom I heard in the early morning holding forth on the staging on the Rigi? "

" Eh, *parfaitemain !* I was pointing out the beauties to the young ladies. Is not the sunrise on the Alps magnificent? "

" *Superbe !* " assented Tartarin, at first without conviction, not wishing to contradict his friend, but wound up after a minute or so; and then it was perfectly bewildering to listen to the two Tarasconnais recalling with enthusiasm the splendours they had seen on the Rigi. It was like Joanne alternated with Bædeker!

Then, in proportion as the meal progressed, the conversation became of a more personal character—full of confidences, gush, protestations, which brought tears into the brilliant Provençal eyes, always retaining in their facile emotion a trace of farce or raillery. This was the only point in which the friends resembled each other: one so dry, salted, tanned, seamed with those peculiar professional wrinkles; the other short, broad-backed, of a sleek appearance, and of fresh complexion.

He had seen so much of it, had this poor Bompard, since he had left the club; that insatiable imagination, which prevented him from retaining any situation, had sent him wandering under so many suns with varied fortune! And he related his adventures, enumerating all the excellent opportunities he had had of enriching himself, such as his latest invention for reducing the amount of the Army Estimates by economising the expense of *godillots*. " Do you know how? Oh, *mon Dieu*, it is very simple—by shoeing the soldiers' feet with iron."

" *Outre !* " remarked Tartarin, astonished.

Bompard continued, calm as ever, with that cool, innocent air of his,—

" A grand idea, was it not? Eh! *bé*, to the War Office—but they never took any notice of me. Ah, my poor Monsieur Tartarin, I have had my bad days. I have eaten the bread of affliction before I entered the service of the Company—"

" The Company? "

Bompard discreetly lowered his voice.

" *Chut !*—by and by—not here! " Then resuming his natural tone, he continued: " And now, what have you all been about at Tarascon? You haven't told me anything of your reasons for coming amid the mountains."

This was the opportunity for Tartarin to unbosom himself. Without anger, but with that melancholy cadence, that *ennui*, which all great artists, beautiful women, and great conquerors of people and hearts, attain when they grow old, he related the defection of his compatriots, the plot that was being concocted to deprive him of the presidency of the club, and the decision he had come to to do something heroic; to make a grand ascent, to plant the banner of Tarascon higher than it had ever yet been fixed—in fine, to prove to the Alpinists of Tarascon that he was ever worthy, always worthy—— Emotion made him pause; he was obliged to cease speaking; then,—

"You know me, Gonzague!" he cried. No one could do justice to the effusiveness, the tenderness, which he threw into this troubadour-like name of Bompard. It was a kind of hand-pressing—of clasping him to his heart. "You know me, *qué !* You know whether I have ever quailed when in quest of the lion; and during the war, when we organised the defence of the club—"

Bompard nodded his head with dreadful mimicry; he could fancy himself there still.

"Well, *mon bon*, what the lions, what the Krupp guns, could not do, the Alps have done—! I am afraid!"

"Don't say that, Tartarin!"

"Why not?" said the hero, with touching simplicity. "I say I am afraid, because I *am !*"

Then quietly, without any attitudinising, he avowed the impression which the engraving from Doré's picture had made upon him,—the catastrophe upon the Matterhorn still haunted him. He was afraid of encountering like perils, and so, hearing of a most extraordinary guide, capable of avoiding such dangers, he had come to confide in him.

Then in the most matter-of-course tone he added,—

"You never have been a guide, have you, Gonzague?"

"*Hé !* yes;" replied Bompard, smiling. "Only I have not done all I said I had."

"Of course," assented Tartarin.

Then his companion said between his teeth,—

"Let us go out into the road, we shall be able to converse more freely there."

Night was coming on: a cool humid breeze was driving the black clouds across the sky wherein the setting sun had left a gleam of dusky grey. They went side by side in the direction of Fluelen, passing mute shadows of famished tourists who were returning to the hotel, shades themselves, not uttering a word, until they reached the long tunnel through which the road is carried, and which opens here and there in " bays," terrace-fashion, over the lake.

" Let us halt here," said Bompard, whose loud voice echoed in the archway like a cannon. Then, seated on the parapet, they contemplated the beautiful view of the lake, the slopes of firs, beeches, black and thick, in the foreground; the indistinct summits of the higher mountains, then others higher still in a confused bluish mass, like clouds; in the middle a white line, scarcely visible, of some glacier frozen into the crevices, which was suddenly illuminated with party-coloured fires, yellow, red, and green. The mountain was being illuminated with Bengal lights.

From Fluelen rockets were sent up, breaking into multi-coloured stars, while Venetian lanterns shone and passed to and fro upon the lake in the invisible boats, carrying musicians and those assisting in the *fête*.

A truly fairy scene it was, framed in the cold, smooth granite of the tunnel walls.

" What a queer country this Switzerland is! " exclaimed Tartarin.

Bompard began to laugh.

" Ah, *vaï !* Switzerland! In the first place there is nothing Swiss in it! "

V

CONFIDENCES IN A TUNNEL

" SWITZERLAND at the present time, *vé !* Monsieur Tartarin, is nothing more than an immense Kursaal, which is open from June till September — a panoramic casino, to which people crowd for amusement, from all parts of the world; and which a tremendously wealthy company possessed of thousands of millions, which has its head-quarters in Geneva, has *exploited*. Money is necessary, you may depend, to farm, harrow, and top-dress all this land, its lakes, forests, mountains and waterfalls, to keep up a staff of *employés*, or supernumeraries, and to build upon all high places monster hotels with gas, telegraphs, and telephones all laid on."

"That is true enough," murmured Tartarin, who recalled the Rigi.

"Yes, it is true; but you have seen nothing of it yet. When you penetrate a little farther into the country, you will not find a corner which is not fixed up and machined like the floor beneath the stage in the Opera: waterfalls lighted up, turnstiles at the entrances of glaciers, and, from ascents of mountains, railways—either hydraulic or funicular. The Company, ever mindful of its clients, the English and American climbers, takes care that some famous mountains, such as the Jungfrau and the Finsteraarhorn, shall always retain their difficult and dangerous aspects, although in reality they are no more dangerous than any others."

"But, my dear fellow, the crevasses! Those horrible crevasses! If you tumble into one of them?"

"You tumble on snow, Monsieur Tartarin, and you will come to no harm: there is always at the bottom a porter—a *chasseur*—somebody who is able to assist you up again, who will brush your clothes, shake off the snow, and respectfully inquire whether 'Monsieur has any luggage?'"

"Whatever is all this you are saying, Gonzague?"

Bompard became twice as serious as before,—

"The keeping up of the crevasses is one of the greatest sources of the Company's expenditure," he replied.

There was a momentary silence in the tunnel: the surroundings were calm and peaceful. No more coloured fires, rockets, or boats on the water; but the moon had risen, and displayed another conventional scene, blue, and liquid, with edges of impenetrable shade.

Tartarin hesitated to believe his companion's mere statement. Nevertheless, he reflected upon all the curious things he had seen in four days: the sun of the Rigi; the farce of William Tell: and the inventions of Bompard seemed to him all the more credible, inasmuch as in every Tarasconnais the faculty of cramming doubles that of swallowing.

"Well, but, my good friend, how do you explain those terrible accidents—that on the Matterhorn, for instance?"

"That was sixteen years ago: the Company was not then in existence, Monsieur Tartarin."

Confidences in a Tunnel

" But only last year there was that accident on the Wetterhorn—two guides were buried with the travellers."

" That must happen sometimes, as a bait for Alpine climbers. The English would not care for a mountain which did not give them the chance of a broken head. The Wetterhorn was going down in people's estimation; but after this little accident the receipts went up immediately."

"Well, but the two guides?"

" They got out, as well as the tourists; but they were obliged to—to disappear—to be maintained abroad for six months. This was a serious expense to the Company; but it is rich enough to stand it."

" Listen, Gonzague."

Tartarin rose, one hand laid on the shoulder of the quondam manager,—

" You do not wish me to come to any harm, *qué?* Well then, tell me frankly; you know my 'form' as a mountaineer—it is but middling."

" Very middling, certainly!"

" Nevertheless, do you think that I can without too great risk attempt the ascent of the Jungfrau?"

" I will answer for it, Monsieur Tartarin, ' with my head in the fire.' You have only to trust yourself to your guide."

" And suppose I get giddy?"

" Shut your eyes."

" If I slip?"

" Let yourself slip. It is just like the theatre. Everything is *practicable*. You run no risk."

" Ah, if I only had you there to tell me all that—to repeat it to me! *Allons*, my brave fellow—a good idea. Come with me!"

Bompard would have asked for nothing better; but he had his Peruvians in tow till the end of the season; and how astonished his friend was to see him performing the services of a courier—a servant!

" What would you have, Monsieur Tartarin? The Company has the right to employ us as it seems good to them."

Then he began to reckon off on his fingers the various situations he had filled during the past three years: guide in the Oberland; horn-player in the Alps; an old chamois-hunter; an old soldier of Charles X.; Protestant pastor on the mountains——

" *Quès aco ?* " asked Tartarin, in surprise.

And the other in his calm way replied,—

" *Bé ! oui.* When you travel in German Switzerland, you may often perceive a pastor in the open air standing on a rock, or on a rustic chair, or on the trunk of a tree. Some shepherds and cheese-makers, with their caps in their hands, and women, habited in the cantonal costume, are grouped around in picturesque attitudes: the country is pretty, the pastures are green or freshly reaped; there are waterfalls along the road; and the cattle, with their heavy bells tinkling, are on all the mountain-slopes. All this, *vé !* is just decoration—puppet-show! The *employés* of the Company—guides, pastors, couriers, hotel-keepers—only are in the secret; and it is their interest not to publish it, for fear of frightening away their customers."

The Alpinist remained astounded, silent, the greatest sign of stupefaction in him. In his heart, any doubt of Bompard's veracity which he had was now removed; he was more calm concerning Alpine ascents, and the conversation soon made him joyous. The friends talked of Tarascon, of their pleasant jokes in the past when they were younger.

" Talking of jokes," said Tartarin suddenly, " they played me a nice trick at the Rigi-Kulm. Just imagine, this morning—" Then he proceeded to relate the incident of the letter fixed to his glass, which began with the emphatic " *Français du diable.*" " That is a mystery, *qué ?*

" Who can say? perhaps—" began Bompard, who seemed to take the incident more seriously. He inquired whether Tartarin during his stay at the Kulm had any conversation with any one, and let fall a word too much.

" Ah! *vaï*, a word too much! How could one even open his mouth with all those English and Germans as mute as fishes by way of being in ' good form ' ! "

On reflection, however, he remembered having " given a clincher " pretty smartly to a sort of Cossack, a certain Mi—Milanoff!

" Maniloff," said Bompard, correcting him.

" You know him, then? Between you and me, I believe that this Maniloff was annoyed with me on account of a little Russian girl."

Confidences in a Tunnel

" Yes, Sonia; " murmured Bompard.

" You know her also? Ah, my friend, what a pearl of price—what a dear little grey partridge she is! "

" Sonia de Wassilief! 'Twas she who shot General Felianine dead in the open street. He was president of the court-martial which had condemned her brother to transportation for life."

Sonia an assassin! that child! that little blonde! Tartarin could not believe it. But Bompard was precise, and gave him the details of the incident, which were well known. For two years, it appeared, Sonia had lived at Zurich, where her brother Boris, who had escaped from Siberia, had joined her. He was consumptive, and all the summer she carried him about in the bracing mountain air. The courier had frequently met them in the company of friends, who were all exiles—conspirators. The Wassiliefs, very intelligent, very energetic, still possessing some means, were at the head of the Nihilist party, with Bolibine, the assassin of the Prefect of Police, and this Maniloff, who the year before had blown up the Winter Palace.

" *Boufre!* " ejaculated Tartarin, " one has queer neighbours on the Rigi."

But there was yet another thing! Bompard was of opinion that the famous letter had come from these young people: he recognised in this the Nihilist mode of proceeding. The Czar every morning found such menaces in his own room; beneath his *serviette*.

" But," said Tartarin, who had become very pale, " why do they send them to me? What have *I* done? "

Bompard thought they must have taken him for a spy.

" A spy! I? "

" *Bé*, yes." In all the Nihilist centres — at Zurich, Lausanne, Geneva—the Russian Government maintained at great cost a number of detectives; some time back she had enlisted the former chief of the French Imperial police with a dozen Corsicans, who followed and watched all exiled Russians, adopting a thousand disguises to entrap them. The costume of our Alpine climber, his spectacles, his accent, they had no doubt mistaken for the disguise of one of these agents.

" *Coquin de sort!* You have given me an idea," said

Tartarin. "They had all the time at their heels an Italian tenor. He is a detective, you may be sure! But what am I to do now?"

"First of all, take care that you do not cross the path of these people, who have warned you that evil will befall you."

"Ah! *vaï*, evil! The first of them who approaches me will get a bullet in his brain!"

And in the obscurity of the tunnel the eyes of the Tarasconnais gleamed. But Bompard, less assured than he, knew that the hatred of these Nihilists was terrible, and overtakes one secretly by underhand plotting. One had better be a rabbit like the president. You must be distrustful of the bed at the inn in which you sleep; the chair you sit upon; of the rail of the steamer, which will suddenly give way, and cause a fatal accident. And the poisoned dishes, and water!

"Beware of the spirits in your flask; of the foaming milk which is brought to you by the cowherd in *sabots*. These people stick at nothing, I can tell you!"

"Then what is left? I am a lost man!" groaned Tartarin; and, seizing the hand of his companion, he said,—

"Advise me, Gonzague."

After a moment's reflection, Bompard traced out his programme. Let him depart early next morning, cross the lake, and the Pass of the Brünig, and sleep at Interlachen. The next day go up to Grindelwald by the Little Scheideck. The day after that, the Jungfrau! Then away to Tarascon, without losing an hour, without even looking back!

"I will start to-morrow, Gonzague," said our hero, in a stout voice, but with an uneasy glance around into the darkness.

VI

THE PASS OF THE BRÜNIG—TARTARIN FALLS INTO THE HANDS OF THE NIHILISTS—DISAPPEARANCE OF AN ITALIAN TENOR AND AN AVIGNON ROPE—NEW EXPLOITS OF A " CHASSEUR DE CASQUETTES "—PAN! PAN!

" Now then, get in! Get in! "
" But where? Where the devil am I to get in? all the places are filled! They won't have me anywhere! "
This conversation took place at the end of the Lake of the Four Cantons, at Alpnach—on that damp, undrained shore, like a delta, whence the diligences and post-carriages start in line for the Brünig Pass.

A fine, needle-pointed rain had been falling since morning, and the worthy Tartarin, impeded by his equipment, bustled about by the porters and the custom-house people, was running from carriage to carriage, noisy, and encumbered like the one-man orchestra at *fêtes*, who at every movement plays a triangle, a big drum, a Chinese hat, and cymbals. At every door our hero was saluted with cries of alarm, and the same " Full " which warned him off in all languages, the same extension motions in order to occupy as much space as possible, and to prevent the entry of such a dangerous and loud-voiced companion.

The unfortunate man perspired and panted, responded by cries of " *Coquin de bon sort,*" and by despairing gestures to the impatient clamour of the convoy: " *En route ;* " " All right; " " *Andiamo ;* " " *Vorwärtz.*" The horses pawed the ground, the drivers swore. At length the mail-guard; an immense red-faced man in a tunic and flat cap, interfered; and opening the door of a half-covered landau pushed Tartarin in like a parcel, and then stood upright and majestic before the splash-board, his large hand extended for a *trinkgeld*.

Humiliated, furious with the people in the carriage, who received him *manu militari*, Tartarin pretended not to look at them, thrust his purse down into his pocket, wedging in his ice-axe beside him with evident ill-humour.

"*Bonjour, monsieur,*" said a sweet and well-known voice.

He looked up, and remained transfixed with terror; opposite to him was the pretty, rosy, round face of Sonia, who was seated under the hood of the landau, and also a great boy wrapped up in shawls and rugs, of whom nothing could be seen but a forehead of livid pallor and some curly hair, thin and golden as the frames of his eye-glasses. The brother, no doubt. A third person, whom Tartarin knew too well, accompanied them; this was Maniloff, the incendiary of the Winter Palace.

Sonia! Maniloff! what a trap he had fallen into!

Now they would carry out their threat in the precipitous Pass of the Brünig, flanked by deep abysses! And our hero, in one of those lightning-flashes of imagination, saw himself stretched on the pebbles in some ravine, or balanced on the high branches of an oak-tree. Fly? Whither? How? At that moment the carriages were beginning to file off at the sound of a horn; a crowd of *gamins* presented bunches of *edelweiss* at the doors. Tartarin, in his infatuation, had a great mind to commence the attack, by spitting, with a blow of his alpenstock, the Cossack who was seated next to him: then, on reflection, he thought it more prudent to refrain. Evidently these people would not make their attack until they had gone some distance, in the uninhabited districts; and perhaps he would have an opportunity of getting out first. Besides, their intentions did not appear to him hostile. Sonia smiled on him sweetly with her pretty turquoise-blue eyes; the big, pale young man looked at him as if interested; and Maniloff, very much softened in manner, obligingly moved up so as to permit Tartarin to put his knapsack between them. Had they discovered their mistake after reading in the register of the Rigi-Kulm Hotel the illustrious name of Tartarin of Tarascon? He wished to assure himself of this, and in a familiar, good-natured way he began,—

" Delighted to meet you again, young lady; allow me to introduce myself: you are unaware with whom you have to do, while I know perfectly well who you are."

"*Chut!*" said the smiling Sonia from behind the tip of her *gant de Suède;* and she pointed to the coach-box, where, by the side of the driver, was the tenor with the sleeve-links,

The Nihilists 143

and the other young Russian, sheltering under the same umbrella, laughing and talking together in Italian.

Between the policemen and the Nihilists Tartarin did not hesitate.

"Do you know who that man is?" he asked in a low voice, putting his face very close to the rosy complexion of Sonia, and seeing himself reflected in her bright eyes, which grew stern and hard in their expression as she answered "Yes," with quivering lashes.

The hero shivered, but as at a theatre, with that delicious sensation in the epidermis which seizes you when the action is strong, and you sit back in your stall to see and hear better. Personally out of the business, delivered from the horrible visions which had haunted him all night, which had prevented his enjoying his coffee, butter, and honey, and, on the boat, had kept him far from the bulwarks, he now breathed freely, found life pleasant, and this little Russian irresistibly charming in her travelling *toque,* her jersey high to her neck, clinging to her arms and moulding her still slim but elegant figure. And such a child! a child in the openness of her laugh, the softness of her cheeks, and the pretty grace with which she spread her shawl over her brother's knees, asking him if he were well and not cold. How could one believe that that little hand, so slender in its chamois glove, had had the moral force and physical courage to kill a man!

Nor did the others appear ferocious either. All had the same ingenuous laugh—a little sad and constrained on the lips of the invalid, more noisy in the case of Maniloff, who, very youthful under his shaggy beard, would explode, like a schoolboy out for a holiday, in roars of exuberant merriment.

The third companion, he whom they called Bolibine, and who was chatting with the Italian, was as much amused, and would often turn round to translate the tales which the pretended singer related of his successes at the St. Petersburg Opera-house; his *bonnes fortunes,* the sleeve-links which lady subscribers had presented to him on his departure; the curious buttons, graven with the three notes *la, do, re,* (*l'adoré*); and this pun, repeated in the landau, caused such amusement that the tenor drew himself up proudly, and twirled his moustache with such a " killing " air as he stared at Sonia, that Tartarin began to ask himself whether he had not to do with ordinary tourists, and a real tenor!

But the carriages, driving rapidly, rolled over the bridges, and alongside the pretty lakes, the flowery meads, the lovely orchards, dripping and deserted, for it was Sunday, and the peasants were dressed in their holiday garments, the women wearing long plaits of hair and silver chains. The travellers were beginning to ascend the zig-zag road amid the woods of oak and beech; by degrees the magnificent horizon unrolled itself on the left hand; and at each turn of the carriage, streams, and valleys, from which uprose church steeples, were seen; and in the distance the snowy peak of the Finsteraarhorn sparkled in the beams of the invisible sun.

After a while the road became shaded, and of a wilder aspect. On one side was gloomy shadow, a chaos of trees planted on the slope, twisted and irregular, amongst which the splashing of a torrent was audible: on the right an immense rock overhung the path, bristling with branches which sprung from the crevices in its sides.

They were not laughing in the landau now: all were admiring the scenery, and with uplifted faces endeavouring to catch sight of the top of the granite tunnel.

"One would almost imagine we were in the forests of the Atlas," remarked Tartarin gravely, and his speech passing unnoticed he added—"Without the roaring of the lions, of course."

"You have heard them then, monsieur?" inquired Sonia.

Heard lions! He! Then, with an indulgent smile, he replied: "I am Tartarin of Tarascon, mademoiselle."

Now see what barbarians they were! If he had said "I am called Dupont," it would have been just the same. They were unacquainted with the name of Tartarin!

However, he did not feel vexed, and replied to the question of the young lady as to whether the roar of the lion frightened him: "No, mademoiselle; my camel trembled greatly as I rode him, but I visited my bait as quietly as if in the neighbourhood of a herd of cows. At a distance, the roar is something like this——"

With a view to give Sonia an exact idea of the thing, he forced from his chest in his most sonorous tones a most formidable "*Meuh*," which rose extending in volume, and was reflected back by the echo of the rock. The horses pranced, the travellers in all the carriages stood up, greatly alarmed, wanting to know what had happened, and the cause of such an awful noise; then recognising the Alpinist, whose capped head and voluminous equipment were visible over the hood of the landau, they asked themselves once more: " What can that creature be? "

He himself, perfectly calm, continued to illustrate the details, the manner of attacking the beast, the conquest, and the despatching of it, the diamond " sight " with which his gun was supplied so as to enable him to fire straight at night. The young girl listened, bending towards him, with the greatest attention, as evidenced by the slight palpitation of her nostrils.

" They say that Bombonnel still hunts," said her brother. " Did you know him? "

" Yes," replied Tartarin, without enthusiasm. " He is by no means unskilful. But we have better than he."

A word to the wise! Then in a melancholy tone he continued: " After all, one's greatest pleasures are in hunting noble game. When one cannot get that life seems void, and one does not know how to fill up existence."

At this juncture, Maniloff, who understood French although he did not speak it, seemed to listen intently to Tartarin, and said some few words laughingly to his friends.

" Maniloff pretends that we are in the same category with you," explained Sonia to Tartarin. " We also hunt big game! "

" Té! Yes, *pardi;* wolves, white bears."

" Yes, wolves; white bears, and other beasts still more detestable! "

The laughing began again, strident, interminable, in fierce and penetrating tones this time; laughs which displayed the teeth, and recalled to Tartarin the peculiar character of the company in which he was travelling.

Suddenly the carriages pulled up. The road was becoming stiff, and in this place made a long circuitous bend to reach the top of the Brünig, which could be reached in twenty minutes by a footpath through the beech-wood. Notwithstanding the morning's rain, and the wet and slippery ground, the tourists, taking advantage of a break in the clouds,

K

nearly all got out, and proceeded in a long file in the narrow path.

From Tartarin's landau, which came last, the men descended; but Sonia, finding the paths very muddy, settled herself in the carriage, and as the Alpinist was following the others, somewhat retarded by his equipment, she said to him in a low tone—and in a very insinuating manner too—
"Remain here, and keep me company!" The poor man stood still, quite overwhelmed, weaving for himself a romance as delicious as unlikely, which made his old heart throb loudly and fast.

He was quickly undeceived when he perceived the young lady bending anxiously to watch Bolibine and the Italian at the entrance of the path, behind Maniloff and Boris who were already ahead. The pretended tenor hesitated. Some instinct seemed to warn him not to trust himself alone with these men. He made up his mind at last, and Sonia watched him ascending, caressing her cheek with a bunch of violet cyclamen—those mountain violets, the leaf of which is toned with the fresh colour of the flowers.

The landau proceeded at a slow pace; the coachman was walking with his comrades, and the train of fifteen carriages proceeded upwards silent and empty.

Tartarin felt disturbed by some presentiment of sinister import, not daring to look at his companion, so greatly did he fear that a word or a glance might make him an actor or an accomplice in the drama which he felt was about to take place. But Sonia paid no attention to him: with abstracted eyes she continued to caress the soft down of her cheek, mechanically, with the bunch of flowers.

Then she said after a long pause: "So you know who we are—I and my friends? Well, what do you think of us? What do the French people think of us?"

The hero grew pale and then red. He did not wish to anger, by any imprudent statements, people so vindictive as these; on the other hand, how could he make a compact with assassins? He got out of the difficulty by using a metaphor,—

"Well, mademoiselle, you told me just now that we were in the same category, hunters of hydras and monsters, of despots and carnivora. So as a *confrère* of St. Hubert I will reply. My opinion is that even when dealing with wild beasts we ought to meet them with honest weapons. Our Jules Gérard—the famous lion-hunter—used explosive bullets. I myself do not recognise such things, and I never used them. When I went in pursuit of the lion or the panther, I stood up before the animal face to face with my double-barrelled gun—and—bang! bang!—went a bullet into each eye!"

"In each eye!" said Sonia.

"Never once did I miss my aim!"

He said so: he still believed it himself.

The young lady regarded him with *naïve* admiration, thinking aloud,—

"It is a good thing that he should have been quite sure of it."

A quick tearing aside of the branches of the briars, and the thicket opened above them so suddenly, in so feline a manner, that Tartarin, whose head was full of hunting adventures, could have believed he was on the watch in the Zaccar. Maniloff leaped from the thicket noiselessly, close to the carriage. His little wrinkled eyes burned; his face was scratched by the brambles, his beard and his hair were dripping with moisture. Panting for breath, his great hands resting on the carriage-door, he said a few words in Russian to Sonia, who, turning to Tartarin, said sharply,—

"Your rope—Quick!"

"My—my rope?"

"Quick, quick! You shall have it again immediately."

Without deigning any other explanation, with her own little gloved hands she assisted him to unfasten the famous rope, made at Avignon. Maniloff took the coil joyfully, and regained the summit of the bank in two bounds, with the activity of a wild cat.

"What is going on? What are they going to do? He looked very ferocious," muttered Tartarin, not daring to speak his thoughts aloud.

Fierce! Maniloff! Ah, it was easily to be seen that he did not know him. No creature could be better, milder, more compassionate; and, as instancing this susceptible nature of his, Sonia, with open blue eyes, told him that her friend, after executing the dangerous mandate of the Revolutionary Committee, leaped into the sleigh which awaited him in his flight, and threatened to throw the coachman from his seat if he continued to beat or over-drive the horses on whose speed his own safety depended!

Tartarin thought this trait worthy of the ancients; then, having speculated on all the human lives sacrificed as indiscriminately as an earthquake, or as an active volcano, by Maniloff, who would not have an animal ill-treated, he asked the young lady with an ingenuous air,—

"Did he kill many people in the explosion of the Winter Palace?"

"Far too many," Sonia replied sadly. "And the only one who deserved to die escaped."

She remained silent, as if displeased; and so pretty—the head bent down, and the long, golden lashes resting upon the damask cheek. Tartarin was vexed that he had annoyed her, and captivated by the charms of youthfulness and freshness which seemed to surround this strange little being.

"So, monsieur, the war we wage appears to you unjust and inhuman?" She asked that question with her face close to his, with a caress in her voice and in her eyes: our hero felt himself giving way.

"Do not you think that any means are good and legitimate to deliver a people who are in the death-throes, who are being strangled?"

"No doubt—no doubt."

The young lady, becoming more pressing as Tartarin became weaker, continued,—

"You are speaking of a void to be filled, just now; does it not occur to you that it would be more noble, more interesting, to stake your life in a great cause than to risk it in killing lions or in climbing glaciers?"

"The fact is—" said Tartarin, who, quite intoxicated, had lost his head, and was tortured by the mad impulse to seize and kiss that dainty, warm, persuasive hand which she had placed upon his arm, as she had that morning up on the Rigi, when he was putting on her shoe. At length he could control himself no longer, and seizing her little gloved hand between his own,—

"Listen, Sonia," he cried, in a soft, familiar, and paternal voice; "Listen, Sonia——"

The Summit of the Brünig 149

The sudden stoppage of the landau interrupted him. They had reached the summit of the Brünig: tourists and drivers were rejoining their respective carriages, to make up for lost time, and to gain the next village—where *déjeuner* and relays were to be had—at a gallop. The three Russians resumed their places, but that of the Italian remained unoccupied.

"The gentleman has got into one of the first carriages," said Boris to the coachman, who made inquiry concerning him; and then, addressing himself to Tartarin, whose anxiety was plainly visible, he said,—

"We must obtain your rope from him; he wished to keep it!"

Upon that, fresh bursts of laughter rose in the landau, and caused Tartarin once again the greatest perplexity: he did not know what to think of this good humour and cheerful disposition of the supposed assassins. While wrapping the invalid in plaids and rugs—for the air at that elevation was sharp, and augmented by the pace of the carriage—Sonia related in Russian to her friends the conversation she had had with Tartarin, throwing upon the "bang! bang!" a gentle emphasis which her countrymen repeated after her, some admiring the hero, while Maniloff shook his head incredulously.

The relays!

There is, in the *place* of a large village, an old inn with a worm-eaten wooden balcony, with a rusty hanging iron signboard. There the file of carriages halted, and while the horses were being changed, the hungry travellers hurried up and crowded into a first-floor room, painted green, which smelt mouldy and damp, where a *table d'hôte* had been laid for twenty people, more or less. There were actually sixty, and for five minutes a regular scramble took place between the Rice and Prune factions round the dishes, to the great alarm of the inn-keeper, who became quite confused, as if the "post" did not pass his door every day at the same time, and he bustled his servants about, who were also seized with a chronic aberration of intellect—an excellent excuse for only serving half the dishes enumerated on the *carte*, and to give a fantastic change of their own, in which the white *sou* pieces of Switzerland count as half-francs!

"Suppose we breakfast in the carriage?" said Sonia, who was tired; and as nobody had time to attend to them the young people undertook to wait. Maniloff returned brandishing a cold leg of mutton, Bolibine with a long roll and sausages; but the best forager of all was Tartarin. No doubt there was an excellent opportunity for him to leave his companions in the hubbub, and to assure himself concerning the fate of the Italian, but he did not think of that: he was entirely occupied by the prospect of breakfasting with "*la petite*," and of showing Maniloff and the others what a native of Tarascon could do in the way of supplies.

When he descended the steps of the hotel, with a grave and resolute face, holding a tray on which were plates, *serviettes*, and different kinds of food, with Swiss champagne in gold foil, Sonia clapped her hands and complimented him,—

"How *did* you manage to get all this?"

"I don't know—one manages it somehow—we are all like that in Tarascon."

Oh! those happy moments. They will be red-letter minutes in the hero's life. That delightful breakfast, seated opposite Sonia, almost on her knees, as in a scene at the opera: the village market-place with its green quincunx, beneath which the silver ornaments and the dresses of the Swiss women glanced brightly as they paced about, two and two like dolls.

How good the bread seemed to be, and what savory sausages! The sky itself was sympathetic,—soft, veiled, but not inclement. There was rain, certainly, but such gentle rain—"lost drops"—just enough to tone down the Swiss champagne, which is dangerous for Southern heads.

Under the veranda of the hotel were four Tyrolese, two giants and two dwarfs, in heavy ragged costumes of staring colours, who, it was said, released by the bankruptcy of a show at a fair, were now mingling their "goose-notes,"— "*aou aou*,"—with the clatter of plates and glasses. They stood there, ugly, stupid, inert, stretching the tendons of their thin necks! Tartarin thought them delightful, and threw them handfuls of coppers, to the great astonishment of the villagers who had assembled round the unhorsed landau.

"*Fife le Vranze!*" exclaimed a tremulous voice from the crowd, out of which pushed his way a tall old man, clothed in a curious blue uniform with silver buttons, the skirts of his coat sweeping the ground behind him. He wore an enormous shako in the shape of a sauerkraut trough, and so heavy with its great plume that the old man was obliged to balance himself with his arms extended as he walked, like a tight-rope dancer.

"*Fieux soltat—carte royale—Charles.tix!*"

The Tarasconnais, still mindful of the tales told him by Bompard, began to laugh, and covertly winked.

"I know you, my friend!" But nevertheless he gave him a piece of silver, and poured him out a bumper, which the old man accepted smilingly and with another wink, without knowing why. Then, taking from the side of his mouth an enormous porcelain pipe, he raised his glass and drank "to the company," a circumstance which confirmed Tartarin in his opinion that the man was a colleague of Bompard.

Never mind: one toast was as good as another!

Then, standing up in the carriage, Tartarin, in a loud voice and with uplifted glass, brought tears to his own eyes, by drinking, first to France, his native land, and afterwards to hospitable Switzerland, which he was happy thus publicly to honour, and to thank, for the generous reception which she bestowed upon all conquered people, and all exiles. Lastly, lowering his voice, the glass inclined towards his travelling companions, he wished them a speedy return to their own land, where he trusted they might find kind relatives and faithful friends, honourable employment, and the termination of all dissensions; for people cannot spend their lives in destroying each other.

While he was enunciating this toast, the brother of Sonia smiled coldly and deprecatingly behind his glasses; Maniloff, with extended neck, his frowning brows making a furrow on his forehead, asked himself if that "*barine*" was never going to stop babbling; while Bolibine, perched on the seat, and screwing up his queer face, which was yellow and wrinkled like a Tartar's, looked like a wretched little monkey perched on the shoulders of Tartarin.

The young lady only listened to him: she was very serious, and endeavouring to understand this curious type of individual. Did he mean all he had said? Had he done all he had related? Is he a fool, or only a braggart, like the deceptive Maniloff, who, in his capacity of a man of action, gave to the word a misleading significance?

The test was about to be applied. His speech concluded, Tartarin was about to resume his seat when a sound of fire-arms was heard—three shots in succession, which at once caused him to rise in some excitement, his ear on the alert; he scented powder.

"Who is firing? where is it? what is happening?"

In his inventive brain quite a little drama was being played—the attack on the convoy by an armed band; an occasion to defend the life and honour of this charming girl. But no; the firing came merely from the stand where the young men of the village practised shooting on Sundays. Tartarin airily suggested that they should go so far. He had his idea in proposing this; Sonia had hers in accepting. Guided by the old soldier of the royal guard, still undulating beneath his heavy shako, the party crossed the market-place, dividing the ranks of the crowd, who followed them with some curiosity.

With its thatched roof and newly-cut fir supports, the stand resembled, in a very rustic fashion, one of the (French) shooting-galleries at fairs, at which amateurs practise with old-fashioned, muzzle-loading weapons, which they handle cleverly enough. Silent, with folded arms, Tartarin watched the shooting, criticising it in a loud voice, giving advice—but he did not shoot. The Russians noticed all this, and made signs to each other.

"Bang! bang!" laughed Bolibine, with a gesture of aiming a gun, and imitating the accent of Tarascon: "Pan! pan!"

Tartarin turned round, scarlet, and bursting with rage,—

"*Parfaitemain*, young man. Pan! pan!—and as many times as you please."

In the time necessary to load a double-barrelled gun, which had served for generations of chamois-hunters, Tartarin was ready. Pan! pan! He had done it! Both bullets were in the mouth of the figure. A hurrah of admiration rose from all sides. Sonia was triumphant. Bolibine did not laugh.

"That is nothing at all," said Tartarin. "You shall see."

The stand did not suffice; he sought a mark, something

to knock over, and the crowd recoiled, dismayed, before this strange Alpinist, with his gun in his hand, who was suggesting to the old guardsman to permit him to knock his pipe from between his teeth at fifty paces. The old man uttered a cry of terror, ran away, and endeavoured to conceal himself in the crowd, over the heads of which his plume nodded continually. Nevertheless Tartarin felt constrained to put the bullet into something. " *Té, pardi!* like at Tarascon!" And the old sportsman—the *chasseur de casquettes*—threw his head-piece into the air with all the strength of his " double muscles," fired, and put the ball through it. "Bravo!" said Sonia, placing in the little hole, made by the bullet in the cloth, the bouquet with which she had lately been caressing her cheek.

With this beautiful trophy, Tartarin got into the carriage again. The horn was blown, the string of carriages started at a rapid pace down the hill along that marvellous *corniche* road cut in the rocks, where only posts six feet apart protect the traveller from a fall of more than a thousand feet. But Tartarin no longer thought of danger; he no longer gazed upon the landscape. Softened by tender reflections, he admired the pretty child opposite, thinking that glory is only doubtful happiness, that it is a sad thing to grow old alone in so great grandeur, like Moses; and that this cold flower of the North, transplanted into the little garden at Tarascon, would dissipate the monotony of the everlasting baobab (*Arbos gigantea*) in its tiny pot. Sonia gazed at him also, and thought—but who can ever tell of what young ladies think!

VII

NIGHT AT TARASCON—WHERE IS HE?—ANXIETY—THE " CIGALES DU COURS " DEMAND TARTARIN—MARTYRDOM OF A TARASCON SAINT—THE ALPINE CLUB—WHAT HAPPENED AT THE CHEMIST'S—HELP! BÉZUQUET

"A LETTER, M. Bézuquet. It comes from Switzerland, *vé!* —from Switzerland," exclaimed the postman joyfully across the little court, as he waved something in the air, and hurried up as the summer evening was closing in.

The chemist, who was enjoying the fresh air in his shirt-sleeves at his door, bounded forward, seized the letter with trembling hands, and carried it into his "den," which was redolent of various elixirs and dried herbs, but he did not open the missive until the postman had gone, refreshed by a glass of the delicious *Sirop de Cadavre* as a reward for his good news.

For fifteen days had Bézuquet been expecting this letter from Switzerland—fifteen days of agonising suspense! Now here it is! And while only looking at the small and determined address on the envelope, the post-mark of Interlachen and the large violet stamp of the "Hotel Jungfrau, kept by Meyer," tears filled his eyes, and caused those heavy Barbary-corsair moustaches to tremble with emotion.

"*Confidential : destroy when read.*"

These words in large letters at the head of the page, and in the telegrammic style of the Pharmacopœia—"For external use only: to be well shaken before being applied,"—troubled the recipient so greatly that he read them aloud as one speaks in bad dreams.

"What has happened to me is appalling!"

In the next room, Madame Bézuquet, his mother, who was in the habit of taking a little nap, after supper, could hear him as well as the pupil who kept braying something in a great mortar in the laboratory. Bézuquet continued his reading in a low voice—began again two or three times, very pale, while his hair literally stood up on his head! Then, with a rapid glance around him—*cra cra*—there was the letter in a thousand little bits tossed into the waste-paper basket: but it could be pieced together again, perhaps! While he was stooping to pick them up, a querulous voice cried,—

"*Vé*, Ferdinand, are you there?"

"Yes, *maman*," replied the unhappy corsair, congealed with fear, all his great body under the desk as he groped for the pieces of the letter.

"What are you doing, my treasure?"

"I am,—*hé*—I am making—the eye-salve for Mademoiselle Tournatoire."

The mother went to sleep again; the pestle of the pupil, suspended for the moment, again resumed the monotonous movement which lulled to sleep the household, already exhausted by the fatigue of the hot summer day. Bézuquet now paced up and down before his door, by turns red or green according as he passed one or other of his bottles. He gesticulated, jerking out words at intervals: " Poor fellow! lost! fatal attachment; how can he be extracted from this?" —and notwithstanding his anxiety he accompanied with a lively whistle the " retreat " played by the dragoons under the plane-trees of the *Tour de ville*.

" *Hé !* adieu, Bézuquet," said a shadow, hurrying through the grey twilight.

" Where are you off to, Pégoulade? "

" To the club; there is a meeting to-night. We are to discuss Tartarin and the presidency. We must attend."

" *Té*, yes! I will come," replied the chemist, suddenly. He had conceived a providential idea. He went inside, put on his overcoat, and searched his pockets to assure himself that his latch key and the American knuckle-duster, without which no native of Tarascon would venture out after " retreat," were safe. Then he called for Pascalon, but in subdued tones, for fear of arousing the old lady.

Almost a youth, and already bald, as if he wore all his hair in his frizzly fair beard, the pupil Pascalon had the elevated soul of a fanatic, a forehead like a dome, eyes like an idiotic gnat, and on his cheeks pimples of various delicate tones, crusty and golden, like a little loaf of Beaucaire. On great days and festivals the club intrusted its banner to this youth who had vowed to the P. C. A. a fierce admiration, the silent, but burning, devotion of the candle which consumes itself upon the altar at Easter-tide.

" Pascalon," whispered the chemist, so close to his pupil's head that the tip of his moustache entered his ear, " I have had news of Tartarin! It is harrowing!"

Then, seeing his assistant grow paler, he continued,—

" Courage, my lad, all may yet be repaired. *Différemment* to you I confide the shop. If any one asks for arsenic, don't let him have it; if any one asks for opium, don't give it to him; nor rhubarb either—nor anything! If I am not back at ten o'clock, shut up and go to bed. Go! "

With intrepid steps he plunged into the darkness of the *Tour de ville* without once looking behind him, a circumstance which gave Pascalon the opportunity to rush to the wastepaper basket, and to search with eager and trembling hands, to turn the contents out at last upon the desk, in his anxiety to ascertain whether some bits of the mysterious letter did not remain.

Any one who knows the exaltation of the Tarasconnais will readily understand the state of excitement the little town had been in since the sudden disappearance of Tartarin. And besides, *pas moins, différemment*, they had all lost their heads, all the more because they were now in the middle of August, and their craniums were broiling under a sun hot enough to boil their kettles. From morning till night nothing was heard in the town but the name of "Tartarin," whether on the pinched lips of the old women with hoods, or in the cherry mouths of the *grisettes* with velvet ribbons in their hair: "Tartarin, Tartarin," and, under the plane-trees of the *Cours*, laden with white dust, the hidden grasshoppers seemed to give vent to the two sounding syllables, "Tar—tar—tar—tar—tar."

As no one knew anything whatever about him, it was only natural that every one should be well-informed, and be able to give an explanation of the departure of the President. There were the most extravagant versions. According to some, he had become a Trappist, he had carried away the Dugazon; others said that he had emigrated to found a colony which would be called Port Tarascon, or even that he had penetrated into Central Africa in search of Doctor Livingstone!

"Ah! *vaï*, Livingstone! Why he died two years ago!"

But the Tarascon imagination defies all considerations of time and space. And the curious part of the matter was that all these tales of La Trappe, colonisation, distant voyages, etc., were ideas of Tartarin himself; visions of that waking dreamer, already communicated to his intimate friends, who did not know what to think; and felt very much annoyed in their secret hearts at not being told; while affecting with others an ostentatious reserve, a knowing and crafty air! Excourbaniès suspected Bravida of knowing all about it, and Bravida on his part said: "Bézuquet must be acquainted with all this. He looks askance like a dog carrying a bone!"

It is a fact that the chemist suffered a thousand deaths with this secret like a hair-shirt, smarting and itching; making him grow pale and red in the same minute, and causing him to squint continually. Just think that the poor wretch was in Tarascon, and say whether, in all the *Book of Martyrs*, there is to be found a torture so terrible as his—the martyrdom of Saint Bézuquet, who knew something and was not permitted to divulge it!

This is the reason why that evening, notwithstanding the terrible news, his step was so light, so free, almost running as he went to the meeting. *Enfein!* He was going to speak: to unbosom himself, to tell what had so long weighed on his mind, and in his haste to free himself he threw out interjectional remarks at the passers-by in the *Tour de ville*. The day had been so hot that notwithstanding the unwonted hour and the terrifying darkness—it was a quarter to eight by the town clock—there was out of doors a merry crowd, tradesmen's families seated on the benches and enjoying the fresh air while their houses were cooling; bands of factory-girls walked five or six abreast, holding each other's arms, in an undulating, chattering, laughing line. In all these groups they were speaking of Tartarin.

"Well, Monsieur Bézuquet, no letter yet?" asked one, stopping the chemist in his walk.

"Yes, indeed, my friend; I beg your pardon! Read the *Forum* to-morrow morning."

He hurried on, but they followed him, pressed upon him, and there ran a murmur along the drive, a trampling of feet, that halted under the windows of the club, which were open, throwing large square patches of light upon the ground.

The meeting was being held in the old card-room, in which the long table covered with green cloth served as a desk. In the centre of it was the President's chair with P. C. A. embroidered on the back; and the chair of the secretary faced it. Behind was displayed the banner, above a long map *in relievo* of the *Alpines*, with their respective names and altitudes. Alpenstocks of honour, mounted in ivory in racks like billiard-cues, embellished the corners, and the glass cases displayed curiosities picked up on the mountains—crystals, flints, petrifactions, two sea-urchins, and a salamander!

In the absence of Tartarin, Costecalde, looking radiant,

rejuvenated, occupied the chair. The secretary's seat was filled by Excourbaniès; but this devil of a fellow, frizzled, shaggy, and bearded, felt the need of noise or of agitation, which did not fit him for performing secretarial duties. On the smallest pretext he would throw up his arms and legs, utter the most alarming cries, and shout " Ha! ha! ha! " in his ferocious joy, which generally terminated in the terrible war-cry of the residents of Tarascon in their idiom—" *Fen dé brut !*—let us make a noise! " They called him " The Gong," because his brazen tones were continually dinning in one's ears.

Here and there about the room the other members of the Committee were seated.

In the first line was the former *capitaine d'habillement*, Bravida, whom every one in Tarascon called the Commandant—a very small man, as neat as a new pin, who compensated himself for his small stature by cultivating the wild and moustached head and face of Vercingetorix.

Then we perceive the long, seamed, and sickly face of Pégoulade, the tax-collector, the sole survivor of the wreck of the *Medusa*. Always, as far as the memory of man extended, there had been in Tarascon a sole survivor of the wreck of the *Medusa*. At one time, indeed, there had been three, who mutually looked upon each other as impostors, and would not associate with each other. Of the three, the true one was Pégoulade. Shipped on board the *Medusa* with his parents, he had experienced the disaster when he was six months old, but this circumstance did not prevent him from recounting, as *an eye-witness*, the minutest details of the famine, the boats, the raft, and he told how he had seized by the neck the captain, who had endeavoured to save himself—" the wretch! " At six months old! *Outre !* Always boring people with his everlasting story, which everybody knew before, filtered through fifty years, and which gave him a pretext for giving himself an injured, desolate air, apart from life, as it were. " After what I have seen," he would say, and very unjustly, since he had retained his position as tax-gatherer through every administration.

Near him were the brothers Rognonas, twins and sexagenarians, never deserting each other, but always quarrelling

The Alpine Club

and making rude remarks to each other. There was so great a resemblance between their two old, worn, and irregularly-shaped heads, that, had they been placed facing in opposite directions for antipathy, they might have figured in a medallion with IANVS BIFRONS as a legend.

In other chairs were scattered President Bédaride, Barjavel the advocate, Cambalalette the notary, and the terrible Doctor Tournatoire, who, Bravida said, " would let blood from a turnip! "

The heat was increasing, being much augmented by the gas, so these gentlemen sat in their shirt-sleeves, a circumstance which rather detracted from the dignity of the meeting. It is true they were in private, and the infamous Costecalde wished to profit by it to advance the date of the election, without waiting for the return of Tartarin. Assured of success, he triumphed in advance, and when, after the reading of the orders of the day by Excourbaniès, he rose to work his plot out, a horrible smile curved his thin lips.

" Beware of him who smiles before speaking," muttered the Commandant.

Costecalde, without flinching, and with a wink to the faithful Tournatoire, began in a thin voice,—

" Gentlemen, the indefensible conduct of our President,— the uncertainty in which he leaves us——"

" It is false! The President has written! "

Bézuquet, trembling, planted himself before the table; but remembering that his attitude was " unparliamentary," he changed his tone, and with uplifted hand, according to custom, requested leave to make a statement on a pressing question.

" Speak! Speak! "

Costecalde, very yellow, and with throat compressed, gave him permission with a nod. Then, and not till then, Bézuquet began,—

" Tartarin is at the foot of the Jungfrau. He is about to ascend it. He requests that the banner may be sent to him."

A silence, broken only by the hard breathing of the audience and the burning of the gas, succeeded. Then a loud hurrah, an uproar of " bravos " and stamping, which overbore the gong of Excourbaniès, who uttered his war-whoop, "Ha! ha! ha! *fen dé brut!*" to which the anxious crowd without responded with cheers.

Costecalde, becoming more and more yellow, rang the presidential bell desperately. At length Bézuquet continued, mopping his forehead and puffing as if he was ascending five stories high.

Now, about this banner, which their President demanded, with a view to planting it on the virgin summit, were they going to tie it up, and send it, packed like an ordinary case, by express?

"Never! Ha! ha! ha!" roared Excourbaniès.

Would it not be better to appoint a delegation by lot?

They would not permit him to finish. While you could say "*Zou!*" the proposition was carried by acclamation, the names of the three delegates were chosen in the following order: (1.) Bravida, (2) Pégoulade, (3) the chemist.

No. 2 protested. The lengthy journey alarmed him, so weak and ill had he been since the accident to the *Medusa*.

"I will go in your place, Pégoulade," roared Excourbaniès, making a semaphore of his limbs. As for Bézuquet, he could not leave his pharmacy. It was necessary for the safety of the town that he should remain. One indiscreet act on the part of the pupil, and Tarascon would be poisoned, decimated!

"*Outre!*" said the Committee, rising as one man.

It was certain that the chemist could not go, because he could not leave Pascalon alone, but he could send Pascalon, who would carry the banner. That he would know how to do. On this, more acclamations, a fresh burst of clangour from the Gong, and outside another popular demonstration, so great that Excourbaniès felt constrained to show himself at the window, and his unrivalled voice was soon heard above the tumult.

"My friends, Tartarin is found. He is in a fair way to cover himself with glory."

Without adding more than "*Vive Tartarin*," his war-whoop was uttered with all the force of his lungs; it dominated the terrible clamour of the great crowd under the trees of the *Cours*, rolling on and echoing in the cloud of dust until it reached the trees whereon it compelled the trembling grasshoppers to pipe up again as if in mid-day!

A Strange and Startling Puzzle 161

Hearing that, Costecalde, who had approached a window, as well as all the others, returned to his chair with unsteady steps.

"*Vé*, Costecalde," said some one, "what is the matter? How yellow he is!"

Every one ran away then, for the terrible Tournatoire was bringing out his lancet, but the gun-maker, writhing in apparent pain, murmured, through a hideous grimace, ingenuously,—

"Nothing—it is nothing. Leave me—it is the envy!"

Poor Costecalde, he had indeed all the appearance of suffering!

While these events were taking place, at the other side of the *Tour de ville*, in the chemist's shop, Bézuquet's pupil, seated on his patron's counter, was patiently collecting and putting together bit by bit the fragments left by the chemist in the waste-paper basket; but numerous pieces could not be re-united. Here was the strange and startling puzzle put before him, very like a map of Central Africa, with spaces— the blanks of *terra incognita*, which the terrified imagination of the simple banner-bearer was exploring,—

	mad for love	
lamp à chalum	*Chicago preserves*	
can scarce tear mys	*Nihilist*	
to death	*condition abom*	*in exchange*
of her	*You know me, Ferdi*	
	know my liberal notions,	
but from that to Czaricide		
	rrible consequences	
Siberia	*hung*	*adore her*
	Ah!	*shake thy faithful han*
	Tar	*Tar*

L

VIII

MEMORABLE DIALOGUE BETWEEN THE JUNGFRAU AND TARTARIN—A NIHILIST SALON—THE DUEL WITH HUNTING-KNIVES—HORRIBLE NIGHTMARE—" 'TIS I WHOM YOU SEEK, GENTLEMEN?"—STRANGE RECEPTION OF THE TARASCON DELEGATES AT THE HÔTEL MEYER

LIKE all the fashionable hotels in Interlachen, the Hôtel Jungfrau, kept by Meyer, is situated on the Hœheweg, a wide promenade between rows of chestnut-trees which vaguely recalled to Tartarin his beloved *Tour de ville* without the sun, the dust, and the grasshoppers, for the rain had not ceased for a week.

He had a capital room, with a balcony, on the first floor; and in the morning, when trimming his beard before a little hand-glass — an old habit of his—the first object that met his gaze, beyond the corn, and the lavender, and the firs, in a frame of dark green, rising by successive stages, was the Jungfrau, its peak-like summit emerging from the clouds, a pure white mass of snow, upon which the rays of an invisible sunrise rested daily. Then, between the red and white Alp and the Alpinist of Tarascon arose a short dialogue which was not wanting in grandeur.

"Tartarin, are we ready?" inquired the Jungfrau severely.

"*Voilà*, I am ready," replied the hero, his thumb beneath his nose, hastening to finish his beard; and very quickly he dressed as far as his check suit, which had not been worn for some days. He passed it by, grumbling,—

"*Coquin de sort!* it is true that is no word——"

But a clear and pleasant voice now arose amid the myrtles which lined the windows of the *rez-de-chaussée*,—

"Good morning," said Sonia, seeing him appear upon the balcony; "the landau is waiting for us—make haste, you lazy man!"

"I am coming; I am coming!"

In "two twos" he had substituted a linen shirt for his

flannel one; for his knickerbockers a serpent-green suit with which he had been in the habit of turning the heads of all the Tarascon ladies on Sundays.

The landau was waiting in front of the hotel. Sonia was already seated beside her brother, who was growing paler and paler day by day, notwithstanding the healthy air of Interlachen; but at the moment of departure Tartarin saw approaching, with all the deliberation of bears, two famous guides of Grindelwald, Rudolf Kaufmann and Christian Inebnit, engaged by him for the ascent of the Jungfrau, and who every morning came to see whether their employer was disposed to attempt it.

The appearance of these two men, wearing strong hobnailed boots, fustian jackets, rubbed on the shoulder by the knapsack and rope, their simple and serious faces, the four words of French which they stumbled over as they twirled their great hats in their hands, was veritable torture for Tartarin. He had better have said,—

"Don't disturb yourselves; I will come to you first."

Every day he found them in the same place, and got rid of them by a "tip" in proportion to the magnitude of his remorse. Very much delighted to do the Jungfrau in such pleasant fashion, the guides pocketed the *trinkgeld* gravely, and with resigned steps returned to their village in the fine rain, leaving Tartarin confused and desperate in his weakness. But the beautiful air, the flowery plains, reflected in the clear pupils of Sonia's bright eyes, the touch of her little foot on his boot in the carriage——To the devil with the Jungfrau! The hero only thought of his love, or rather of the mission which had been assigned to him to turn into the right way this poor little Sonia—an unconscious criminal, cast, in consequence of her devotion to her brother, beyond the pale of the law and of nature.

This was the motive which kept him in Interlachen, in the same hotel as the Wassiliefs. At his age, with his fatherly air, he could not—it was out of the question that he should—fall in love with this child; only he perceived she was so gentle, so kind, so generous towards all the miserable people of her party, so devoted to her brother, who had returned from the Siberian mines covered with ulcers, poisoned with verdigris, condemned to death by consumption more surely than by any number of courts-martial! There was something to touch him in all this, *allons!*

Tartarin suggested that they should come to Tarascon, and he would accommodate them in a cottage full of sunlight at the gates of the town, that charming little town where it never rains, where life passes in singing and *fêtes*. He got excited, pretended to play a tambourine on his hat, and hummed the gay national air to a *farandole*,—

> *Lagadigadeù*
> *La Tarasco, La Tarasco,*
> *Lagadigadeù*
> *La Tarasco de Casteù.*

But while an ironical smile thinned the lips of the invalid, Sonia shook her head. No *fêtes*, no sun for her, so long as the Russian people groaned beneath the tyrant. So soon as her brother had recovered—his sunken eyes told another tale—nothing would prevent her from returning to Russia to suffer and to die for the sacred cause.

"But, *coquin de bon sort!*" exclaimed Tartarin, "after this present tyrant has been blown up, there will be another! You will then have to begin all over again! And so time passes—*vé!* the time for happiness and love." His manner of pronouncing *amour*, in the Tarascon dialect, with three *r*'s, and his eyes starting out of his head, amused the young girl: but then, seriously, she could never love any man but one who would save her native land. Yes, were he as ugly as Bolibine, more rustic and rough-looking than Maniloff, she was prepared to give herself up to him, to live with him *en libre grâce*, so long as her youth lasted, or until he was tired of her!

"*En libre grâce!*" is the term used by the Nihilists to describe the unions illegally contracted between them by mutual consent. And of this primitive style of marriage Sonia spoke calmly, with her maiden face opposite Tartarin, a good citizen, a peaceable elector,—but quite disposed, nevertheless, to end his days with this adorable girl in the said state of "free grace" if she had not saddled it with so many murders, and such-like horrible conditions.

While they were discussing these exceedingly delicate topics, the fields, the lakes, the woods, the mountains were being unfolded before them, and ever, at every turning, through every shower of the perpetual wet days which followed the hero in his excursions, the Jungfrau uplifted her white peak as if to sharpen the edge of his remorse for that beautiful excursion. The party returned to *déjeuner*, and seated themselves at the long table, where the Rice and Prune factions preserved their hostile attitude, and silent as ever; but Tartarin was perfectly unconcerned about them, as he sat beside Sonia, watching to see that Boris did not have a window open behind him, solicitous, attentive, paternal, airing all his seductions as a man of the world, and his domestic qualities as an excellent domestic rabbit!

Afterwards they took tea in the Russian apartments, in the little *salon* on the ground floor at the end of the garden, by the side of the promenade. Another charming hour of intimate conversation in a low tone for Tartarin, while Boris slept on a sofa. The hot water bubbled in the *samovar*, a smell of watered flowers came in through the half-open door, with the blue tint of the glass frame. A little more sun and heat, and it would have been the realisation of Tartarin's dream—his little Russian seated by him, tending the small garden in which the baobab grew!

Suddenly Sonia jumped up,—

"Two o'clock! And the letters?"

"Here goes," cried the worthy Tartarin, and by nothing but his accent, the manner in which he buttoned up his coat, and balanced his cane, could you have guessed the gravity of his errand, so simple in appearance, viz., to go to the post-office to find the Wassiliefs' letters.

Very closely watched by the local authorities and the Russian police, the Nihilists, particularly the chiefs, were compelled to take certain precautions, such as having their letters addressed to the *poste restante*, and with initials only.

Since their arrival at Interlachen, Boris had scarcely been able to get about. Tartarin, with a view to spare Sonia the long wait at the *guichet*, under the gaze of many eyes, was charged with the risks and perils of the correspondence. The post-office is only ten minutes' walk from the hotel, in the wide street which is a continuation of the promenade, and bordered with *cafés*, beer-shops, shops for tourists' alpenstocks, gaiters, straps, opera-glasses, tinted spectacles, flasks, travelling-bags, everything that would serve to make a renegade climber ashamed of himself. Tourists passed in caravans—horses, guides, mules, blue veils, green veils, with the rattling of canteens, and the ambling of animals, the iron tips of sticks marking the steps; but this *fête*, ever renewed, left Tartarin indifferent. He did not even feel the *bise* and the puffs of snow which came down from the mountains, being only attentive to throw off the scent the spies whom he believed were on his track.

The first soldier of the advance guard, the first skirmisher skirting the wall of an enemy's town, does not advance with more circumspection than did our hero during his short excursion from the hotel to the post-office. At the least sound of footsteps behind him, he stopped attentively at the photographic shops, or turned a few pages of an English or German book, in order to compel the detective to pass him; or sometimes he would turn suddenly round, to perceive, with his fierce eyes, a girl from one of the inns carrying or going for provisions; or some inoffensive tourist, an old Prune from the *table d'hôte*, who would step off the pavement astonished, taking him for an idiot.

When he reached the "*poste*," the pigeon-hole of which opens right upon the street, Tartarin passed and repassed before he approached; then suddenly he hastened forward, pushed his head and shoulders into the aperture, muttering some indistinct words, which they always asked him to repeat, a course which made him savage, and at length, having received his letters, he regained the hotel by a long *détour* by the kitchens, his hand clenched in his pocket upon the packet of letters and papers, ready to tear them up and swallow them on the least alarm.

Maniloff and Bolibine nearly always waited for the news in their friends' apartments. From motives of prudence and economy they did not lodge in the hotel. Bolibine had found work in a printing-office, and Maniloff, a very skilful cabinet-maker, worked for contractors. The Tarasconnais did not love these men; the one bored him with his grimaces and his bantering manner, the other haunted him with his fierce airs. Besides, they occupied too much of Sonia's heart.

"He is a hero," she had said to him when talking of Bolibine, and she related how, during three years, he had, unaided, printed a revolutionary paper in St. Petersburg. Three years he did this, without coming down stairs once, and without showing himself at a window, sleeping in a large cupboard, where the woman with whom he lodged concealed him every evening with his clandestine printing-machine.

And, again, the life of Maniloff during six months in the underground cellars of the Winter Palace, biding his time, sleeping every night upon his store of dynamite, which gave him intolerable headaches, and nervous attacks, still more enhanced by the ceaseless anguish, the sudden appearances of the police vaguely conscious that a mine was being prepared, and coming suddenly to surprise the workmen employed in the Palace. At his rare exits, Maniloff would be accosted on the Admiralty Square by a delegate of the Revolutionary Committee, who demanded, in a whisper,—

" Is it done? "

" No, nothing yet," the other would reply, without moving his lips. At length, one evening in February, the same question was put in the same terms; he replied with the greatest coolness,—

" It is done."

Almost immediately afterwards a bewildering uproar confirmed his words, and all the lights in the Palace were suddenly extinguished, the square was plunged in the deepest obscurity, which was pierced only by the cries of pain and terror, the sounding of trumpets, the galloping of orderlies, and of the fire-brigade hurrying up with their engines. . . .

Sonia paused in her recital,—

" Is this horrible, so many human lives sacrificed? is so much effort, courage, and intelligence useless? No, no; yet, these butcheries *en masse* are bad. The man they aim at always escapes. The true way to proceed, the most humane, would be to go to the Czar as you would approach a lion, determined, well armed, post yourself at a window, or at the door of his carriage, and when he passes——"

" *Bé oui!* certainly," said Tartarin, who felt much embarrassed, feigning not to understand the allusion; and suddenly launched into some discussion, philosophic or humanitarian, with some of the others present. For

Bolibine and Maniloff were not the only visitors to the Wassiliefs. Every day some new faces came in, young people, men or women dressed as poor students or fanatical teachers, blonde and rosy, with the obstinate foreheads and the fierce childishness of Sonia, law-breakers, exiles, some of them even under sentence of death, which could in no way detract from their youthful expansiveness.

They laughed, chatting loudly too, and as the greater number spoke French, Tartarin quickly found himself at his ease. They called him "uncle," divining in him something infantine, *naïf*, which pleased them. Perhaps he rather carried his recitals of his exploits a little too far, baring his arm above the elbow to show where the panther had wounded him, or displaying beneath his beard the holes which the claws of the lion of the Atlas had made; perhaps, also, he became familiar with his friends too soon, putting his arm round them, slapping them on the shoulders, calling them by their Christian names in about five minutes after being introduced, as thus,—

"Listen, Dmitri," "You know me, Fedor Ivanovitch," or at any rate within a very short time; but he "went down" with them all the same, by his plain-dealing, his amiability, his confident air, and by his desire to please. They read their letters in his presence, discussed their plans and passwords to blindfold the police—a purely conspirators' view which tickled Tartarin's imagination very much; and although he was by nature opposed to acts of violence, he could not at times help discussing their homicidal projects, approving, criticising, offering advice dictated by the experience of a great chief who has been upon the war-path, accustomed to the management of all kinds of weapons, and to personal encounters with wild beasts.

One day, when they were talking in his presence of the assassination of a police officer by a Nihilist at the theatre, he demonstrated to them that the thrust had been badly given, and then he gave them a lesson on the use of the knife,—

"Like this, *vé!* from below upwards. Thus you do not run any risk of wounding yourself."

Then, exciting himself to his acting level, he said,—

"Suppose, *te!* that I have your despot *entre quartre-*

z'yeux at a bear-hunt. He is where you are, Fedor; I am here near the round table, and each has a hunting-knife. We two, *monseigneur*, we must have a turn!"

Planted in the middle of the room, bending his short legs ready for a spring, stripped like a woodcutter, he imitated for them a real combat, terminating with his cry of triumph when he had plunged his weapon to the hilt upwards, *coquin de sort!* in the entrails of his adversary!

" That is how it is done, young people," he said.

But what retribution, what terrors he endured when he was no longer under the influence of Sonia's blue eyes, after the mental intoxication which had produced this bouquet of follies, he found himself alone, in his night-cap, face to face with his reflections and his usual nightly glass of *eau sucrée*.

After all, in what was he meddling? The Czar was not his Czar; and all these tales scarcely concerned him. Suppose that, one of these days, he was imprisoned, banished, delivered up to Muscovite justice!

Boufre! all these Cossacks did not joke about that! And in the darkness of his own room, with that horrible faculty of imagination that the horizontal position increases, now was opened out before him, like one of those sets of unfolding pictures which he used to have given him when a child, the varied and terrible punishments to which he was rendering himself liable; Tartarin in the copper-mines, as Boris had been, working in water up to his waist, his body being slowly eaten away — poisoned. He escapes! hides himself in the midst of snowy forests, pursued by Tartars and dogs trained to hunt fugitives. Worn out by cold and hunger, he is recaptured, and finally hanged between two convicts, embraced by a priest with shiny hair, smelling strongly of brandy and seal-oil, while far away yonder at Tarascon, in the sunlight, sound the *fanfares* of trumpets on a fine Sunday: the crowd—the ungrateful and oblivious populace—are installing the triumphant Costecalde in the chair of the P. C. A.!

It was in the agony of one of these terrible dreams that he shouted, " *A moi, Bézuquet!* " He sent to the chemist that confidential letter under the influence of that horrible nightmare. But the gentle " Good morning " of Sonia again bewitched him, and threw him once again into all the weakness of indecision.

One evening, when returning from the Kursaal to the hotel with the Wassiliefs and Bolibine, after two hours of enthralling music, the miserable man forgot all prudence, and the words "Sonia, I love you!" which he had so long restrained, he at length pronounced, grasping the little arm which rested on his own. She made no sign of emotion, but looked at him fixedly, very pale, under the gas-light where they had stopped: "Well then, deserve me," she said, with a charming but puzzling smile, which displayed all her beautiful teeth. Tartarin was about to reply, binding himself, by an oath, to perform any deadly deed, when the *chasseur* of the hotel came up and said,—

"There are some people for you, upstairs,—some gentlemen. They are looking for you!"

"Looking for me! *Outre!* What for?" Then Number 1 of his dioramic views came before his mind's eye: Tartarin imprisoned—exiled! Certainly he was afraid, but his attitude was heroic. Separating himself quickly from Sonia, he said in a choking voice, "Fly! save yourself!" Then he ascended the stairs, with head erect, and proud mien, as if he were going to execution; but so nervous, nevertheless, that he was obliged to grasp the banisters for support.

When he gained the corridor, he perceived a group of men at the door of his apartment, looking through the keyhole, knocking, and calling to him.

He advanced two paces, and then with parched lips managed to say, "Do you want me, gentlemen?"

"*Té, pardi!* yes, my President!"

A little elderly man, brisk and bony, dressed in a grey suit, and who seemed to be carrying on his coat, his hat, his gaiters, his long pendent moustaches, all the dust of the *Tour de ville*, fell upon the neck of our hero, rubbing against his soft and chubby cheeks the tough hide of the old captain.

"Bravida! it is impossible! Excourbaniès, too!—and who is that yonder?"

A bleating voice replied, "Dear ma-as-ter!" Then the pupil advanced, knocking against the wall as he came a

Strange Reception of the Delegates 171

species of long fishing-rod, thick at the top, and swathed in silver paper and oil-cloth.

"Hé! vé, it is Pascalon. Let us embrace, petitot! But what are you carrying? Put it down!"

"The paper—undo the paper," puffed the Commandant. The youth unrolled it quickly, and the Tarascon banner was displayed to the eyes of the astonished Tartarin.

The delegates took off their hats.

"My President"—Bravida's voice was trembling, solemn, and husky—"you demanded the banner; we have brought it to you—té!"

The President opened his eyes until they became as large as apples,—

"I! *I* asked for it?"

"What! didn't you ask for it?"

"Ah! yes, *parfaitemain*," replied Tartarin, suddenly enlightened by the name of Bézuquet.[1]

Now he understood it all, and guessed what had happened; and feeling overcome by the ingenious deception which Bézuquet had practised with a view to recall him to his duty and to honour, he choked, and muttered in his beard: "Ah, my children, this is kind—what good you do me!"

"*Vive le Présidain!*" squeaked Pascalon, brandishing his "oriflamme." The Gong sounded loudly, and shouted his war-whoop, "Ha! ha! ha! *fen dé brut!*" which penetrated to the cellars of the hotel. Doors were opened, curious faces appeared on every floor. These disappeared quickly at the sight of the standard and of the dark and shaggy men who hurled out strange defiances with extended arms. Never had such a row been heard in the peaceful Jungfrau hotel before.

"Come into my room," said Tartarin, somewhat ashamed. They were feeling their way in the darkness, seeking the match-box, when an authoritative rap at the door caused it to open and disclose the arrogant, yellow, puffed visage of Meyer, the hotel proprietor. He was about to enter the room, but stopped in the darkness, in which his fiery eyes gleamed, on the sill, his teeth clenched on his hard Teutonic accents,—

[1] Bézuquet is not mentioned.—*Trans.*

"Mind you keep quiet, or I will have you all taken up by the police."

A bellow as from a buffalo followed this discourteous speech, and the brutal use of the word "*ramasser.*" The landlord retreated a pace, but flung another sentence into the room,—

"We know who you are! Be off! We have our eyes upon you; and I do not want any more people like you in the house!"

"Monsieur Meyer," replied Tartarin calmly, politely, but very firmly, "get my bill made out; these gentlemen and I will leave for the Jungfrau to-morrow morning."

O, native land, O, little country in the great one, what influence is thine! It was sufficient to hear the Tarascon dialect rustling, with the country air, the blue folds of the banner—when, lo! there is Tartarin delivered from his love, and from the snares which surrounded him, restored to his friends, his mission, and to glory!

Now, *zou !*

XI

AT THE SIGN OF "THE FAITHFUL CHAMOIS"

NEXT day it was delightful to take the footpath from Interlachen to Grindelwald, which the tourists were obliged to pass to pick up the guides for the Little Scheideck; delightful, the triumphal march of the P. C. A., once more equipped in his mountaineering habiliments, supported on one side by the thin shoulder of the Commandant Bravida, on the other by the robust arm of Excourbaniès, both proud to escort him, to sustain their dear President, to carry his ice-axe, his sac, his alpenstock; while sometimes in front, and sometimes behind, or on the flank, Pascalon gamboled like a little dog, carrying his banner, wisely packed up, so as to avoid any demonstration such as they had had the evening before.

The high spirits of his companions, the sentiment of duty done, the snowy Jungfrau yonder, were not sufficient to make the hero forget what he had left behind him, perhaps for ever, and without a farewell! As he passed the last houses of Interlachen, his eyes filled with tears, and while he was walking he unbosomed himself, turn about, to Excourbaniès with " Listen, Spiridion," or to Bravida with " You know me, Placide "—for, by the irony of fate, the invincible soldier was called Placide, and the rough " buffalo," with material instincts, Spiridion.

Unfortunately, the Tarascon race, more brave than sentimental, never could take love affairs seriously. " Whoever loses a woman and fifteen pence, is to be condoled with for the loss of the money," replied the sententious Placide, and Spiridion quite agreed with him: As for the innocent Pascalon, he held women in fear, and blushed to the eyes when they pronounced the name of *la Petite Scheideck* in his hearing, having a kind of notion that it referred to a lady of somewhat free-and-easy manners. The poor lover was, therefore, obliged to keep his thoughts to himself, and to console himself alone, which is, after all, the safest course.

Besides, what worries could resist the attractions of the route across the narrow, deep, and shaded valley, where the tourists skirted a winding river, white with foam, and roaring like thunder amid the echoing pines which overhung and surrounded it on both its sloping sides!

The Tarasconnais delegates, with their heads held high, advanced with a feeling akin to terror in " religious " admiration; like the companions of Sindbad the Sailor, when they saw the mangroves and other gigantic flora of the Indian coasts. Only hitherto acquainted with their little bare and stony hills, they had no idea that there could possibly grow so many trees at once, on such very high mountains too!

" Oh, that is nothing; wait until you see the Jungfrau," remarked the P. C. A., who quite enjoyed their surprise, and felt himself growing bigger in their estimation.

At the same time, to enliven the scene and to humanise its imposing strain, many parties of people passed them *en route* —large landaus at full trot, with veils floating from the doors—heads were bent in curiosity to see the President surrounded by the delegation; while from time to time woodcarvers' stalls were passed; little girls standing by the wayside, looking very wooden-y in their straw hats with wide ribbons, and party-coloured skirts, singing in chorus of three voices, and offering bouquets of raspberry-sprays and *edelweiss*. Sometimes the Alpine horn would echo through the mountains its melancholy notes, swelling up, and repeated by the gorges, then slowly dying away after the manner of a cloud resolving into vapour.

"It is beautiful. One might fancy it the notes of an organ," murmured Pascalon, who, with moist eyes, was in ecstasy like a saint in a stained-glass window. Excourbaniès shouted without any fear, and the echo repeated itself in his Tarascon dialect until it finally died away: "Ha! ha! ha! *fen dé brut!*"

But they got tired of this in about two hours, proceeding through the same scenery—was it all arranged?—green on blue; glaciers at the bottom; and as sonorous as a musical clock. The roar of the torrents, the three-voice choruses, the sellers of wood-carvings, the little flower-girls, became insupportable to our friends: the dampness, too, the steam at the bottom of this gorge, the humid ground, full of water-plants, into which the sun never penetrates.

"It is enough to give one pleurisy," remarked Bravida, pulling up his coat-collar. Then fatigue, hunger, and ill-humour all attacked him at once. They could find no inn, and, being stuffed with raspberries, Excourbaniès and Bravida began to suffer cruelly. Even Pascalon himself—that angel—laden not only with the flag, but with the ice-axe, the sac, and the alpenstock, of which the others had by turns disembarrassed themselves, had lost his sprightliness and activity.

At a turn of the road, as they were about to cross the Lutschine on one of the covered bridges which are found in very snowy districts, a very formidable blowing of a horn reached their ears.

"Ah! *vé!* enough! enough!" screamed the exasperated delegation.

The blower—a giant ambushed by the side of the road—put down an enormous pine-trumpet, which rested on the ground and was terminated by a sounding-box which gave to this prehistoric instrument the loudness of a piece of artillery.

"Ask him whether he knows where there is an inn?"

said the President to Excourbaniès, who with great dignity, and with a very small pocket-dictionary, pretended to act as interpreter to the delegation since they were in German Switzerland. But before he could produce his dictionary, the horn-blower replied in very good French,—

"An inn, gentlemen? why, certainly: the *Chamois fidèle* is quite close by: allow me to show you the way?"

And while he accompanied them thither he informed them that he had lived in Paris many years as commissionaire at the corner of the Rue Vivienne.

"Another of the Company's people, *parbleu !*" thought Tartarin, leaving his friends to be amazed. The *confrère* of Bompard also made himself very useful, for although the sign of the house was in French, the people of the *Chamois fidèle* only spoke a horrible German *patois*.

The delegates, seated before an enormous potato omelette, soon recovered their health and good humour, which are essential to the Southerner as the sun is to his country. They drank deeply, and ate well. After toasts drunk to the President and to his ascent, Tartarin, who had been much exercised in his mind concerning the sign, turned to the horn-player, who was breaking a crust in the same room with them, and said,—

"So you have some chamois hereabouts? I thought none were left in Switzerland."

The man winked his eyes,—

"There are not many of them, but we could manage to let you see one all the same!"

"He wants to shoot at one, *vé !*" said Pascalon enthusiastically, "and the President never misses his aim."

Tartarin was sorry he had not brought his gun.

"Wait a minute; I will speak to the 'patron.'"

He ascertained that the innkeeper was an old chamois-hunter; he offered his gun, powder, his buckshot, and even his services as guide to the gentlemen, towards a lair which he knew.

"*En avant ; zou !*" cried Tartarin, yielding to his Alpinists, who were delighted to witness their chief's skill. It was only a trifling delay after all; and the Jungfrau would lose nothing by waiting.

Leaving the inn by the back door, they had only to push

through a path in an orchard scarcely larger than the little garden of a station-master on a railway, to find themselves on the mountain side, cut up by great crevasses between the pines and the bushes.

The innkeeper had gone on ahead, and the delegates could perceive him gesticulating and throwing stones, no doubt with a view to startling the animal. They had considerable trouble to rejoin him on the rocky and difficult slopes, particularly for people who have just got up from table, and who are no more accustomed to climbing than the worthy Tarasconnais were. There was, besides, a heavy air, a pressage of storm, which rolled the clouds slowly across the peaks overhead.

" *Boufre !* " whined Bravida.

Excourbaniès groaned,—

" *Outre !* "

" Let me tell you—" added the tame and bleating Pascalon.

But as the guide motioned them to be silent and to stay where they were, they obeyed. " One should never speak when carrying arms," said Tartarin of Tarascon with a severity of which each took his share, although the President was the only one armed. They remained standing and holding their breath; suddenly Pascalon exclaimed: " *Vé !* the chamois! *Vé !* "

At a hundred yards above them there stood the pretty animal, his horns upright, his coat a pretty fawn colour, the four feet planted together upon a rock. It was plainly visible against the sky, looking around without any appearance of fear. Tartarin methodically shouldered his gun as usual: he was going to fire, when the chamois disappeared!

" It is your fault," said the Commandant to Pascalon. " You whistled—that frightened it."

" I whistled! I! "

" Then it was Spiridion."

" Ah! *vaï ;* I never whistled in my life."

There had nevertheless been a whistle, shrill and long. The President put them all at their ease by informing them that the chamois at the approach of an enemy utters a whistling noise through his nostrils. What a devil of a fellow Tartarin was! he knew all the details of chamois-hunting as well as of all the other sports. At the guide's suggestion they continued their way; but the slope became more and more steep, the rocks more uneven, with sloughs and gullies to right and left. Tartarin kept his presence of mind, turning round every moment to assist the delegates, to hold out his hand or his gun to them.

"The hand, the hand! if it's all the same to you," exclaimed the brave Bravida, who had a mortal horror of loaded firearms.

Another sign from the guide—another halt.

"I think I felt a drop of rain," muttered the Commandant, who was very anxious. At the same time it thundered, and louder than the thunder rose the voice of Excourbaniès: "Look out, Tartarin!" The chamois came on, bounding between them like a flash—too quick for even Tartarin to shoulder his gun, not quick enough though to prevent them from hearing the loud whistling of his nostrils.

"I will give an account of him, *coquin de sort!*" said the President; but the delegates protested. Excourbaniès suddenly very sharply asked him if he had sworn to exterminate them.

"Dear ma-as-ter," bleated Pascalon, timidly, "I have heard it said that the chamois when driven to bay turns against the hunter, and becomes very dangerous."

"Don't let us bring him to bay, then," said Bravida the terrible.

Tartarin called them chicken-hearted milksops. Then suddenly, while they were disputing, they lost sight of each other in a thick, warm cloud which smelt of sulphur, and through which they kept searching for each other, calling out,—

"*Hé!* Tartarin!"

"Are you there, Placide!"

"Ma-as-ter!"

"Keep cool! keep cool!"

There was a regular panic. Then a gust of wind dispersed the cloud, carried it away like a veil torn off the bushes, and from it came a forked flash of lightning, followed by an awful crash of thunder under their very feet as it seemed.

"My cap!" exclaimed Spiridion, whose hair was standing up quite electrified, his headgear having been carried off by the tempest. They were in the heart of the storm—in

M

Vulcan's forge itself. Bravida first fled at full speed; the remainder of the delegation followed him; but one cry from the P. C. A., who thought for them all, restrained them,—

"*Malheureux!* beware of the lightning!"

Besides, outside of the real dangers which threatened them, they could scarcely run upon the steep slopes, across ravines now transformed into torrents and cascades by the rain. Their return was disastrous, at a slow pace, amid the lightning, the thunder, their tumbles, *glissades*, and forced halts. Pascalon crossed himself, and appealed aloud as at Tarascon to Saint Martha, Saint Helena, and Saint Mary Magdalen, while Excourbaniès swore "*Coquin de sort!*" and Bravida, who brought up the rear, turning round in a nervous state, said,—

"What is that I hear coming behind us? that sniffing, that gallop,—there—it has stopped!" The idea of the maddened chamois throwing itself upon the hunters could not be banished from the mind of the old warrior. In a low tone, so as not to alarm the others, he imparted his fears to Tartarin, who bravely changed places with him, and marched last with head held high, wet to the skin, yet with the inward determination which imminent danger bestows! But when they had regained the inn, and when he saw his dear Alpinists in shelter, in a fair way to dry themselves around an enormous faïence stove, in a room on the first floor, whence was ascending the odour of hot grog and wine, then the President felt himself shiver, and he declared with a very pale face: "I really believe I am taken ill."

Taken ill! an expression of sinister meaning in its vagueness and brevity, which hinted at all kinds of maladies——plague, cholera, yellow fever, "blue devils," jaundice, and lightning-strokes, the thought of which always occurred to the Tarasconnais at the least indisposition.

Tartarin was taken ill! There could, therefore, be no question of continuing the journey, and the delegates only cared for rest. Quickly they warmed his bed, plied him with wine, and at the second glass the President felt a grateful warmth permeate his body: a good omen! Two pillows at his back, an eider-down on his feet, his comforter tied over his head, he experienced a delicious satisfaction in listening to the roarings of the storm; in the pleasant smell of the pines;

in the little rustic, wooden inn, with latticed windows; in regarding his friends, the dear Alpinists, who pressed around his bed, glasses in hand, looking such queer figures in their odd costumes of curtains and such materials, with their Gallic, Saracen, or Roman types of features, while their clothes were drying before the stove. Forgetting himself, he questioned them in a doleful voice,—

"Are you quite well, Placide? Spiridion, you seemed to be unwell just now."

No, Spiridion suffered no longer, it had all passed away when the President was taken so ill. Bravida, who suited the moral to the proverbs of his country, added cynically: "The sickness of a neighbour comforts and even cures us." Then they spoke of their hunting, warming at the recollection of certain dangerous incidents, such as when the animal had turned upon them furiously; and without any complicity of lying, they very ingeniously fabricated a fable which they would relate on their return.

Suddenly, Pascalon, who had gone downstairs for another modicum of grog, reappeared in the greatest alarm—a naked arm outside his blue-flowered curtain, which he gathered around him with modest gesture *à la Polyeucte*. He was more than a second in the room before he could utter in a low voice and with quick breathing,—

" The chamois! "
" Well, what about it? "
" It is downstairs, in the kitchen! "
" Ah, go along! "
" You are joking! "
" Will you go and see, Placide? "

Bravida hesitated; so Excourbaniès descended on tip-toe; and then returned almost immediately, with a scared face. More extraordinary news still—

The chamois was drinking warm wine!

They owed him as much, poor beast, after the pretended hunt he had afforded them on the mountain, all the time started off or recalled by his master, who usually contented himself with putting it through its paces in the *salle* to show tourists how easily it had been tamed.

"This is crushing," said Bravida, not caring to understand any more about it, while Tartarin pulled the comforter over his face to hide from the delegates the gentle mirth which overspread his features, when at any stage of his journey he encountered the all-satisfying Switzerland of Bompard, with its mechanism and its supernumeraries!

X

THE ASCENT OF THE JUNGFRAU—VE! THE OXEN!—THE KENNEDY "CRAMPONS" DO NOT ANSWER; NEITHER DOES THE LAMP—APPEARANCE OF MASKED MEN AT THE CHALET—THE PRESIDENT IN THE CREVASSE—HE LEAVES HIS SPECTACLES BEHIND HIM—ON THE PEAKS—TARTARIN A DEITY

THERE was a tremendous crowd that morning at the Belle Vue Hotel on the Little Scheideck. Notwithstanding the rain and the squalls, the tables had been laid out of doors, under the shelter of the veranda, amongst an assemblage of alpenstocks, flasks, telescopes, cuckoo-clocks, etc.; and the tourists could, while breakfasting, gaze to the left upon the valley of Grindelwald, some 6000 feet below; on the right the Lauterbrunnen valley, and in front of them, at what seemed within gun-shot distance, the pure and stupendous slopes of the Jungfrau, with its *névé*, its glaciers, the whiteness of it all illuminating the air around, making the glasses still more transparent and the table-linen still more snowy.

But for the moment the attention of the company was directed to a noisy bearded party of tourists, who were coming up on mule-back, on donkey-back, one man even in a *chaise à porteurs*, who prepared themselves for the ascent, by a copious breakfast; they were in high spirits, and the noise they made contrasted greatly with the worn-out and solemn airs of the Rice and Prune factions, some illustrious members of which had assembled at the Scheideck: Lord Chippendale, the Belgian Senator and his family, the Austro-Hungarian diplomatist and his family. It seemed as if all these bearded people were about to attempt the ascent, for they occupied themselves in turn with the preparations for departure, rose,

The Ascent of the Jungfrau

hurried off to give instructions to the guides; to inspect the provisions, and from one end of the terrace to the other they shouted to each other in discordant accents,—

"*Hé!* Placide, see if the frying-pan is in the bag, and don't forget the spirit-lamp, mind!"

When the starting time arrived, however, it was perceived that all this was on account of one, and that of all the party one individual alone was going to undertake the ascent! But what an individual!

"Children, are we ready?" said the good Tartarin, in a triumphant and joyful tone, which did not tremble with the shadow of a fear for the possible perils of the journey, his last doubt concerning the "machinery" of the Swiss having been dissipated that morning before the two Grindelwald glaciers, each provided with a turn-stile and a *guichet* with an inscription, "Entrance to the glacier, one franc and a half."

He could then enjoy this departure without regret: the delight of feeling himself the observed of all observers; envied, admired, by those cheeky little girls with the close-cropped hair, who had laughed at him so quietly on the Rigi-Kulm; and who were at that very moment in raptures, comparing that little man with that enormous mountain which he was going to ascend. One was sketching him in her album, another was requesting the honour of holding his alpenstock. "Tchimppegne—Tchimppegne," suddenly cried a lanky, melancholy Englishman, of bricktint, who was approaching with a bottle and a glass in his hands. Then, after having compelled the hero to drink, he said,—

"Lord Chippendale, sir; *et vô?*"

"Tartarin de Tarascon."

"Oh, yes,—Tarterine. It's a capital name for a horse," said his lordship, who must have been a great sportsman on the other side of the Channel!

The Austro-Hungarian diplomatist also came forward to shake the mountaineer by the hand between his mittens—having a vague recollection of having met him somewhere. "Delighted, delighted," he repeated many times, and, not knowing how to get out of it, he added: "My compliments to Madame,"—his society formula, by which he concluded all introductions.

But the guides were becoming impatient. The cabin of the Alpine Club must be reached before dark; there they would sleep, and there was not a moment to lose. Tartarin quite understood this, and saluted the company with a wave of his hand, smiled paternally at the malicious " misses," and then, in a voice of thunder, cried,—

"Pascalon, the banner!"

It was displayed, the Southerners had unfolded it, for they like theatrical display; and at the thirtieth repetition of *"Vive le Président!" "Vive Tartarin!"* "Ha! ha! *jen dé brut,*" the party started—the two guides in front carrying the *sac*, the provisions, and some wood; then Pascalon, holding the "oriflamme;" and the P. C. A. with the delegates, who were to escort him to the Guggi glacier, brought up the rear. So the procession deployed, the folds of the flag flapping upon the swampy ground, or on the naked or snowy crests, the *cortège* in a vague way recalling *le jour des morts* in country places.

Suddenly, the Commandant cried out in great alarm,—

"*Vé!* oxen!"

They perceived some cattle grazing amid the undulations of the ground. The old warrior had a nervous terror of cows —an insurmountable fear; and as his friends could not leave him alone, the delegation was obliged to halt. Pascalon handed the banner to one of the guides; then a last embrace, a few hurried words of warning, with their eyes on the cows,—

"Adieu, *qué!*"

"No imprudence, mind!"

And they parted.

As for any one proposing to ascend with the President, it was not to be thought of. The ascent was too high, *boufre!* As one got nearer to it, it seemed more difficult, the ravines increased, the peaks bristled up in a white chaos which seemed impossible to traverse. It was much better worth while to watch the ascent from the Scheideck.

Naturally, Tartarin in all his life had never set foot on a glacier. There were no such things upon the hillocks of Tarascon, which were as perfumed and dry as a bundle of bent-grass. Yet the surroundings of the Guggi gave him a sensation of familiarity, as if he had seen them before— arousing the memory of the chase in Provence, all around the

The Kennedy Crampons

Camargue, towards the sea. It was the same grass, but shorter and burnt up as if scorched by fire. Here and there were pools of water, infiltrations, indicated by slim reeds; then the moraine, like a mobile hill of sand, broken shells, and cinders; then the glacier, with its blue-green waves, tipped with white, undulating as a silent and frozen sea. The wind also had all the coolness and freshness of the sea-breeze.

"No, thanks; I have my *crampons*," said Tartarin, as the guide offered him woollen foot-protectors to wear over his boots: "Kennedy's pattern *crampons*—first-rate—very convenient." He shouted all this at the top of his voice as if the guide were deaf, so as to make him understand better, for Christian Inebnit knew no more French than his comrade Kaufmann. Then Tartarin seated himself upon the moraine and fixed upon his boots with irons the species of large pointed iron socks called *crampons*.

He had experimented a hundred times with these "Kennedy *crampons*," and had tried them in the garden where the baobab grew; nevertheless the result was unexpected. Beneath the hero's weight the spikes buried themselves in the ice to such a depth that all attempts to extricate them were vain! Behold Tartarin nailed to the ice, springing, swearing, making semaphores of his arms and alpenstock; and finally reduced to recall his guides, who had gone on ahead in the full belief that they had to do with an experienced climber!

Finding it impossible to pull him up, they unfastened the *crampons* from him, and left them in the ice, replacing them by a pair of worsted boot-coverings. The President continued his way, not without toil and fatigue. Unaccustomed to use his *bâton*, he knocked it against his legs; the iron slid away from him, dragging him with it, when he leaned on it too heavily; then he tried the ice-axe, which proved even more difficult to manage; the swellings of the glacier increased, casting up its motionless waves into the appearance of a furious ocean suddenly petrified.

Apparently motionless only—for the loud crackings, the interior rumblings, the enormous blocks of ice slowly displaced like the revolving scenes at a theatre, displayed the action, the treacherousness, of this immense glacial mass;

and before the climber's eyes, within reach of his axe, crevasses opened—bottomless pits into which the pieces of ice rolled to infinity. The hero fell into many of these traps —once up to his waist into one of the green gulfs, wherein his broad shoulders alone prevented him from being buried.

Seeing him so unskilful, and at the same time so calm and collected—laughing, singing, gesticulating, just as he had been doing at breakfast—the guides began to think that the Swiss champagne had got into his head. Could they think anything else of a President of an Alpine Club, of a mountaineer so renowned, of whom his companions never spoke without "Ah!" and expressive gestures? Having, therefore, seized him under his arms after the respectful fashion of policemen putting a well-born but elevated young gentleman into a cab, the guides, by the aid of monosyllables and gestures, endeavoured to arouse his reason to the dangers of the route; the threatening appearance of the crevasses, the cold, and the avalanches. With the points of their ice-axes they indicated the enormous accumulations of ice, the sloping wall of *névé* in front, rising to the zenith in a blinding glare.

But the worthy Tartarin laughed at all this. "*Ah! vaï, les crevasses!* Ah! get out with your avalanches!" and he choked with laughter, winked at the guides, and nudged them playfully in the ribs, to make them understand that he was in the secret as well as they!

The men ended by joining in the fun, carried away by Tarascon melody; and when they rested a moment upon a block of ice to permit "*monsieur*" to take breath, they "jodelled" in Swiss fashion, but not loudly, for fear of avalanches, nor for long, because time was passing apace. Evening was evidently coming on, the cold was becoming more intense, and the singular discoloration of the snows and the ice, heaped up and overhanging in masses, which, even under a cloudy sky, glitter and sparkle, but when daylight is dying out, gone up towards the tapering peaks, take the livid, spectral tints of the lunar world. Pallor, congelation, silence—all is dead. And the good Tartarin, so warm, so lively, began at length to lose his *verve*, when at the distant cry of a bird, the call of the " snow partridge " (ptarmigan) resounding amid the desolation, before his eyes there passed

The Alpine Club Hut 185

a vision of a burnt-up country, browned under a setting sun, sportsmen of Tarascon, wiping their foreheads, seated upon their empty game-bags, beneath the shade of an olive-tree! This reminiscence comforted him.

At the same time Kaufmann was pointing out to him something above them which looked like a faggot on the snow. This was the hut. It seemed as if a few paces would suffice to reach it, but it was a good half-hour ere they got there. One of the guides went on in front to light the fire. It was dark by this time; the east wind came piercingly off the death-like ground, and Tartarin, no longer troubling himself about anything, firmly sustained by the arm of the guide, jumped and bounded about until there was not a dry thread on him, notwithstanding the lowness of the temperature. Suddenly, a savoury odour of onion-soup assailed their nostrils.

They had reached the hut.

Nothing can be more simple than these stopping-places established on the mountains by the forethought of the Swiss Alpine Cub; a single room, in which a sloping plank, serving as bed-place, occupies nearly all the space, leaving very little for the stove and the long table, which is nailed to the floor, as well as the benches which surround it. The supper was already laid when the men arrived; three bowls, tin spoons, the " Etna " for the coffee, two tins of Chicago preserved meats opened. Tartarin found the dinner excellent, although the onion-soup was rather smoked, and the famous patent lamp, which ought to have produced a quart of coffee in three minutes, failed to work.

For dessert they sang: it was the only way to converse with the guides. He sang his country's songs: *la Tarasque, les Filles d'Avignon.* The guides responded with local songs in their German *patois:* " *Mi Vater isch en Appenzeller; aou, aou !* " Fine fellows these—hard as rock, with soft flowing beards like moss, clear eyes, accustomed to move in space, as sailors' are; and this sensation of the sea and space, which he had lately experienced while ascending the Guggi, Tartarin again experienced here in the company of these glacier-pilots in that narrow cabin, low and smoky, a veritable " 'tween-decks," in the dripping of the snow which the heat had melted on the roof, and the wild gusts of wind, like masses of falling water, shaking everything, making the planks creak and the lamp flicker: then suddenly stopping in a silence as if all the world were dead.

Dinner was finished, when heavy steps were heard approaching, and voices were distinguished. A violent knocking at the door! Tartarin, somewhat alarmed, gazed at the guides. A nocturnal attack at such an elevation as this? The blows redoubled in intensity. "Who is there?" cried the hero, seizing his ice-axe: but the cabin was already invaded by two tall Americans masked in white linen, their clothing saturated with perspiration and snow-water, and behind them guides and porters—quite a caravan coming down from the summit of the Jungfrau.

"Welcome, my lords," cried Tartarin, with a hospitable and patronising wave of his hand, but "milords" had no compunction as to making themselves quite at home. In a few seconds the table was relaid, the bowls and spoons passed through some hot water to serve for the new-comers, according to the rules existing in all Alpine huts, the boots of "milords" were drying at the stove, while they, with their feet wrapped in straw, were disposing of a new supply of onion-soup.

These Americans were father and son—two ruddy giants, with the heads of pioneers, hard and practical. The older of the two seemed to have white eyes; and after a while the manner in which he tapped and felt around him, and the care which his son took of him, assured Tartarin that he was the famous blind mountaineer of whom he had heard at the Belle Vue Hotel, a fact he could scarcely credit, a famous climber in his youth, and who, notwithstanding his sixty years, had recommenced his ascents again with his son. He had in this manner already made the ascent of the Wetterhorn and the Jungfrau, and reckoned upon attacking the Cervin and Mont Blanc, declaring that the mountain air gave him intense enjoyment, and recalled all his former vigour.

"But," said Tartarin to one of the porters—for the Yankees were not communicative, and only replied "Yes" or "No" to all advances—"but, if he cannot see, how can he manage to cross dangerous places?"

"Oh, he has the foot of a true mountaineer, and his son

Continuation of the Ascent 187

looks after him, places his feet in the proper positions, etc. The fact is, he never has an accident."

" More especially as accidents are never very deplorable, *qué ?* " After a knowing smile to the astonished porter, the Tarasconnais, more and more persuaded that all this was *blague*, stretched himself on the plank, rolled himself in his rug, his comforter up to his eyes, and fell asleep, notwithstanding the light, the chatter, the smoke of pipes, and the smell of the onion-soup.

" *Mossié ! Mossié !* " (Monsieur.)

One of the guides was shaking him by the shoulder, while the other was pouring out some boiling coffee into the bowls.

There were a few oaths and some grumbling from the sleepers, as Tartarin pushed past them in his way to the table and to the door. All of a sudden, he found himself in the open air, shivering with cold, and puzzled by the moonlight upon the white plains, the frozen cascades, which the shadows of the peaks, *aiguilles*, and *séracs*, cut with intense blackness. There was not the bewildering scintillation of the afternoon, nor the livid grey tinge of the evening, but a town cut by dark alleys, mysterious passages, dubious angles between the marble monuments and crumbled ruins—a dead town with its wide deserted squares.

Two o'clock! With good walking they ought to reach the summit by mid-day. " *Zou*," said the P. C. A. quite gaily, and pressed forward to the assault. But the guides stopped him: it was necessary to rope themselves.

" Ah! go along with your tying up! Very well, then; if it amuses you, be it so! "

Christian Inebnit took the lead, leaving six feet of rope between him and Tartarin, and the same length between Tartarin and the other guide, who was carrying the provisions and the banner. The Tarasconnais got on better than the day before, and really he did not seem to appreciate the difficulties of the path—if the way along that terrible *arête* of ice can be called a path—over which they were advancing with the greatest caution. It was a few inches wide, and so slippery that Christian had to cut steps in it.

The *arête* glittered between profound abysses. But do you think Tartarin was afraid? Not a bit of it! Scarcely did he experience the little tremor of the newly-made Freemason who has to submit to the ordeal! He placed his feet exactly in the holes cut by the guide, doing everything as he saw him do it, as coolly as if he were in the baobab garden, walking on the edge of the fountain, to the great terror of the gold-fish. At one time, the crest became so narrow that they were compelled to proceed on all-fours, and while they were advancing slowly a tremendous detonation was heard on the right beneath them. "An avalanche!" said Inebnit, stopping quite still so long as the uproar lasted, while the reverberations, grandly repeated, terminated by a lengthened thunder-roll, which slowly died away in echoes. After that the former terrible silence succeeded, covering all things like a winding-sheet.

The *arête* passed, they reached the *névé*, which sloped easily, but was terribly long. They had climbed for more than an hour, when a thin streak of rosy hue began to touch the peaks high—very high—over their heads. Day was announcing its arrival. As a good Southerner, cherishing an enmity to darkness, Tartarin trolled out his cheerful song,—

Grand souleù de la Provenço
Gai compaire dou mistrau.[1]

A tug at the cord both before and behind stopped him short in the middle of his verse: "Hush! hush!" cried Inebnit, indicating with the handle of his ice-axe the menacing line of immense and clustered *séracs* which the least shock would send down upon the travellers. But the Tarasconnais knew what he was about—they were not going to humbug him; so he recommenced in a resonant voice,—

Tu qu'escoulès la Duranço
Commo un flot dé vin de Crau.[2]

The guides, perceiving that they could not keep the headstrong singer within due bounds, made a wide *détour* to avoid the *séracs*, and soon were brought to a standstill by an enormous *crevasse*, which was lighted in its green depths by the first rays of daylight. A snow bridge crossed it, but so thin and fragile, that at the very first step it disappeared in a whirlwind of fine snow, dragging with it the head guide and

---

[1] Grand soleil de la Provence,—Gai compère du mistral.
Toi qui siffles la Durance—Comme un coup de vin de Crau.

Tartarin in the Crevasse

Tartarin, who hung by the cord, which Rudolf Kaufmann, the rear guide, gripped with all his force, his axe firmly fixed in the snow to sustain the tension. But though he could hold up the men, he could not haul them out, and he stood crouching down, with clenched teeth and straining muscles, too far from the *crevasse* to perceive what was passing within it.

Astounded by the fall, and half blinded by the snow, Tartarin for a minute threw his legs and arms about like a puppet: but then, righting himself by means of the rope, he hung over the chasm, his nose touching the icy wall, which thawed beneath his breathing, in the posture of a plumber mending a water-pipe. He saw the sky paling above him, the last stars were disappearing; beneath him a chasm of intense darkness, whence ascended a cold air.

Nevertheless, his first astonishment over, he regained his coolness and good humour,—

" Eh! up there! Father Kaufmann, don't let us get mouldy here, *qué !* There is a draught, and this cursed cord is bruising our ribs."

Kaufmann was not able to reply. If he unlocked his teeth he would lose some of his strength. But Inebnit hailed from below,—

" *Mossié ! Mossié !* ice-axe! "—for he had lost his own in the *crevasse;* and the heavy instrument passed from Tartarin's hands into those of the guide—a difficult operation because of the length of cord which separated them. The guide wanted it to cut steps in the ice in front of him, or to cling by it foot and hand.

The strain upon the rope being thus lessened by one half, Rudolf Kaufmann, with carefully calculated force and infinite precautions, commenced to drag up the President, whose cap at length appeared over the edge of the *crevasse*. Inebnit came up in his turn, and the two mountaineers met with effusion, but with the few words which are exchanged after great dangers by people of a slow habit of speaking. They were much moved, and trembling with their exertions. Tartarin passed them his flask to restore them. He seemed quite composed and calm, and while he was beating the snow from his dress rhythmically, he kept humming a tune, under the very noses of the astonished guides.

"*Brav ! brav ! Franzose,*" said Kaufmann, patting him on the shoulder, and Tartarin, with his jolly laugh, replied,—

"*Farceur,* I knew quite well there was no danger!"

Within the memory of guide, never had there been such an Alpinist as this!

They continued their way, climbing a gigantic wall of ice eighteen hundred or two thousand feet high, in which they cut steps, which occupied much time.

The man of Tarascon began to feel his strength failing him under the blazing sun, which reflected all the whiteness of the landscape, all the more trying for his eyes as he had dropped his spectacles into the *crevasse*. Soon afterwards a terrible faintness seized upon him, that "*mal de montagnes*" which has the same effect as sea-sickness. Utterly done up, and light-headed, with dragging limbs, he stumbled about, so that the guides had to haul him along, one on each side, as they had done the day before, sustaining him, even drawing him up the ice-wall. Scarcely three hundred feet intervened between them and the top of the Jungfrau; but although the snow was firm and the way easy, this last stage occupied an "interminable" time, while the fatigue and the sensation of suffocation increased with Tartarin continually.

Suddenly, the guides let him go, and waving their hats began to "jodel" with delight. They had reached the summit. This point in immaculate space, this white crest somewhat rounded, was the end, and for poor Tartarin the end of the torpor in which he had been walking, as in his sleep, for the last hour.

"Scheideck! Scheideck!" exclaimed the guides, pointing out to him far below on a verdant plateau, standing out from the mists of the valley, the Hôtel Belle Vue, looking a very toy-house.

From there they had a magnificent panorama spread before them, a snow slope tinged with an orange glow by the sun, or a cold deep blue; a mass of ice fantastically sculptured into towers, steeples, needles, *arêtes ;* gigantic mounds, like graves of the mastodon and the megatherium. All the colours of the rainbow played upon them, uniting again in the beds of the great glaciers, with their motionless icefalls, crossed by tiny streams which the sun was warming into life again. But at that great elevation the reflections were

After the Ascent

toned down, a light was floating in the air, a cold ecliptic light, which made Tartarin shiver as much as the sensation of the silence and solitude of the white desert and its mysterious recesses.

A little smoke was perceived, and some detonations were heard from the hotel. They had seen the tourists, and were firing cannon in their honour, and the conviction that they saw him, that his Alpinists were there, the young ladies, the illustrious Rices and Prunes, with their opera-glasses, recalled Tartarin to the importance of his mission. He snatched the Tarascon banner from the hands of the guide, and waved it two or three times; then, fixing his ice-axe in the snow, he seated himself, upon the iron of the pick, flag in hand, superb, facing the public. And without his perceiving it—by one of those spectral images frequent at the tops of mountains, the result of sun, and of mist which was rising behind him—a gigantic Tartarin was outlined on the sky, enlarged and shortened, the beard bristling out of the comforter, like one of the Scandinavian deities, which tradition presents to us as enthroned in the midst of the clouds.

XI

EN ROUTE FOR TARASCON!—THE LAKE OF GENEVA—TARTARIN SUGGESTS A VISIT TO BONNIVARD'S CELL—A SHORT DIALOGUE AMID THE ROSES—ALL THE BAND UNDER LOCK AND KEY—THE UNFORTUNATE BONNIVARD—A CERTAIN ROPE MADE IN AVIGNON COMES TO LIGHT

AFTER the ascent, Tartarin's nose peeled and became pimpled, his cheeks cracked. He was obliged to remain in his room for five days at the Belle Vue. Five days of compresses, pomades of which he whiled away the cloying mawkishness and boredom by making little whist parties with the delegates, or dictating to them a long detailed account, most circumstantial in incidents, of his expedition, to be read in full meeting at the club, and published in the *Forum*. Then, when his general fatigue had abated, and

there remained upon the noble features of the P. C. A. a few
blisters, scars, and cracks, with a beautiful Etruscan vase
tint, the delegation and its President took the route for
Tarascon *viâ* Geneva.

Let us pass over the incidents of the journey: the terror
which the Southern party aroused in the narrow railway-
carriages, the steamers, the *tables d'hôte*, by their songs, cries,
and their exuberant affection for each other; their banner,
and their alpenstocks, for since the ascent of the P. C. A.
they had all furnished themselves with stocks, on which the
records of celebrated ascents were burnt in black letters.

Montreux!

Here the delegates, at the suggestion of their leader, decided
to halt for two or three days, to see the celebrated shores of
the Lake Leman—particularly Chillon, and the legendary
prison in which languished the great patriot Bonnivard, as
related by Byron and Delacroix.

As for Tartarin, he cared very little for Bonnivard; his
adventure with William Tell had enlightened him concerning Swiss legends; but while passing through Interlachen
he had learnt that Sonia was about to leave for Montreux
with her brother, whose condition had become more serious,
and this invention of a pilgrimage served him as a pretext to
see the young lady once more, and—who knows?—to persuade her to follow him to Tarascon.

It must be understood that his followers all believed in the
good faith of their leader when he said he came to render
homage to the celebrated citizen of Geneva, whose story
the P. C. A. had related; even now, with their taste for
theatrical display, they would have marched in line to
Chillon, with the banner displayed, crying " *Vive Bonnivard !* " But the President was obliged to restrain them.
" Let us first breakfast," he said, " and then we shall see."

They filled the omnibus of a *pension* Müller, situated, like
many others, near the landing-stage by the lake.

" *Vé ! le gendarme !* How he stares at us," said Pascalon,
as last of all he got into the omnibus with the banner, which
was very much in the way; and Bravida, who was nervous,
said: " That's true; what can that *gendarme* want with us
that he examines us so closely? "

" Perhaps he recognises me, *pardi !* " said the good Tar-

Market-Day in Montreux

tarin, and he smiled a far-off smile at the Vaudois policeman, whose long blue *capote* was persistently turned towards the omnibus, which was proceeding along the poplar-lined road by the lake side.

That was market-day in Montreux. Rows of little shops in the open air were ranged along the lake, filled with fruit, vegetables, cheap lace, and with the silver jewellery, chains, *plaques*, brooches, etc., which embellish the Swiss female costume like "worked" snow or ice-pearls. Amid these shops flowed the stream of people from the little harbour, which sheltered a flotilla of boats of brilliant colours, and where the disembarkation of bags and barrels from the vessels with antennæ-like sails, the shrill whistling, the bells of the steamers, the bustle of the *cafés*, the beer-shops, the florists, and the second-hand dealers which line the quay, were continually mingling. With a little sun, one might have fancied one's self in some Mediterranean port, between Mentone and Bordighera. But the sun was wanting, and the natives of Tarascon looked at this pretty country through a veil of water which rose from the blue lake, climbed up the stony streets, united above the houses with other clouds, massed amid the dark verdure of the mountains, charged with rain, and ready to burst.

"*Coquin de sort!* I am not a lake-man," said Spiridion Excourbaniès, rubbing the glass of the omnibus window to see the views of the glaciers.

"No more am I," sighed Pascalon; "this fog, this dead water, makes one inclined to weep."

Bravida complained also: he was afraid of his sciatica.

Tartarin reprimanded them severely. Was it, then, nothing that they would be able to say, when they returned, that they had seen the prison of Bonnivard, written their names on the historic walls beside the signatures of Rousseau, Byron, Victor Hugo, George Sand, Eugène Sue? Suddenly, in the middle of this tirade, the President interrupted himself — changed colour. He had seen a little *toque*, resting on blonde hair, passing by. Without even stopping the omnibus, just then slackening for the ascent, he leaped out, saying, "Go on to the hotel," to the stupefied Alpinists.

"Sonia! Sonia!"

He was afraid he would not be able to overtake her, so

hurried was she, her slim shadow flitting along the wall
of the road. She turned and waited for him: "Ah! 'tis
you!" Immediately their hands clasped she resumed her
walk. He placed himself beside her, out of breath, excusing
himself for having quitted her in such sudden fashion—the
arrival of his friends—the necessity for the ascent, of which
his face still bore the traces. She listened without saying
a word, hurrying on, her eyes fixed and wide open. Judging
by her profile, she seemed to him pale, her features deprived
of their infantine candour, with something hard, resolute,
which until then had not existed, but in her voice—her
imperious will; but still her juvenile gracefulness, her waving,
golden hair!

"And Boris—how is he?" asked Tartarin, a little put
out by her silence, by the coldness which was creeping over
him.

"Boris?" She trembled. "Ah! yes, it is true; you
didn't know. Well, then, come with me; come."

They proceeded along a little path, bordered with vines
hanging almost over the lake, and villas, gardens—sanded,
elegant, the terraces planted with the virgin vine, roses,
petunias, and myrtle. From time to time they passed
some strange face, with troubled features and mournful
looks, their steps slow and melancholy, such as one meets
with at Mentone or Monaco: only there the light devours
all, absorbs everything; while beneath the cloudy sky
suffering is more apparent, while the flowers appear fresher.

"Come in," said Sonia, pushing open a gate beneath a
pediment of white masonry, inscribed with Russian characters
in golden letters.

Tartarin did not at first understand where he was. A
little garden with carefully tended walks, pebbly, full of
climbing roses amid the green bushes, great clusters of
yellow and white blossoms filled the place with their aroma
and bloom. Amongst these garlands, this marvellous display of blossom, were some stones standing up or lying down,
with dates and names upon them,—this one, quite new,—

"*Boris de Wassilief, aged 22 years.*"

He had been laid there for some days, having died almost
immediately after he had reached Montreux; and, in this

cemetery of strangers, he found a trace of his native land amongst the Russians, Poles, Swedes, buried beneath the flowers—consumptive patients who are sent to this northern Nice, because the sunny South is too hot, and the transition too sudden for them.

The pair remained motionless and silent for a moment before the new white headstone on the dark ground of the freshly-turned earth: the young girl, with bowed head, breathing the odour of the abundant roses, and thus resting her swollen eyes.

"Poor little thing!" said Tartarin, much affected; and, taking in his strong rough hands the tips of Sonia's fingers, he continued: "And you? What will become of you, now?"

She looked him full in the face with dry and brilliant eyes, in which no tear trembled,—

"I? I leave here in an hour!"

"You are going away?"

"Bolibine is already in St. Petersburg. Maniloff is waiting for me to pass the frontier. I am about to enter the furnace. People will hear us talked about." Then, in an undertone, she added, with a half smile, fixing her blue eyes full on the face of Tartarin, who blanched and avoided her gaze: "Who loves me will follow me!"

Ah! *vaï*, follow her! This enthusiast made him afraid; besides, this funeral scene had cooled his ardour. He struggled, nevertheless, not to run away like a contemptible wretch. So, with his hand on his heart, and a gesture worthy of Abenceragus, the hero began: "You know me, Sonia——"

She did not wish to hear any more.

"Babbler!" she replied, shrugging her shoulders. And then she left him, upright and proud, passing between the rose bushes without once turning round. "Babbler!" not another word, but the intonation was so contemptuous that the good Tartarin blushed under his beard, and convinced himself that they were alone in the garden, and that no one had heard them.

Fortunately, impressions did not survive long with our Tarasconnais. Five minutes later, he ascended the terraces of Montreux with a light step, in quest of the *pension* Müller, where the Alpinists were waiting *déjeuner* for him, and he felt a great relief at the termination of this dangerous *liaison*. As he proceeded, he nodded vigorously, and explained eloquently to himself the reason which Sonia would not listen to. *Bé!* yes, it was certainly a despotism—he would not deny that; but to pass from the idea to action! *Boufre!* And then, what an employment for him, to fire upon despots! Suppose every oppressed nation came to him, as the Arabs did to Bombonnel when the panther prowled around the *douar*, all his efforts would not suffice. *Allons!*

A passing carriage quickly cut short his monologue. He had only just time to leap aside: "Look out, you animal!" But his angry exclamation was at once changed into an exclamation of surprise: "*Quès aco! Boudiou!* Impossible!" I give you a thousand guesses to divine what he saw in the landau. The delegation! The delegation in full—Bravida, Pascalon, Excourbaniès—crowded in at one side, pale, exhausted, dishevelled, after a struggle with two *gendarmes*, muskets in hand, seated opposite to them. All their profiles, motionless, mute, in the narrow frame of the doorway, seemed like a bad dream; and Tartarin stood rooted to the spot as firmly as he ever was by the "Kennedy" *crampons*. He saw the carriage gallop off, behind it a crowd of school-boys, satchels on back, just released from school, when a voice sounded in his ear: "Here is the fourth man!" In a moment he was seized, handcuffed, bound: he was hustled into a hackney carriage with the *gendarmes* and an officer armed with his gigantic *latte*, which he held between his knees, the handle touching the top of the cab.

Tartarin wanted to speak, to explain himself. There was evidently some mistake.

He told them his name. He appealed to his Consul, to a dealer in Swiss honey who had known him at Beaucaire. Then, in face of the persistent silence of his attendants, he began to look upon this arrest as a new move of Bompard's and, addressing himself to the officer, he said, with a waggish air: "This is all a joke, *qué! Ah! vaï, farceur!* I know very well it is all for fun!"

"If you speak any more I will gag you. Not a word!"

said the officer, rolling his terrible eyes, so that it seemed as if he was going to impale the prisoner on his staff.

The other kept quiet, and did not stir any more; he kept looking out of window at the borders of the lake, the high mountains—of a damp green hue—the hotels, with their varied roofs, with gilded signs visible a league away; and on the slopes, as on the Rigi, was a coming and going of men carrying up and down baskets and hods of provisions, etc.; as at the Rigi, also, a toy railway, squeaking along, and climbing up as far as Glion; and, to complete the resemblance to the *Regina montium*, a heavy beating rain was falling—an exchange of water and fog between the lake and the sky, the sky and the lake, the clouds touching the waves.

The carriage rolled over a drawbridge between some little shops where knick-knacks were sold—penknives, button-hooks, and such things; passed through a low postern, and stopped in the courtyard of an old castle, grass-grown, and flanked by round "pepper-box" towers, with black *moucharabis* supported by beams. Where was he? Tartarin understood it when he heard the officer of *gendarmes* conversing with the *concierge* of the castle, a fat man in a Grecian cap, shaking a huge bunch of rusty keys.

"In solitary confinement? But I have no room! The others occupy all—unless we put him in the Bonnivard prison."

"Put him in Bonnivard's chamber, then—it is quite good enough for him," said the captain, authoritatively. And his orders were carried out.

The Castle of Chillon, about which the President had continually been speaking to his friends the Alpinists, and in which, by the irony of fate, he found himself suddenly imprisoned without knowing why, is one of the historical monuments of Switzerland. After having served as a summer residence of the Counts of Savoy, then as a State prison, a depot of arms and stores, it is now only an excuse for an excursion, like the Rigi-Kulm or Tellsplatte. There is, however, a guard there, and a lock-up for drunkards and the wilder lads of the district; but such inmates are rare, as the Vaud is a most peaceful canton; thus the lock-up is usually untenanted, and the keeper keeps his store of fuel in it. So the arrival of all these prisoners had put him in a bad temper, particularly when he thought that people would not be able to see the celebrated dungeon, which was at that season of considerable profit.

Furious, he led the way, and Tartarin followed him, timidly, and without making any resistance. A few worn steps, a damp corridor feeling like a cave, a high door like a wall, with enormous hinges, and they found themselves in a vast subterranean vault, with deeply trodden floor, and heavy Roman pillars on which hang the rings of iron to which the State prisoners were formerly chained. A semi-daylight flickers in, and the rippling lake is reflected through the narrow apertures which permit naught but the sky to be seen.

"This is your place," said the gaoler. "Mind you don't go to the end, the *oubliettes* are there."

Tartarin recoiled in terror.

"*Les oubliettes! Boudiou!*" he exclaimed.

"What would you have, *mon garçon?* They have ordered me to put you in Bonnivard's dungeon. I have put you in Bonnivard's dungeon! Now, if you have means, I can supply you with some luxuries, such as a mattress and coverlet for the night."

"Let me have something to eat first," said Tartarin, who very fortunately had not left his purse behind him.

The *concierge* came back with some fresh bread, some beer, and a saveloy, which were all devoured eagerly by the prisoner of Chillon, who had not broken his fast since the day before, and was worn out by fatigue and emotion. While he was eating it on his stone bench in the gleam of the embrasure, the gaoler kept examining him with a good-natured air.

"*Ma foi!*" he said, "I don't know what you have done, nor why they treat you so severely.

"Eh! *coquin de sort*, no more do I! I know nothing whatever about it," replied Tartarin, with his mouth full.

"At any rate, one thing is certain—you have not the appearance of a criminal, and I am sure you would never prevent a poor father of a family from gaining his living? Eh? Well, then, I have upstairs all the people who have come to see Bonnivard's dungeon. If you will promise me to remain quiet, and not attempt to escape——"

The worthy Tartarin promised at once, and five minutes

The Unfortunate Bonnivard 199

afterwards he saw his dungeon invaded by his old acquaintances of the Rigi-Kulm and the Tellsplatte: the ass Schwanthaler, the most inept Astier-Réhu, the member of the Jockey Club with his niece, all the Cook's tourists! Ashamed, and fearful of being recognised, the unhappy man hid behind the pillars, retiring and stealing away as they approached him, the tourists preceding the gaoler, who uttered his claptrap in a melancholy tone: "This is where the unfortunate Bonnivard was imprisoned."

They advanced slowly, retarded by the disputes of the two *savants*, who were always quarrelling, ready to fly at each other, one waving his camp-stool, the other his *sac de voyage*, in fantastic attitudes, which the half-light magnified along the vaulted dungeon roof.

By the mere exigency of retreat, Tartarin found himself at last near the opening of the *oubliettes*—a black pit, open level with the ground, breathing an odour of many centuries, damp and cold. Alarmed, he stopped, crouched in a corner, his cap over his eyes; but the damp saltpetre of the walls affected him, and suddenly a loud sneeze, which made the tourists recoil, betrayed him!

"*Tiens*, Bonnivard!" exclaimed the fast little Parisienne in the Directoire hat, whom the member of the Jockey Club called his niece.

The Tarasconnais did not permit himself to show any signs of being disturbed.

"It is really very interesting, these *oubliettes!*" he remarked in the most natural tone in the world, as if he also was a mere visitor for pleasure to the dungeon. Then he mingled with the other tourists, who smiled on recognising the Alpinist of the Rigi-Kulm, the mainspring of that famous ball.

"*Hé! mossié! ballir, dantsir!*"

The comical outline of the little fairy Schwanthaler presented itself before him, ready to dance. Truly, he had a great mind to dance with her. Then, not knowing how to disembarrass himself of this excited little bit of a woman, he offered her his arm, and gallantly showed her his dungeon: the ring whereon the captive's chain had been riveted, the traces of his footsteps worn in the rock around the same pillar; and, never having heard Tartarin speak with such

facility, the good lady never suspected that he who was
walking with her was also a State prisoner—a victim to the
injustice and the wickedness of men. Terrible, for instance,
was the parting, when the unfortunate " Bonnivard," having
led her to the door, took leave of her with the smile of a man
of the world, saying:—" No, thank you, *vé !* I remain here
a moment longer." She bowed, he bowed; and the gaoler,
who was on the alert, locked and bolted the door, to the
great astonishment of all.

What an insult! He was bathed in agonised perspiration
as he listened to the exclamations of the departing visitors.
Fortunately such torture as this could not be repeated that
day. The bad weather would deter tourists. A terrible
wind was blowing under the old planks; cries arose from the
oubliettes, like the plaints of unburied bodies, and the ripple
of the lake, dotted with the rain, beat against the walls to
the edges of the embrasures whence the spray was dashed
over the prisoner. At intervals the bell of a steamer, and
the patter of its wheels, broke upon the reverie of poor Tartarin,
while the evening descended grey and mournful on
the dungeon, which seemed to grow larger.

How could this arrest be explained? How could his imprisonment
be justified? Costecalde, perhaps—an electoral
manœuvre at the last moment. Or had the Russian police
been informed of his imprudent utterances, his proposal
to Sonia, and had demanded his extradition? But then,
why arrest the delegates? What could be alleged against
these unfortunate men, whose alarm and despair he could
picture, although they were not in the dungeon of Bonnivard,
in these stony vaults, traversed at night by rats of enormous
size, by crayfish, and silent spiders with hairy, uncanny
feet.

Now you see what it is to have a good conscience. Notwithstanding
the rats, the cold, and the spiders, the great
Tartarin found, amid all the horrors of the State prison,
haunted by the shades of martyrs, a rude sound sleep,
with mouth open and hands clenched, as he had slept
between the sky and the abysses in the hut of the Alpine
Club. He thought he was still dreaming, when he heard
his gaoler enter in the morning.

"Get up," said he; " the prefect of the district is here:

he will question you;" and he added, with some respect: "You must be a famous criminal for the prefect to put himself out about you as he has done."

Criminal! No, but one may look like one after a night in a damp and dusty dungeon, without having any opportunity to make one's *toilette*, however quickly. And in the old stable of the castle, now transformed into a guard-house, embellished with muskets in racks—when Tartarin, after a reassuring glance at the Alpinists, who were seated amongst the *gendarmes*, appeared before the prefect of the district, he had the pleasure of feeling he was in the presence of a tidy, well-dressed magistrate, one who questioned him severely,—

"You are named Maniloff, is not that so?—a Russian subject, an incendiary, a fugitive assassin from Siberia?"

"Never in my life! It is an error—a misprision!"

"Hold your tongue, or I will gag you," interrupted the captain.

The neat prefect continued: "Well, to cut short your denials—do you know this rope?"

His rope! *Coquin de sort!* His rope, with the iron fibre, made at Avignon. He bowed his head, to the stupefaction of the delegates, and replied, "I know it!"

"With this rope a man has been hanged in the Canton of Unterwald!"

Tartarin, trembling, swore that he knew nothing about that.

"We shall soon see." Then he introduced the Italian tenor, the detective, whom the Nihilists had hanged to the oak on the Brünig, but whom the woodcutters had miraculously delivered from death.

The spy looked at Tartarin: "That is not the man—nor," he added, looking at the delegates, "are those the others. There has been a mistake here."

The prefect was furious: then, to Tartarin, "Well, then, what *have* you done?"

"That is just what I want to know, *vé!*" replied the President, with all the assurance of innocence.

After some explanations, the Alpinists of Tarascon, set at liberty, hurried away from Chillon, of which place no one has experienced the romantic and melancholy oppression more strongly than they. They stopped at the *pension* Müller, to get their luggage, the banner, and to pay the bill of the *déjeuner* they had not had time to eat: then they departed for Geneva by train. Rain was falling. Through the steaming windows they could see the names of the stations, Clarens, Vevay, Lausanne; the red *chalets*, the gardens of rare shrubs—all lying under a damp veil, which dropped from the branches of the trees, the roofs of the houses, and the terraces of the hotels.

Installed in a corner of the long Swiss railway carriage, two seats face to face, the Alpinists looked defeated and discomfited. Bravida, very bitter, complained of pain, and all the time kept asking Tartarin, with fierce irony: "Eh, *bé!* you haven't seen Bonnivard's dungeon, have you? You wished to see it so much, too! I believe you *have* seen it, after all, *qué?*" Excourbaniès, voiceless for the first time in his life, gazed piteously at the lake, which the line skirted: "There is water enough, *Boudiou!* After this, I shall never take another bath as long as I live!"

Upset by a shock from which he had not yet recovered, Pascalon, the banner between his knees, hid himself behind it, looking right and left, like a hare. And Tartarin? Oh! he; always calm and dignified, he was improving his mind reading the papers from southern France, a packet of journals forwarded to the *pension* Müller, which had all copied from the *Forum* the narrative of his ascent—which he had dictated and enlarged—embellished by startling eulogies. All of a sudden, our hero uttered a cry—a loud cry which pervaded the carriage. All the travellers rose: they thought an accident had occurred. It was only that these words had caught Tartarin's eyes in the *Forum*—"Listen to this!" he cried to the Alpinists: "'It is reported that V. P. C. A. Costecalde, who has scarcely recovered from the jaundice which has afflicted him for some days, is about to leave here with a view to ascend Mont Blanc—to go higher up than Tartarin!' Ah! the bandit! He wants to destroy the effect of my Jungfrau! Well, wait a little; I will take the wind out of you and your mountain! Chamonix is only a few miles from Geneva—I will do Mont Blanc before him! Are you agreed, my boys?"

Bravida protested. *Outre!* He had had adventures

enough. "Enough, and more than enough," growled Excourbaniès in a low tone, in his husky voice.

"And you, Pascalon?" asked Tartarin, gently.

The pupil bleated without raising his eyes: "Ma-as-ter!" He also denied him!

"Very well," said the hero, solemnly and sorrowfully. "Then I will go alone. I shall have all the honour. *Zou!* Give me the banner!"

XII

THE HÔTEL BALTET AT CHAMONIX—THAT SMELL OF GARLIC!—CONCERNING THE USES OF THE CORD IN ALPINE EXCURSIONS—SHAKE HANDS!—A PUPIL OF SCHOPENHAUER'S—AT THE GRANDS-MULETS—"TARTARIN, I MUST SPEAK TO YOU"

THE clock of Chamonix was striking nine on a chilly, wet evening. All the streets were dark, all the houses shut up, except where occasionally the gas of the hotels blazed out and made the surroundings still more sombre in the vague reflection of the snow, a star of white under a night of sky.

At the Hôtel Baltet, one of the best and most frequented in the Alpine village, the numerous travellers and excursionists had dispersed by degrees, tired out by the fatigues of the day, so there remained in the grand *salon* only an English parson playing draughts with his wife, while his innumerable daughters in pinafore aprons were engaged in copying the notices for the next services; and seated, in front of the hearth, on which blazed a good fire of logs, a young Swede, hollow-cheeked and pale, who was regarding the fire with a mournful air while he drank *kirsch* and seltzer-water. Occasionally a belated tourist traversed the *salon* with soaked gaiters and glistening waterproof; went up to a big barometer hanging on the wall, tapped it, watched the mercury for the next day's weather, and turned away in consternation. Not a word, no other manifestation of life save the crackling of the fire, the dashing of the sleet against the windows, and the roaring of the Arve beneath the wooden bridge, a few yards from the hotel.

Suddenly the door of the *salon* was opened, a silver-laced porter entered laden with *valises* and rugs, with four Alpinists, shivering, and bewildered by the sudden change from darkness and cold to light and warmth.

"*Boudiou!* what weather!"

"Something to eat, *zou!*"

"Warm the beds, *qué!*"

They all spoke together beneath their comforters and wraps and ear protectors, and no one knew which to listen to, until a short fat man, whom they called the President, imposed silence upon them by crying louder than all, in a commanding tone,—

"Bring me the visitors' book first."

Then, turning the leaves with a benumbed hand, he read aloud the names of the travellers who, during the last eight days, had sojourned at the hotel. Doctor Schwanthaler and Frau—again! Astier-Réhu, of the French Academy! He turned over two or three pages, growing pale when he saw a name resembling that of which he was in search. Then at length, as he threw the book on the table with a triumphant laugh, the little man cut a caper—an extraordinary performance for such a fat little fellow—and cried: "He is not here, *vé!* he has not come! He must come down here, at any rate. Bother Costecalde! *lagadigadeou!* Quick with the soup, lads!" And the worthy Tartarin, having bowed to the ladies, marched towards the *salle à manger*, followed by the delegates, hungry and noisy.

Eh? Yes; the delegates—all of them—Bravida himself amongst them! Is it possible! What would they have said yonder if they had gone home without Tartarin? Each one had felt the same. And in the moment of separation at the railway-station at Geneva the *buffet* was witness to a most heartrending scene of tears, embraces, and distressing farewells to the banner,—the result of which adieux was that the whole party crowded into the landau which the President had engaged to carry him to Chamonix. A superb route to which they firmly closed their eyes, swathed in wraps, snoring sonorously, without admiring the

A Smell of Garlic

magnificent landscape which from Sallanches displayed itself through the rain: chasms, forests, foaming cascades, and, according to the windings of the valley, alternately visible or shrouded, the crest of Mont Blanc above the clouds. Fatigued by this kind of natural beauty, the Tarasconnais only sought how to make up for the bad night they had passed under lock and key at Chillon. And now, once more, at the end of the long, deserted *salle à manger* of the Hôtel Baltet, while being served with the re-heated soup and removes of the *table d'hôte*, they ate ravenously, without speaking, only preoccupied in their desire to get to bed as quickly as possible.

Suddenly, Spiridion Excourbaniès, who had been eating like a man in his sleep, rose up out of his place, and, sniffing the air, said,—

"*Outre!* what a smell of garlic!"

"That's true, that is the smell," remarked Bravida; and all the party, aroused by this recall to their native land, this smell of the national dishes, which Tartarin had not breathed for a long while, turned in their chairs with gastronomic anxiety. The odour came from the other end of the *salle*, from a small room wherein was a traveller supping alone—no doubt a personage of importance, for every minute the cap of the *chef* was visible at the grating opening to the kitchen, to pass up a pile of little covered dishes, which were carried by the waitress to the little room.

"Some one from the South," murmured the gentle Pascalon; and the President, who had become pale at the idea of Costecalde, commanded,—

"Go and see, Spiridion; you know what to say."

A loud burst of laughter arose from the room which the brave man had penetrated to by his chief's commands, whence he led in by the hand a long-nosed individual with comic eyes, his *serviette* tucked under his chin, like the gastronomous horse.

"*Vé!* Bompard!"

"*Té!* The Impostor!"

"*Hé!* Adieu, Gonzague. *Comment te va?*"

"Pretty well, gentlemen; I am your most obedient," said the courier, shaking hands all round, and seating himself at the table with the Tarasconnais to partake with them a dish of *cèpes à l'ail*, prepared by Mère Baltet, who, as well as her husband, had a horror of the *table d'hôte* fare.

Whether it was the *fricot* or the delight of finding a resting-place, the delightful Bompard was inexhaustibly imaginative. Immediately fatigue and the desire for sleep were dissipated; champagne was gulped in bumpers, and with moustaches glistening with bubbles, they laughed, screamed, gesticulated, embraced each other, full of effusiveness.

"I will not leave you any more," Bompard was saying. "My Peruvians have gone away. I am at liberty."

"At liberty! Then you can make the ascent of Mont Blanc with me to-morrow?"

"Ah, you are going to do Mont Blanc, *demeïn ?*" replied Bompard without enthusiasm.

"Yes, I am going to put Costecalde's nose out of joint. When he comes, *uit !* No more Mont Blanc! You are with me, Gonzague?"

"I'm there, I'm there; if the weather suits. It is an ascent which is not always pleasant at this season."

"Ah! *vai* with your 'not pleasant!'" said the worthy Tartarin, winking with a meaning which Bompard, on his part, did not seem to understand.

"Let us have our coffee in the *salon*. We will consult with Père Baltet. He knows all about it. He is an old guide who has made the ascent twenty-seven times."

The delegates cried simultaneously,—

"Twenty-seven times! *Boufre !*"

"Bompard is always exaggerating," said the P. C. A. severely, with a touch of envy.

In the *salon* they found the parson's family still bent over the church notices, the father and mother nodding over their game of draughts, and the long Swede stirring his *kirsch* and seltzer with the same listless gesture. But the invasion of the Tarasconnais, brightened up by the champagne, gave some little entertainment, as we may imagine, to the young church-women. These charming young girls had never seen coffee taken with so much mimicry and so much rolling of eyes.

"Sugar, Tartarin?"

"Well, no, Commandant. You know that since I was in Africa——"

"True, pardon! *Té!* Here is M. Baltet."
"Sit down there, *qué*, M. Baltet."
"Long live M. Baltet! Ha! ha! *fen dé brut!*"
Surrounded and pressed upon by these people whom he had never seen in his life Père Baltet smiled calmly. A robust Savoyard, tall and broad-shouldered, his back rounded, his step slow, his thick and shaven face was lighted up by a pair of cunning eyes still youthful, contrasting with his baldness caused by a frost-bite one early morning on the snow-fields.

"These gentlemen wish to ascend Mont Blanc?" said he, gauging the Tarasconnais with a look at once humble and ironical. Tartarin was about to reply, but Bompard anticipated him,—

"Is not the season rather advanced?"

"No," replied the old guide. "Here is a Swedish gentleman who will go up to-morrow; and I am expecting, at the end of the week, two American gentlemen to ascend also. One of them is blind."

"I know—I met him on the Guggi."

"Ah! monsieur has been to the Guggi?"

"Eight days ago, going up the Jungfrau."

There was a flutter among the Evangelical ladies, their plumes rustled, and they raised their heads to look at Tartarin, which action, for Englishwomen, who are great climbers, and experts in all sports, carried considerable authority. He had been up the Jungfrau!

"A good expedition," said Père Baltet, looking at the P. C. A. with astonishment; while Pascalon, alarmed by the ladies, blushed, and bleated,—

"Ma-a-ster, tell them the—the *crevasse*."

The President smiled: "Child!" But all the same he commenced his recital of his fall; first with a touch-and-go listless air, then he warmed up and illustrated the narrative with action, such as kicking at the end of the cord, over the chasm, appeals with stiffened hands, etc. The ladies shivered, devouring him with their cold English eyes—those eyes which open so widely and round.

In the silence that followed, the voice of Bompard rose loudly,—

"Up on Chimborazo we do not tie ourselves to cross the *crevasses.*"

The delegates looked at him. As a *Tarasconnade*, this beat everything! "Oh, that Bompard!" murmured Pascalon, with ingenuous admiration.

But Père Baltet, taking Chimborazo quite seriously, protested against the non-employment of the rope. According to his view, no ascent was possible on ice without ropes—a good Manilla rope. At least, then, if one slipped, the others could hold him up.

"Supposing the rope does not break, Monsieur Baltet," said Tartarin, recalling the catastrophe on the Matterhorn.

But the hotel-keeper replied deliberately: "The rope did not break on the Matterhorn. The rear guide cut it with his axe."

As Tartarin became angry at this, he continued: "You must excuse me, monsieur; the guide was within his rights. He perceived the impossibility of holding the others, and he detached them to save the lives of himself, his son, and the traveller who had accompanied them. Had it not been for his determination, there would have been seven victims instead of four."

Then a discussion commenced. Tartarin maintained that, once attached to the line, it was a matter of honourable engagement to live or die together; and then, influenced by the presence of ladies, he rose to the occasion. He applied his words to facts, to people present. "Thus," said he, "when to-morrow, *té*, in attaching myself to Bompard, it would not be only a precaution that I would take, but an oath before Heaven and my fellow-men only to live with my companion, and to die rather than return without him, *coquin de sort!*"

"I accept the pledge for myself, as well as for you, Tartarin," exclaimed Bompard, from the other side of the round table.

This was an affecting moment.

The parson, as if electrified, rose and inflicted on our hero a pumping hand-grip, English fashion. His wife followed his example; while all his daughters continued to shake hands with a vigour which, properly applied, would have pumped water to the fifth story of the hotel. The delegates, I am bound to state, displayed less enthusiasm.

"Eh, *bé!* I am of M. Baltet's opinion," said Bravida.

"In cases like these, it's every one for himself, *pardi!* and I can quite understand that stroke of the axe."

"You astonish me, Placide," said Tartarin, severely; then quite privately he added: "Hold, you miserable man—England is watching us!"

The old warrior, who decidedly had kept a store of bitterness in his heart since the excursion to Chillon, made a gesture which signified his contempt for "England," and perhaps he would have drawn upon himself a severe reprimand from the President, irritated by so much cynicism, when the young man with the melancholy mien, full of grog and sadness, introduced his bad French into the conversation. He also maintained that the guide was right to cut the rope—to put an end to the existence of four unhappy individuals still young, that is to say, condemned to live a certain time —to lay them to rest by one stroke—such an action was both noble and generous!

Tartarin at this exclaimed,—

"How, young man! at your age, do you speak of life with this abandonment—this anger! What harm has existence done you?"

"Nothing; it merely bores me."

He was studying philosophy at Christiania, he had imbibed ideas from Schopenhauer and Hartmann, and found life gloomy, foolish, chaotic. Very near suicide, he had closed his books at his parents' urgent prayers, and had gone to travel; still meeting everywhere with the same *ennui*, the gloomy misery of the world. Tartarin and his friends appeared to him the only people contented to live whom he had hitherto met.

The good P. C. A. began to laugh. "The race comes out there, young man. We are all the same at Tarascon, the country of *le Bon Dieu*. From morn till night we laugh, we sing, and the rest of the time we dance the *farandole*, like this —*té!*" Then he cut an *entrechat* with the grace and lightness of a great cockchafer spreading his wings.

But the delegates had not nerves of steel, or the indefatigable energy of their chief. Excourbaniès growled: "The *Présidain* is dancing, and it is close on midnight!"

Bravida rose in a rage: "Let us go to bed, *vé!* I shall not have any more of my sciatica there."

Tartarin consented, thinking of the ascent on the morrow; and the Tarasconnais went, candlestick in hand, up the wide granite staircase to their rooms, while the Père Baltet proceeded to busy himself about provisions and to engage guides and mules.

"*Té!* it snows!"

These were the first words which escaped Tartarin as he saw the frosted windows next morning, and perceived that the room was bathed in a white reflection; but when he hung up his little shaving-glass, he understood that he had been mistaken, and that Mont Blanc was glittering opposite in a bright sun and making all this light. He opened his window to the breeze from the glacier, fresh and comforting, which carried to his ears all the tinkling of the cow-bells and the long bellowings of the shepherds' horns. Something strong and pastoral, which he had not breathed in Switzerland, filled the air.

Downstairs an assemblage of guides and porters awaited him. The Swede already had mounted, and, mingled with the spectators, who formed a circle, was the parson's family; all these brisk damsels, in morning *toilettes*, had come down to shake hands again with the hero who had haunted their dreams.

"A splendid morning! make haste!" cried the hotel-keeper, whose bald head shone in the sun like a pebble. Tartarin had need to hurry, for it was no light task to awake the delegates, who were to accompany him as far as the Pierre-Pointue, where the mule-path stops. Neither prayers nor expostulations could induce the Commandant to get up; with his nightcap down to his ears, and his nose against the wall, he contented himself with replying to the objurgations of the President by a cynical Tarasconnais proverb: "He who has a character for early rising may sleep till noon." As for Bompard, he kept repeating all the time: "Ah! get out with your Mont Blanc! what rubbish!" and he would not get up until formally commanded to do so by the President of the Alpine Club.

At length the party started, and crossed the little streets of Chamonix in a most imposing array—Pascalon in front, on a mule, the banner unfurled; and last, grave as a mandarin,

A Philosophic Discussion

amongst the guides and porters who surrounded his mule, Tartarin himself, a more curious Alpinist than ever, with a new pair of spectacles of smoked glass, and his famous rope made in Avignon, recovered we know at how great a price.

Stared at almost as much as the banner, he was delighted beneath that mask of importance, pleased with the picturesqueness of the streets of the Savoyard village, so different from the Swiss village—too clean, too varnished, like a new toy, the bazaar *chalet*—the contrast of these buildings scarcely above ground, in which the stable occupies nearly all the space, with the large, sumptuous hotels, five stories high, whose glaring signs strike one equally as do the silver-banded cap of a porter, the black suit and the pumps of the *maître d'hôtel*, in the midst of the Savoyard costumes, the caps, the fustian, and the coalheavers' hats with large flaps. On the *place* are some unhorsed vehicles, travelling-carriages side by side with dung-carts; a drove of pigs basking in the sun before the post-office, whence exits an Englishman with his packet of letters and his *Times*, which he reads as he walks, before opening his correspondence. The cavalcade traversed all this, accompanied by the whinnying of the mules, the war-cry of Excourbaniès, to whom the sun has restored the use of his "gong," the pastoral carillon on the slopes, and the roaring of the glacier-torrent—quite white, shining as if it were carrying with it sun and snow.

At the end of the village, Bompard approached his mule to that of the President, and said to him, as he rolled his extraordinary eyes: "Tartar*éin*, I must speak to you!"

"By and by," said the P. C. A., who was deep in a philosophic discussion with the young Swede, from whom he was endeavouring to drive out the black pessimism by means of the marvellous spectacle which surrounded them—the pastures with their wide zones of light and shade, those forests of dark green crested with the whiteness of the glittering *névé*.

After two attempts to approach Tartarin, Bompard gave up the idea perforce. After crossing the Arve by a little bridge, the caravan found itself on one of those narrow pathways which wind through the pine-woods, on which the mules, one by one, shave all the turns of the track above the abysses, and the Tarasconnais had quite enough to do to keep their equilibrium by the aid of " *Allons !* " " *Douce-main !* " " *Outre !* " by which they managed their animals.

At the hut on the Pierre-Pointue, in which Pascalon and Excourbaniès were to await the return of the climbers, Tartarin, very much occupied in ordering breakfast and in looking after the guides and porters, turned still a deaf ear to Bompard. But it was a curious thing, which no one remarked until later, that notwithstanding the fine weather and the good wine, the pure air, 6000 feet above the sea, the *déjeuner* was melancholy. While the guides were laughing and joking on their side, the Tarasconnais were silent, occupied solely with the table, and the only noise being the clinking of glasses and the rattling of dishes on the wooden board. Was it the presence of the mournful Swede, or the anxiety visible in the face of Gonzague, or some presentiment? The party continued the journey, as melancholy as a regiment without music, towards the glacier Des Bossons where the real ascent begins.

When putting his foot on the ice, Tartarin could not help smiling at the recollection of the Guggi, and his patent *crampons*. What a contrast between the neophyte he there had been, and the first-class Alpine climber he felt he had become! Firm on his heavy boots, which the porter at the hotel had spiked with four big nails, expert in the use of his axe, he scarcely required the assistance of the guides, and less to sustain himself than to have the route indicated. The smoked glasses tempered the glare of the glacier, which a recent avalanche had powdered with fresh snow, where the little " lakes " of sea-green tint appeared here and there slippery and treacherous; and quite calm, assured by experience that there was no danger whatever, Tartarin strode alongside the smooth shining *crevasses*, infinitely deep, passing amidst *séracs*, only careful to place his feet behind the Swedish student, an intrepid climber, whose silver-buckled gaiters continued to step out short and clean, and at the same distance from the point of his alpenstock, which seemed a third limb. Their philosophical discussion continued in spite of the difficulties of the route, and people could hear in the frozen air a sonorous sound as of a river, a hearty, familiar voice puffing out, " You know me, Otto! "

At the Grands-Mulets

Bompard, all this time, was experiencing many adventures. Firmly convinced till that morning that Tartarin would never proceed with his boast, and that he (Bompard) would never do Mont Blanc any more than he had done the Jungfrau, the unhappy courier was clothed in his ordinary costume, without nailing his boots, nor even utilising his famous invention for shoeing the feet of soldiers; he had no alpenstock either—the mountaineers of Chimborazo did not require them! Armed only with the cane which suited well his round hat and his ulster, the approach to the glaciers terrified him, for, notwithstanding all his tales, the others knew pretty well that the Impostor had never made an ascent. He consoled himself, however, when he perceived from the *moraine* how well Tartarin got on on the ice, and he decided to follow him up to the Grands-Mulets, where they intended to pass the night. At the first step, he fell on his back, and the second time on his hands and knees. "No, no," he said to the guide who offered to assist him, "it is done on purpose. The American fashion, *vé!* as at Chimborazo!" This attitude seemed to him comfortable, so he retained it, advancing on all fours, his hat on the back of his head, and his ulster training behind him like the coat of a white bear; very calm withal, and telling those near him how, amid the Cordilleras of the Andes, he had climbed in this fashion a mountain 30,000 feet high. He did not say how long it look him, by the by, but it must have been a very considerable time, judging by the stage up to the Grands-Mulets, where he arrived an hour after Tartarin, dripping with snow, while his hands were half-frozen under his worsted, knitted gloves.

Compared with the hut on the Guggi, the cabin erected by the commune of Chamonix at the Grands-Mulets, is truly comfortable. When Bompard came into the kitchen, in which a bright wood fire was burning, he found Tartarin and the Swede drying their boots, while the hut-keeper, an old shrivelled-up individual, with long white hair falling in curls, was exhibiting to them the treasures of his little museum.

Somewhat sad was this museum of *souvenirs* of catastrophes on Mont Blanc for a space of forty years, during which period the old man had kept the inn (hut); and, while taking the objects from their cases, he told their lamentable history. That morsel of cloth, those waistcoat-buttons, preserved the memory of a Russian *savant*, precipitated by a whirlwind over the glacier of the Brenva. Those teeth were the remains of a guide of the famous party of eleven travellers and porters who disappeared in a snow-storm. In the light of the dying day, and the pale reflection of the *névé* against the glass, the surroundings of these relics, the monotonous recital of them had something painful in them, so much so that the old man's voice trembled in the pathetic parts, and he was even moved to tears in displaying the green veil of an English lady who perished in an avalanche in 1827.

Tartarin had only to compare dates to convince himself that at that time the Company was not in existence to arrange non-dangerous ascents, yet this *vocero* Savoyard touched him, and he went to the door for a little fresh air.

Night came on, and shrouded the depths. The Bossons stood out livid, and seemed very near, while Mont Blanc rose high, still caressed by the ruddy beams of the setting sun. The Southern traveller was recovering himself at the sight of this smile of Nature, when the shade of Bompard came behind him.

"Ah! 'tis you, Gonzague? you see I am enjoying the pure air. That old man rather made me feel foolish with his reminiscences."

"Tartar*éin*," said Bompard, catching hold of his companion's arm forcibly, "I hope that you have had enough of this, and that you are going to end this ridiculous expedition here."

The great man opened his eyes with some anxiety in them,—

"What *are* you chattering about?"

Then Bompard drew a picture of the thousand terrible deaths which menaced them—the *crevasses*, the avalanches, the storms, the whirlwinds of snow!

Tartarin interrupted him,—

"Ah! *vaï*, you joker! And the Company? Is not Mont Blanc managed in the same manner as the rest?"

"Managed! the Company!" exclaimed Bompard, who remembered nothing of his *Tarasconnade*; and when the other repeated it word for word—the Swiss Society, the "farming" out of the mountains, the clap-trap *crevasses*, etc.,—the former manager began to laugh,—

"What! did you believe all that? Why, it was only a *galéjade*. Between people of Tarascon, of course—we know that what we say is—is——"

"Then the Jungfrau *was not prepared?*" said Tartarin, very much excited.

"By no means."

"And if the rope had broken?"

"Ah! my poor friend!"

The hero shut his eyes, pale with the horrifying retrospection, and for a moment he did not speak. This landscape, like a polar cataclysm—cold, sombre, undulated, broken; those lamentations of the old inn-keeper still ringing in his ears. "*Outre!* What made you tell me so?" Then, suddenly, he thought of the *gensses* at Tarascon, of the banner which he had flung out above, and he said to himself that, with good guides, a companion of such proved experience as Bompard——well, he had accomplished the Jungfrau—why not attempt Mont Blanc?

Then, placing his large hand on the shoulder of his friend, he said in a manly voice,—

"Listen, Gonzague!"

XIII

THE CATASTROPHE

IN a dark night, a moonless darkness, no stars, no visible sky, on the white quivering surface of an immense snow slope, is unrolled a long rope, to which some fearful shadows, and all small ones, are attached in single file, preceded a hundred yards in advance by a lantern, with a red disk, almost at the level of the ground. Blows of an ice-axe ring in the hard snow, the rattling of the detached lumps of ice alone break the silence of the snow-field, as the steps are cut for the travellers; then from time to time a cry, a stifled complaint, the fall of a body on the ice, and suddenly a stout voice, which answers from the end of the rope, " Go gently, Gonzague!" For the poor Bompard has made up his mind to follow his friend Tartarin to the summit of Mont Blanc. Since two o'clock in the morning—it is now four by the President's repeater—the unhappy courier has been advancing, groping in the dark, a very convict on the chain, dragged forward, pushed up, swaying, and stumbling; compelled to restrain the varied exclamations which his mishaps would have wrung from him; for the avalanche threatened on all sides, the least disturbance—a little vibration of the clear air —would determine the fall of the snow or the ice. To suffer in silence—what a torture for a man of Tarascon!

But the party had halted: Tartarin asked why. A discussion was heard in a low voice, in animated whispers: " It is your companion who does not wish to advance any farther," said the Swede. The order of march was changed, the human chaplet extended, turned back on itself, and the party found itself on the edge of an enormous *crevasse*, one which mountaineers call a " *roture*." The previous ones had been crossed by means of a ladder placed across them, over which the climbers crawled on hands and knees: in this case, the *crevasse* was much too wide, and the other lip raised itself eighty to a hundred feet high. The descent had to be made to the bottom of the hole, which narrowed very much, and then the ascent on the opposite side in like manner. But Bompard obstinately declined.

Leaning over the chasm, which the darkness caused to appear unfathomable, he watched the guides making the necessary preparations by the light of the lantern. Tartarin, who was himself by no means easy in his mind, gave himself courage by exhorting his friend: " Come, Gonzague, *zou!*" and then, in a lower tone, he appealed to his honour; he invoked Tarascon, the banner, and the Alpine Club.

" Ah! *vaï*, the Club—I no longer belong to it," he replied, cynically.

Then Tartarin explained to him where to put his feet, than which nothing could be more easy.

" Yes, for you perhaps, but not for me! "

" Why not? You say you have been in the habit——"

The Catastrophe

"*Bé!* yes, certainly the habit,—but of what? I have so many habits. The habit of smoking or sleeping——"

"Particularly of lying!" interrupted the President.

"Of exaggerating, if you will," replied Bompard, without moving a muscle.

However, after much hesitation, the threat to leave him all alone decided him in descending slowly and carefully this terrible Jacob's ladder. To ascend was more difficult, as the opposite wall is as slippery and smooth as marble, and higher than the Réné Tower at Tarascon. From below, the guide's lamp looked a very glow-worm. It was necessary to make up one's mind, nevertheless. The snow under foot was not solid; the dropping of a spring, and running water, were making a large fissure, which the men could guess at better than they could see, at the foot of the ice-wall, and which sent up a cold breath from the abyss.

"Go gently, Gonzague, for fear of falling!"

This phrase, which Tartarin enunciated in an almost supplicatory manner, lent a solemn significance, to the respective positions of the ascensionists, hanging now by hands and feet, one over the other, tied by a rope, and by the similarity of their movements; so that the fall or the awkwardness of one would put all in danger. And what danger, *coquin de sort!* It was quiet enough to listen to the falling and the disintegration of the *débris* of the ice-blocks, and the echo of the fall in the *crevasses* and the unknown depths, to imagine what a monster's throat you would fall into should you happen to make a false step.

But what happened? The long Swede, who immediately preceded Tartarin, stopped, and touched the cap of the P. C. A. with his iron-shod heel. The guides kept crying, "*En avant!*" and the President, "*Avancez donc, jeune homme.*" But he never stirred. Hanging to his full length, and holding with a negligent hand, the Swede looked down, as the breaking day lightened his fair beard, and illumined the curious expression of his dilated eyes, while he made a sign to Tartarin,—

"What a fall, eh, if one let go!"

"*Outre!* I believe you. You would carry us all down with you. Go on!"

The other continued, without moving,—

"A splendid opportunity to have done with life, to re-enter nothingness through the bowels of the earth, to roll from *crevasse* to *crevasse*, like this piece of ice I kick away." As he spoke, he bent over, fearfully, to watch the piece he had detached, which bounded—apparently going on for ever—through the night.

"Unhappy man, take care!" exclaimed Tartarin, pale from fear; and, desperately clinging to the wall, he resumed his argument of the day before, concerning the advantages of existence: "It is good—at your age—a fine fellow like you. You have never known what love is, *qué ?*"

No; the Swede knew nothing of it. Ideal love is the falsehood of poets; the other, a want which he had never experienced.

"*Bé oui! bé oui!* It is true that the poets are something Tarasconic. They very often say more than they need; but, at any rate, the *femellan*—as they call women in our district—is *gentil*. Then one has children—pretty little things, who resemble one!"

"Ah! yes, the children—a source of misery! Since I was born, my mother has not ceased to weep!"

"Listen, Otto; you know me, my good friend."

Then with all the valorous expansion of his soul, Tartarin set about to reanimate, to rub back to life, this victim of Schopenhauer and Hartmann; two punchinellos, who ought to be banished as a punishment for all the evil they have done to young men.

Let us remember, during this philosophic discussion, the high wall of ice—cold, sea-green, glistening with a pale yellow light—and the human bodies spotted on its surface, with the sinister gurglings which kept ascending from the abyss; the oaths of the guides, and their threats to detach themselves and leave the tourists, were all accompaniments.

At length, Tartarin, perceiving that no reasoning could convince this madman, or dissipate his infatuation, suggested to him the idea of throwing himself from the extreme summit of Mont Blanc. That would really be worth the trouble! A splendid finish in space. But to die here, at the bottom of of a cave! Ah! *vaï*, what *foutaise!* He put into the word so much persuasiveness of accent and such conviction that

The Catastrophe

the Swede permitted himself to yield, and then at length, one by one, they gained the summit of this terrible *roture*.

They untied themselves, and waited to drink and eat a little. Day was breaking—a cold pallid day—upon a magnificent amphitheatre of peaks and pinnacles, dominated by Mont Blanc, still 4500 feet above. The guides gesticulated and conversed apart, with many nods of their heads. On the white ground the round-backed, heavy men looked like marmots. Bompard and Tartarin were restless and anxious, and left the Swede to eat by himself, while they came up to the group just as the chief guide was saying,—

"When he smokes his pipe we must only say, 'No.'"

"Who is smoking his pipe?" asked Tartarin.

"*Le Mont Blanc, monsieur.* Look!"

The man indicated, at the highest peak, a white smoke which was blowing towards Italy.

"Well, my good friend, and when Mont Blanc smokes his pipe what does it portend?"

"It means, monsieur, that a storm is raging at the summit —a snowstorm — which will be upon us ere long. And, *dame!* it is dangerous!"

"Let us return," said Bompard, turning green; and Tartarin added,—

"Yes, yes, certainly; no foolish swagger!"

But the Swede came up and struck in. He had paid to go up Mont Blanc, and nothing would prevent him from going. He would ascend alone if no one would accompany him. "Cowards! cowards!" he added, turning to the guides; and he repeated the insult in the same ghostly voice with which he had been urging himself to suicide just before.

"You will very soon see whether we are cowards! Attach yourselves! *En route!*" exclaimed the chief guide. This time it was Bompard who protested energetically. He had had enough; he wished that they would take him back. Tartarin seconded him strongly,—

"You see quite well that this young man is mad!" he exclaimed, indicating the Swede, who had already strode off amid the wisps of snow which the wind was throwing in all directions. But nothing would stop these men, who had been called "cowards." The marmots had been aroused, and Tartarin could not obtain a guide to lead him and Bompard to the Grands-Mulets. However, the direction was easy. Three hours' walking, allowing a *détour* of twenty minutes to " turn " the great *roture*, if they were afraid to pass it alone.

" *Outre !* yes, we are afraid," said Bompard, without any shame; and the two parties separated.

Now the Tarasconnais were alone. They advanced with precaution over the desert of snow, attached to the same cord, Tartarin in advance, prodding with his alpenstock gravely, imbued with the responsibility which devolved upon him, searching for some comfort.

" Courage and coolness! We shall extricate ourselves! " he said every instant to Bompard. Thus the officer in battle chases away the fear he feels by brandishing his sword and crying out to his men,—

" *En avant !* all bullets do not kill! "

At length, behold our travellers at the edge of the horrible *crevasse*. Thence there were no grave obstacles; but the wind blew, and blinded them with little snowstorms. Advance became impossible without danger of losing their way.

" Let us wait here a moment," said Tartarin. A gigantic *sérac* gave them shelter at its base; they crept in, stretched over them the doubled waterproof of the President, and emptied the rum-flask, the only provision which had been left them by the guides. They thus obtained a little heat and comfort, while the sound of the step-cutting above them, growing feebler and feebler, gave them an idea of the progress of the expedition. The sound echoed in the heart of the President like a regret for not having ascended to the summit of Mont Blanc.

" Who will know that? " remarked Bompard, cynically. " The porters have retained the banner, and the people at Chamonix will think it is you."

" You are right; the honour of Tarascon is safe," concluded Tartarin, in a tone of conviction.

But the elements became furious—the *bise* in a storm, the snow in masses. The two friends remained silent, haunted by sinister thoughts: they recalled the museum of the old man at the Mulets, his lamentable narratives, the tale of the American tourist, who was found petrified with cold and hunger, holding in his frozen hand a note-book, in which his

The Catastrophe

last thoughts were inscribed till the last convulsion which shook the pencil and caused his signature to swerve.

"Have *you* a note-book, Gonzague?"

And the other, who understood without any explanation, replied,—

"Ah! *vaï*, a note-book! Do you think I am going to let myself die like that American? *Vite!* let us be off; come away."

"Impossible! At the first step we shall be carried away like straws, and dashed into some chasm!"

"But then we must shout; the inn is not far from here." And Bompard, on his knees, his head protruding from the *sérac* in the attitude of a cow lowing, shouted: "Help! Help!"

"*Aux armes!*" cried Tartarin in his turn, in his most sonorous voice, which the grotto echoed like thunder.

Bompard seized him by the arm: "Miserable man, the *sérac!*" Positively the whole block trembled; another breath, and the mass of accumulated ice-blocks would fall upon them. They remained frozen, motionless, wrapped in a terrible silence, which was soon broken by a distant rumbling, which came nearer and nearer, increased, spread over the horizon, and finally died away underground in the gulfs of the ice.

"Poor fellows!" murmured Tartarin, thinking of the Swede and his guides, carried away by the avalanche, no doubt. Bompard shook his head: "We shall scarcely fare better next time," he said. In fact, their situation had become very critical; they did not dare to move in their ice-grotto, nor could they venture out in the storm.

To complete their terror of mind, from the valley now arose the baying of a dog—a death-wail. Suddenly, Tartarin, with staring eyes and trembling lips, seized the hands of his companion, and, looking at him kindly, said,—

"Forgive me, Gonzague; yes, yes, forgive me. I have often been unkind to you. I treated you as a liar——"

"Ah! *vaï*, what does that matter?"

"I have as little right as any one to do so, for I have told many lies in my life, and at this supreme hour I feel the necessity to confess—to relieve my feelings—to publicly avow my impostures!"

"Impostures! You?"

"Listen to me, friend; in the first place, I never killed that lion!"

"That does not surprise me at all," replied Bompard, quickly. "But why should you worry yourself about so little? It is the sun which causes it; we are born with the lying faculty. *Vé!* myself—have I ever told the truth since I came into the world? As soon as I open my mouth, my Southern blood ascends. The people of whom I speak —well, I do not know them! The countries? I have never been in them! and all this makes such a tissue of invention that I can't even unravel it myself!"

"It is imagination, *pechère!*" sighed Tartarin. "We are liars in imagination!"

"And such lies have never done any one any harm; while an envious person, such a one as Costecalde——"

"Let us not speak of the wretch!" interrupted the P. C. A., seized with sudden rage. "*Coquin de bon sort!* It is, all the same, a little annoying——" He suddenly stopped at a gesture from Bompard. "Ah! yes, the *sérac*," and lowering his voice, forced to swallow his anger, poor Tartarin continued his imprecations in a low voice, with an enormous and comical disarticulation of his mouth: "It is rather annoying to die in the flower of one's age by the fault of a scoundrel who at this moment is taking his *demi-tasse* comfortably in the *Tour de ville!*"

But while he was fulminating, the sky was clearing by degrees. The snow ceased, the wind dropped, blue rifts appeared above the grey of the clouds. Quick—away! They had re-tied themselves, when Tartarin, who had taken the lead as before, turned round and said, finger on his mouth,—

"You know, Gonzague, all that has been said is quite between ourselves."

"*Té, pardi!*"

Full of ardour, they resumed their way, plunging up to their knees into the newly-fallen snow, which had obliterated all traces of the party's ascent, so Tartarin consulted his compass every moment. But this Tarascon compass, accustomed to a hot climate, had been frozen since its arrival in Switzerland. The needle played puss-in-the-corner, agitated

The Catastrophe

and trembling; so the men proceeded straight before them, expecting to see suddenly the black rocks of the Grands-Mulets, calm amongst the uniform whiteness, amid the peaks, needles, and towers, which surrounded them; which dazzled and alarmed them too, for dangerous *crevasses* might be hidden under their feet.

" Coolness, Gonzague, coolness!"

" That is just what I require," replied Bompard lamentably. Then he groaned: " Oh, my foot,—oh, my leg—we are lost: we never shall get home again!"

They walked for two hours towards the middle of a snow-slope very hard to climb. Then Bompard cried, alarmed,—

" Tartar*ein*, this ascends!"

" Eh! I can see that very well," replied the President, who seemed disturbed.

" But in my opinion we ought to be going down!"

" *Bé!* yes; but what do you want me to do? If we keep ascending, we may get down the other side!"

That was descending indeed, and terribly, by a succession of *névés*, almost pointed glaciers, and beyond all this dangerous expanse of white a hut was perceived perched on a rock at a depth that seemed inaccessible. It would be a refuge for the night if they could reach it, as they had lost the direction of the Grands-Mulets—but at the cost of what efforts, what perils, perhaps!

" Whatever you do, don't let me go, Gonzague!"

" Neither you me, Tartarin!"

They exchanged these assurances without seeing each other, being separated by an *arête* behind which Tartarin had disappeared, the one advancing to ascend, the other to descend, slowly and in fear. They said no more, concentrating all their strength for fear of a false step, or a slip. Suddenly, when he was not more than a yard from the crest, Bompard heard a fearful cry from his companion. At the same time, he felt the rope give way with violence, and with an irregular severance. He endeavoured to resist, to fix himself, in order to sustain his companion over the abyss. But the rope was old, no doubt, for at last it snapped suddenly under the strain.

" *Outre!*"

" *Boufre!*"

These two cries arose, wild and despairing, in the silence and the solitude. Then succeeded a terrible calm—the calmness of death, which nothing could trouble more, in the vastness of the immaculate snows!

Towards evening, a man vaguely resembling Bompard—a spectre, dishevelled, wounded, in profuse perspiration—reached the *auberge* of the Grands-Mulets, where they rubbed him, warmed him, and put him to bed, ere he could pronounce the words—almost choked with tears, and interrupted by the clenching of his hands towards heaven: "Tartarin—lost—rope broke!" At length they understood the great disaster which had happened.

While the old inn-keeper was lamenting, and adding a new chapter to his accidents on the mountain, pending the arrival of new relics, the Swede and his guides, who had returned from their expedition, set out in search of the unfortunate Tartarin, with ropes, ladders, and all the apparatus, alas! without effect. Bompard remained as if stupefied, and was unable to furnish any precise information as to the place where the accident took place. They only found on the Dôme du Goûter an end of rope which remained in a fissure of the ice. But, curiously enough, this rope was cut as with a sharp instrument, so as to leave two ends. The newspapers of Chambéry gave a *facsimile* of it. At length, after eight days' searching, conscientiously undertaken, when every one was convinced that the poor *Présidain* was lost without hope of recovery, the delegates, despairing, returned to Tarascon, carrying Bompard with them—for his skull showed traces of a terrible fall.

"Don't talk to me about it," he would say, whenever the accident was mentioned to him. "Never speak to me on the subject!"

Decidedly, Mont Blanc now reckoned one more victim! And what a victim!

XIV

EPILOGUE

A MORE impressive place than Tarascon cannot be found under the sun. Sometimes, in high *fête*, on Sundays, when all the town is out of doors—the drums beating, the *Cours* festive and noisy, dotted with green and red costumes, and on the great party-coloured posters the announcements of the wrestling matches for men and youths, and the bull-rings—it is enough for a practical joker to call out "Mad dog!" or "Escaped bull!" for the whole population to run in-doors, bolt themselves in, the outside Venetian blinds clattering as if in a storm, and lo! there is Tarascon deserted, silent, not a cat visible, not a sound audible, even the grasshoppers themselves are cowering and attentive listeners.

Such was the appearance of Tarascon on this particular morning, when it was neither *fête* day nor Sunday. The shops were closed, the houses shut up, squares and courts seemingly larger in the solitude. "*Vasta silentio*," said Tacitus, when describing Rome on the occasion of the funeral of Germanicus; and the comparison of Rome in mourning would apply so much better to Tarascon, inasmuch as a funeral service was being performed for the soul of Tartarin at that time in the metropolitan church, where the population *en masse* was weeping for its hero, its divinity, its invincible one with the double muscles, who lay amid the glaciers of Mont Blanc.

Now, while the tolling bell was showering its sad notes upon the deserted streets, Mlle. Tournatoire, the Doctor's sister, who in consequence of her delicate health always remained in-doors, shivering in her great arm-chair by the window, was looking out as she listened to the bells. The Tournatoires' house was on the Avignon road, almost opposite to Tartarin's house, and the sight of that illustrious domicile, to which the proprietor would never return, the garden-gate for ever closed—all, even to the boot-brushing boxes of the two little Savoyards by the door, made the heart of the poor lady swell; a secret passion for the hero having

devoured her for more than thirty years! O mysteries of the
heart of an old maid! It had been her happiness to see him
pass at his regular time, and to say, "Where are you going?"
to watch the alterations in his costume, whether he dressed
in his Alpine habiliments or in the green coat! Now, she
would never see him more! And even the consolation of
praying for him with the other ladies of the town was denied
to her.

Suddenly, the long, white cheeks of Mlle. Tournatoire
coloured slightly; her pale eyes, rimmed with rose-colour,
dilated considerably; while her thin hand, with its prominent
wrinkles, formed the sign of the cross. He! 'twas he!
sidling along the wall at the other side of the street. At
first she was under the impression that she had seen an
apparition. No, it was Tartarin himself in flesh and blood;
only pale, piteous-looking, shabby; sidling along the wall
like a poor man or a thief. But to explain his furtive presence
at Tarascon we must return to Mont Blanc, to the Dôme du
Goûter, at the precise time when the two friends found themselves one on each side of the Dôme, Bompard feeling the
rope which attached him to his friend suddenly stretched, as
if by the falling of a body!

In fact, the rope had caught between two masses of ice;
and Tartarin, feeling the same shock, also believed that his
companion had fallen, and would drag him with him! So,
in that supreme moment—how am I to tell it? *mon Dieu!*—
in the agony of fear, both men, forgetting the solemn oath
at the Hôtel Baltet, by a simultaneous movement and the
same instinctive gesture, cut the rope! Bompard with his
hunting-knife, and Tartarin with his ice-axe; then, overwhelmed by their crime, both convinced that they had
sacrificed their friend, fled in opposite directions!

When the spectre of Bompard appeared at the Grands-
Mulets, that of Tartarin reached the canteen of d'Avesailles.
How, by what miracle, after so many falls and *glissades?*
Mont Blanc alone can tell; for the poor P. C. A. remained
two days in complete insensibility, incapable of uttering the
slightest sound. As soon as he was fit, he came down to
Courmayeur, the Italian Chamonix. At the hotel he heard
nothing but the report of the melancholy catastrophe on
Mont Blanc, quite a pendant to that on the Cervin: another

Epilogue

Alpine climber killed in consequence of the fracture of the rope.

In the conviction which he experienced concerning Bompard, Tartarin, torn by remorse, did not dare to rejoin the delegates nor return home. He anticipated in all eyes and on every lip: "Cain, where is thy brother?" However, the want of funds, the condition of his wardrobe, the cold of September, which emptied the hotels, compelled him to proceed homewards. After all, no one had seen him commit the crime. Nothing need prevent him from inventing no matter what tale; and, the distractions of the journey assisting, he commenced to pull himself together again. But as he approached Tarascon, when he saw the fine lines of the *Alpines* standing forth against the blue sky, all the shame, remorse, and fear of being brought to justice seized upon him again; and, to avoid the scandal of an arrival on the railway-station, he quitted the train at the last station before the town was reached.

Ah! on this fine Tarascon road, all white and crackling with dust, without any other shade than the posts and the telegraph-wires, on this triumphal way where so many times he had marched at the head of his Alpinists or his cap-shooters, who would have recognised him, the valiant, the spruce, under those torn and dirty clothes, with that defiant, restless gaze watching the *gendarmes*? The day was very warm though the season was declining, and the water-melon which he purchased from a hawker, and ate in the shade of the cart, seemed to him delicious, while the peasant declaimed against the want of custom in Tarascon that morning, "because a mass for the dead was being said, for a person found away there in a hole in the mountains! *Té!* the bells were tolling—they could hear them where they stood!"

There was no longer room for doubt: it was for Bompard, who had fallen, that this lugubrious carillon of death was carried by the wind over the lonely surounding districts.

What an accompaniment to the return of a great man to his native place!

One minute, the door of the little garden was suddenly opened and shut. Tartarin found himself again at home— he saw the narrow paths bordered with trim box edging, and quite tidy; the basin, the fountain, the gold-fish darting

away as the sand crackled under his feet, and the giant
baobab in the flower-pot — a touching appearance of
comfort; the warmth of his home as a domestic rabbit
enveloped him like a cloak of safety after all his dangers
and adventures. But the bells—the cursèd bells—redoubled
their clangour, and their deep notes crushed into his heart
anew. They kept saying to him in funereal tones: " Cain,
where is thy brother? Tartarin, what hast thou done with
Bompard?" Then, without having the courage to move,
he seated himself on the sunny edge of the little basin, and
remained there exhausted and pensive, to the great disturbance of the gold-fish.

The bells have ceased. The church porch, lately so
animated, is given up to the beggar-woman seated there as
motionless as the stone saints. The religious ceremony is
over, all Tarascon has proceeded to the Alpine Club, where
in solemn session Bompard is about to give an account of the
catastrophe, and to detail the incidents connected with the
last moments of the President. Besides the members, many
privileged persons, military, clerical, noble, and mercantile,
had taken their places in the conference hall, of which the
large open windows permitted the band stationed below on
the steps, to mingle some heroic chords with the discourses
of these gentlemen. An enormous crowd pressed around the
musicians, standing on tip-toe and stretching their necks in
the attempt to catch some fragments of the discourse; but
the windows were too high up, and they could obtain no
impressions as to what was passing within, except from two
or three youngsters perched in a tree hard by, who threw
scraps of information as one throws nuts or cherries from
the top of a tree.

" *Vé* Costecalde, who is trying to make himself weep!
Ah! the blackguard, he holds the chair at present. And
poor Bézuquet, how he blows his nose, how red his eyes are!
Té! they have put *crêpe* on the banner. And Bompard
is coming to the table with the three delegates. He puts
something on the desk. He speaks now. That must be
beautiful! Look, how the tears are falling!"

As a matter of fact, the tenderness became general as
Bompard advanced in his fantastic recital. Ah! memory
came back to him again—also imagination! After relating

how he and his illustrious companions got to the summit of Mont Blanc, without guides, for all had refused to follow them, being alarmed by the bad weather, and how they alone, with the banner displayed, for five minutes stood upon the highest peak in Europe, he proceeded to recount—and, with what emotion!—the perilous descent and the fall—Tartarin rolling to the bottom of a *crevasse*, and he, Bompard, attaching himself to a rope two hundred feet in length, had explored the hideous chasm throughout its whole length!

" More than twenty times, gentlemen—what do I say?—more than ninety times did I sound that abyss of ice without being able to reach our poor *Présidain*, whose fall, nevertheless, I could trace in consequence of some *débris* left in the crevices of the ice."

As he spoke, he laid on the table a fragment of a jaw-bone, some hairs from a beard, a piece of a waistcoat, and a buckle from a pair of braces—one would have declared they came from the relic-cases at the Grands-Mulets!

In face of this testimony, the transports of grief could no longer be restrained; even the hardest hearts, the partisans of Costecalde and the gravest persons—Cambalalette the notary, Doctor Tournatoire—shed, most effectively, some tears as large as decanter stoppers. The ladies present uttered piercing cries, which dominated even the sobbing howls of Excourbaniès and the bleatings of Pascalon, while the funeral march, played by the band, accompanied all with a slow and lugubrious bass.

Then, when he perceived the emotion and distress his peroration had caused, Bompard ended his speech with a fine gesture of pity towards the remains, as conclusive evidence: " There, dear friends and fellow-citizens, is all I could discover of our illustrious and well-beloved President. The remains the glacier will render up to us—in forty years! "

He was about to explain, for the benefit of ignorant people, the recent discovery of the regular progress of glaciers; but the creaking of the little door at the end interrupted him—some one was coming in. Tartarin, paler than a spirit of Hume's raising, stood before the speaker!

" *Vé!* Tartarin! "

" *Té!* Gonzague! "

And this race is so singular, so *facile*, in the matter of

improbable stories, audacious falsehoods and quick refutations, that the arrival of the great man, whose fragments still lay on the table, did not create any particular astonishment throughout the hall.

"It is a misapprehension, *allons !*" said Tartarin, very much relieved—radiant—with his hand on the shoulder of the man he had believed he had killed. "I did the Mont Blanc on two sides—ascended on one, descended on the other—and this quite accounts for my disappearance."

He did not confess that he had passed the second slope on his back!

"*Sacré Bompard !*" said Bézuquet; "he came back to us with his story all the same!" Then they all laughed, and rubbed their hands, while outside, the band, which they in vain attempted to silence, furiously attacked the Funeral March of Tartarin of Tarascon.

"*Vé* Costecalde, how yellow he is!" murmured Pascalon to Bravida, indicating the armourer, who had risen to cede his chair to the old President, whose good face shone brightly. Bravida, always sententious, replied in a whisper, as he perceived Costecalde superseded—relegated to the rank of subaltern: "The luck of the Abbé Mandaire; from parish priest he was relegated to curate." [1]

And then the meeting resumed.

[1] "La fortune de l'abbé Mandaire—
De curé il devint vicaire! "—H.F.

www.ingramcontent.com/pod-product-compliance
Lightning Source LLC
Chambersburg PA
CBHW031638040426
42453CB00006B/145